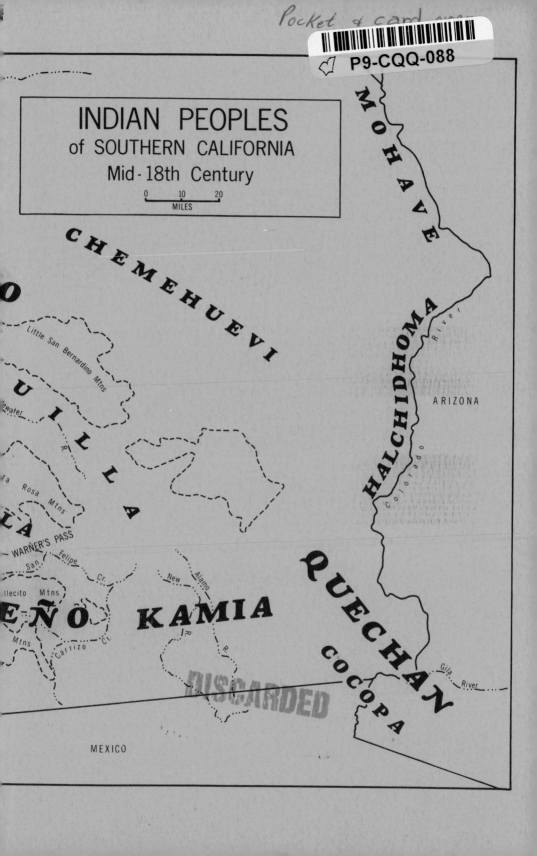

INDIAN PEOPLES
of SOUTHERN CALIFORNIA
Mid-18th Century

0   10   20
MILES

CHEMEHUEVI

MOHAVE

HALCHIDHOMA

ARIZONA

Little San Bernardino Mtns

O

UILLA

ewater

R.

a Rosa Mtns

LA

WARNER'S PASS

San   Felipe   Cr.

llecito   Mtns

New   Alamo

EÑO   KAMIA

Mtns   Carrizo   Cr.

R.

R.

Colorado

River

QUECHAN

COCOPA

Gila   River

MEXICO

CHIEFS AND CHALLENGERS

CHIEFS

AND

CHALLENGERS

*Indian Resistance
and Cooperation
in Southern California*

George Harwood Phillips

UNIVERSITY OF CALIFORNIA PRESS
Berkeley · Los Angeles · London
1975

UNIVERSITY OF CALIFORNIA PRESS
BERKELEY AND LOS ANGELES, CALIFORNIA

UNIVERSITY OF CALIFORNIA PRESS, LTD.
LONDON, ENGLAND

FOR THE INDIAN PEOPLES
OF SOUTHERN CALIFORNIA,
WHOSE ANCESTORS MADE HISTORY

Contents

Preface

With the completion of this project, I found myself indebted to so many individuals that space will not permit the special acknowledgment each one deserves. Collectively, however, I would like to thank those members of the California Room of the San Diego County Library, the National Archives, the Bancroft Library, the California State Archives, the Office of the Church Historian in Salt Lake City, Whaley House in San Diego, the Huntington Library, Mission Santa Barbara Archives, the Serra Museum and Library of San Diego, and the Department of Special Collection at the University of California, Los Angeles, who gave me much-needed and much-appreciated assistance. Individually, I would especially like to thank Norris Hundley who first encouraged me to undertake an Indian project, Lowell Bean who made me aware that a historical study of southern California Indians was a feasible undertaking, and Emre Sutton who put in long hours without pay in designing the fine maps. Those who read the manuscript and offered encouragement and advice include Norris Hundley, William Bright, Lowell Bean, and Clifton Kroeber. For their time and effort, I am very grateful. I would also like to thank Marlene and Ted Zeigler, Mrs. Donna Bea Noble, and my mother, Mrs. Maxine Phillips, all of whom typed one version or another of the work. Appreciation is also extended to Michael Stannard who drew the maps, to Lucy Kluckhohn who gave the manuscript its final and most thorough reading, and to Shirley Warren of the University of California Press.

Although mainly concerned with Indian response to
white pressure, this study, unfortunately, relies almost exclusively on white-produced evidence. This could not be
helped since the lineage-organized peoples of southern
California lacked well-developed institutions for the preservation of detailed historical traditions and since it was
extremely difficult for them to transmit historically valid
information during two hundred years of intensive colonization. Indians interviewed remembered only bits and
pieces of the events here considered, and I suspect that
most of their information came not from traditions but
from published sources.

Presenting something of a problem were Indian language, societal, village, and personal names. The Spanish
identified many southern California Indians after the missions into which they were grouped. Anthropologists have
applied these terms to a linguistic classification system,
each labeling a distinct language within a larger language
family. "Luiseño," therefore, refers both to a precontact
language division within the Shoshonean language family
and to a postcontact people who were associated with
Mission San Luis Rey. Not all the Indians of southern
California were linked with the Spanish missions, however, so some traditional terms have been preserved. "Cahuilla," for example, is an original Indian word that identifies a people and their language. "Cupeño" also refers to
a people and their language, but it only came into common written use around the beginning of the twentieth
century. In the mid-nineteenth century, when many of
the events in this study took place, white men called the
Cupeños the Agua Caliente Indians after the Spanish
name of their main village. In fact, nearly every village in
the region came to possess both a Spanish and an Indian
name. This is also true for many individual Indians. They
used their Spanish names when dealing with white men
and their Indian names when interacting among themselves. While no attempt has been made to standardize
Indian terminology, consistency of usage has been main-

tained. If anything dictated how terms were selected, it was the frequency of their appearance in the historical documentation and the anthropological literature.

How best to organize the data also posed some difficulties. While I wanted to present a straightforward narrative, I sought neither to overwhelm the reader with an endless sequence of names and dates nor to shun the responsibility of issuing judgments and making analyses. I therefore decided to arrange the book along thematic, rather than strictly chronological, lines. For instance, chapters 4, 5, and 6, cover approximately the same time period, but each is concerned with a different aspect of Indian-white interaction. I also decided to save my analyses for a concluding chapter, thus keeping the narrative free from judgmental interruptions and allowing the reader clearly to discern when "the facts are speaking for themselves" and when I am speaking for myself. But separated by time and culture from the events and people here discussed, I realize that my conclusions are not infallible and that some will be open to challenge.

G. H. P.

Introduction

Much of what constitutes the historical literature of Indian-white relations in North America is concerned with the mistreatment of the Indian by the white man. Beginning in 1881 with the publication of Helen Hunt Jackson's *A Century of Dishonor* and increasing voluminously in succeeding years, this literature documents beyond a doubt that the white man was guilty of the most heinous crimes against the Indian. But while the historian has the right, and perhaps even the obligation, to issue moral judgments, his preoccupation with the theme of mistreatment has often distorted rather than clarified the nature of Indian-white relations. By concentrating on how Indians were massacred, why treaties were broken, or when the Indian Bureau failed in its responsibilities, historians tell us much more about the white man than about the Indian. Whites, therefore, are too often viewed as the elites of American history, the only ones whose activity is worthy of serious investigation.

White activity, of course, cannot be overlooked in any study of Indian-white relations, since it usually resulted in the destruction or colonization of Indian societies. But if the work is to acknowledge the historical importance of the Indian, the approach must be shifted from one that concentrates exclusively on white activity to one that shows Indians responding to the foreigners in ways that were logical and valid in light of their own experiences and aspirations. Only from this perspective will the Indian emerge as a truly important agent in the shaping of American history.

Active Indian response varied considerably from group to group, from region to region, and from period to period, but Indian leaders and societies had only three basic options open to them when faced with incoming whites—to resist, to withdraw, or to cooperate. Since each option was designed to achieve the same goals, namely the preservation of political sovereignty, corporate unity, and cultural integrity, it was not unusual for a leader or a society to implement all three policies over a period of time. And while none could guarantee success, each was not doomed to immediate failure. In the course of four hundred years, Indians achieved numerous military victories and often succeeded in either withdrawing from or maintaining peaceful relations with the white foreigners.[1]

It seems that most Indian leaders implemented policies of cooperation when first confronted by white men. Some cooperative relationships, based on commercial or military ties, lasted for decades and greatly increased the wealth and power of the participating Indian societies. For many leaders, especially those of small and relatively weak societies or those who had acquired their positions through white support, cooperation was perhaps their best policy. This was particularly true if political or geographical conditions prevented withdrawal. Cooperation, however, does not necessarily indicate collaboration or helplessness. As the foreign policy of a society's politics of survival, it had many degrees of implementation. An astute Indian leader could be very cooperative on one occasion and only partially so on another. Moreover, cooperating with the whites did not preclude making demands upon them.

Of course, cooperative relationships often degenerated into hostilities. When this happened, the nature of Indian resistance was determined at least in part by the length of time the society had been in contact with the whites. When a society's territory was first being probed by white men, Indian leaders usually engaged in what amounted to traditional warfare. Tactics and goals were much the same as when fighting a neighboring Indian group—to push the enemy from the immediate area in a short campaign that utilized well-tested strategies and techniques. Because white pressure was still relatively weak, there was little if any effort to introduce new methods of warfare, to develop new military or political alliances, or to formulate new and long-range objectives.

When whites were in the process of consolidating their colonial rule, however, the nature of the resistance was sometimes significantly different. Often undertaken by a society that had centralized its political structure in response to white pressure, the resistance movement was sometimes the creation of an individual who had years of experience in dealing with white men and who knew, therefore, the danger they posed to Indian sovereignty. No longer content to accept Indian political fragmentation as a permanent condition, the leader sought to forge an Indian alliance that would present a united and powerful front to the whites. He often introduced new military tactics, undertook prolonged campaigns, and advocated bold and long-range objectives, such as the elimination of all white men within a particular region.

The decision to implement either policies of resistance or cooperation was determined both by the state of inter-Indian and Indian-white affairs within a particular region; that is, the way an Indian leader dealt with the whites stemmed in part by the nature of his relations with neighboring Indian rulers. And the way he dealt with neighboring Indian rulers was partly determined by the quality of his relations with the whites. Consequently, it would not be unusual for a leader to be continually altering his foreign policy regarding both whites and Indians. On one occasion he might assist the whites against an Indian ruler that both considered to be dangerous, while on another he might seek an alliance with neighboring Indian leaders to counter the growing strength of the whites. This diplomatic shifting became even more complex when members of different white nations were involved. At one time, a particular white group might be preferred over another, but this preference could be reversed at a later date.[2]

Although the Indian is given credit for helping to determine historical trends in other regions of North America, few studies to date have investigated the Indian's role in California history.[3] Anthropologists have been reluctant to utilize documentary materials or even to generate an interest in postcontact, prereservation Indian history. Most have directed their energies to reconstructing different aspects of aboriginal existence. But since the Indians of California did not always build, create, and organize on as large a scale or in as elaborate a manner as other Indian peoples, the anthropologist has created the impression that in social organization, technology, art, ceremony, and warfare they were somehow lacking. Indeed, as hunters and gatherers they have been ranked by some anthropologists at the lowest level in the hierarchy of social and cultural evolution.[4]

Anthropologists, however, at least have considered the California Indian worthy of serious investigation. Historians, in contrast, have rarely paid any attention to the Indian, finding Spaniards, *Californios* (Mexicans), and Anglo-Americans more to their scholastic liking.[5] While often sympathetic to the Indians for the mistreatment they have received, seldom has the historian viewed them as anything more than passive spectators of their own destruction, doing nothing to solve the problems created by invading white men and thereby playing only an insignificant role in the historical process.

The Indians of California, it seems, suffer from two negative images—that of being backward in their aboriginal state and that of always being helpless during postcontact times. Fortunately, through the efforts of present-day California anthropologists, the former image is being corrected.[6] The latter, however, persists and stems in large part from the writings of late-nineteenth-century white observers who saw the Indians when they had lost most of their lands to American settlers and when they were often without the will or means to alter their situation. In the 1870s and 1880s several reports were issued on the so-called Mission Indians of southern California, all pointing out the deplorable conditions under which they were then laboring.[7] Two of the most widely read were written by an early crusader for Indian rights, Helen Hunt Jackson, who in 1884 also published her novel *Ramona*. Designed to bring national attention to the Indians of southern California, the book was widely read and did in fiction what the reports did in fact. But it was also largely responsible for creating and spreading the negative image of the docile, helpless, passive California Indian.[8] Because this image is often applied to the Indians in all stages of their postcontact existence, it fits in nicely with the historian's Eurocentric approach to California history. For if Indians are seen to be passive and helpless, no matter what time period is being investigated, the historian can easily justify excluding them from his works. After all, history is made by active, not passive, individuals and societies.

Correlated to the idea of Indian helplessness is the view that white men nearly always prevailed in their dealings with the California Indian. This is not true, for the Spaniards never dominated but a small portion of California's total Indian population. During the Mexican period, the Californios suffered greatly at the hands of Indian horse and cattle raiders. And in many instances, especially in southern California, the early Anglo-Americans were so poorly armed and organized and were so numerically inferior that they lived in perpetual dread of Indian hostility.

Lacking a "frontier" where Indians and whites were clearly separated on either side of some geographical or political boundary, California was a region where distinct groups of peoples were forced to interact on very intimate terms. That the Indians were profoundly affected by the white man is most apparent. But Indian activity also had a great impact on the whites. Often it sent shock waves far beyond the local setting where the events took place, forcing the whites into initiating counteraction that sometimes affected themselves as much as it did the Indians. Of course, as time passed, the white man eventually got the upper hand, and the Indians were either exterminated, decimated, or subordinated. But until this happened, the interaction of Indians and whites was often of crucial historical importance.

This study is an investigation of how, why, and with what consequences southern California Indians interacted with one another and with Spaniards, Californios, and Anglo-Americans from the late 1760s to the early 1860s. Specifically, it examines the activities of three chiefs—Juan Antonio, Antonio Garra, and Manuelito Cota—as each in his own way responded to the imposition and consolidation of American rule.[9] The importance of these Indian leaders rests not so much on what they actually achieved for themselves and their followers but in what they attempted to achieve. Whether expressed in resistance or cooperation, their initiative was manifested in action that was part of the making of California history.

The Cahuilla, Luiseño, and Cupeño

By the middle of the eighteenth century, the region of North America now known as California was a vast conglomeration of Indian linguistic units. No less than six major language families were represented,[1] although the linguistic diversity was most complex in the northern two-thirds of the region. In the extreme south (see endpaper map), the majority of the Indians belonged to the Uto-Aztecan language family, especially the Shoshonean subfamily. These Indians were further separated into numerous language divisions, including Cahuilla, Luiseño, Cupeño, Serrano, Chemehuevi, Gabrielino, Fernandino, and Juaneño. Located to the south and east of the Shoshonean-speakers were Indians who spoke languages of the Hokan-Siouian family of which Yuman was the subfamily. They were also separated into several language divisions, including Quechan (Yuma), Halchidhoma, Cocopa, Mohave, Kamia, and Diegueño.[2]

Despite their linguistic fragmentation, most of southern California's Indians, especially those located west of the Colorado Desert, shared many common cultural characteristics. By the middle of the eighteenth century, they were practicing a highly specialized hunting and food-gathering economy based on a vast ecological knowledge. From their most important staple, the acorn, they made a gruel, but they also consumed many other kinds of wild food plants, such as lambs celery, different kinds of rushes, the stalks of sage and yucca, currants, wild plums, and several varieties of berries. Big game was hunted, especially the greatly desired deer, but small game such as rats, mice, ground squirrels, quail, ducks, songbirds, and rabbits, was their usual source of meat.[3] Compared with many other North American Indians, those of southern California had a very diversified and healthy diet.[4]

Because of the warm climate and generally abundant food sources, the material needs of these Indians were not great. Their houses consisted of pole frames covered with bark, brush, cattail, or woven mats. Clothing was limited to a skin breechclout for the men and fiber skirts for the women. Yucca fiber sandals were worn on long journeys, but most of the time people went barefoot. In winter, cloaks made from the skins of sea otter, rabbit, or deer were worn about the shoulders.[5]

Skill in basket-making was highly developed and a woman's task. Most women used the coiling method, winding a rope of grass or twigs in circular layers and then sewing the coils together. Baskets were used as plates and cups, for storage, and for carrying seeds and other materials. Women of some groups also knew the art of pottery-making. Smooth clay, free from sand and stones, was pounded and mixed with fine, crushed rock. Long strips were rolled and then coiled into the desired shape.[6] Knowledge of pottery manufacture was probably introduced from the Yuman-speakers of the Colorado River region.[7]

One of the tasks of the men was the fashioning of nets, some six feet high and thirty or more feet long. Manufactured from Indian hemp, milkweed, or nettles, they were mainly used to snare rabbits on communal hunts. The men also shaped knives and arrowheads from stone and carved bows from willow, elder, or ash. A flat, curved throwing stick, used to bring down small animals, was also made. And those who lived along the coast built plank boats by lashing the boards together with thongs and covering the cracks with asphalt.[8]

For recreation several games were played. Men and boys especially enjoyed batting a wooden ball about with curved sticks. Women and girls preferred a game in which

rings made of acorn cups were threaded on a string attached to a pointed stick. The idea was to throw the cups
in the air and ring as many as possible on the stick. Older
people played a dice game, using four wooden boards that
were painted with different designs. On which side the
boards landed decided the score. Perhaps the most popular game was *peon*. Usually eight men were engaged, four
to a team, each side facing the other on its knees. One
team was given eight small pieces of bone, a black and
white one for each member. While keeping their hands
under a cover, the bones were passed between members
of the team. At the same time they and their supporters
chanted to confuse the other side. When the cover was
dropped, the leader of the other team had to guess in
whose hands the white bones were concealed. An umpire
kept score with sticks, and the game sometimes would go
through the night before one side was declared the win-
ner.[9]

Many ceremonies centered on important transitional
periods in the life of the individual: coming-of-age, marrying, and dying. Attaining adulthood, usually at about
thirteen or fourteen, was an extremely significant period for the individual and the society. At a coming-of-
age ceremony, a group of girls, to ensure enduring health
so they would have many strong children, were placed in
beds of hot sand and covered with mats. For at least three
days they lay there, taking only water and gruel. Women
and men sang them special songs about the society's traditions and about the importance of adulthood. Their relatives made baskets and prepared gifts of food which they
gave to members of other groups who participated in the
ceremony. When the initiation was completed, the girls
remained in their houses for several days where they
were further instructed in the traditions of the society.[10]

The coming-of-age ceremony for boys was also very important. Because the society needed their skill and
strength, the boys sought to exhibit great "power" during
the ceremony. At night, away from the village in a spe-

cially prepared clearing, the boys were assembled. Singing softly, an elder pounded the root of the jimsonweed into a powder that was then sifted through a basket and mixed with water. The drink was given to the boys to produce visions, the source of the desired power. The party then returned to the village to dance. When the boys became dizzy from the drink, they were taken back to the clearing, while the men continued to sing and dance through the night. For the next few days, the boys, existing on a little gruel, were taught special songs and were instructed through sand paintings in the ways of the universe. The conclusion of the ceremony signaled that the boys had become men and now assumed all the duties, responsibilities, and benefits of adulthood.[11]

The marriage ceremony was also an important event. It brought members of different societies together for a feast that lasted several days. During this time, elders lectured the young couple on the responsibilities of marriage. If the marriage failed, however, the girl merely returned to her own people. She and her former husband would eventually find new partners. If the wife died, the husband usually married one of her sisters or cousins, thereby keeping the two families united.[12]

Several ceremonies were concerned with death. There was a strong belief in a future life, although the other world was thought to be similar to the present one. There, the individual would go about his daily tasks but would be successful in every undertaking.[13] Death was not just the concern of the immediate family but of the entire society and related groups as well. With many of his possessions, the deceased was either cremated or buried the day after death. A week later the remainder of his possessions were burned and gifts distributed. This ceremony was designed to speed the departed on his way to the afterworld. A year later a mourning ceremony was held. The deceased's family spent weeks preparing for this event, collecting food and making baskets to give away.

For a week, members of related groups conducted special rites.[14]

While coming-of-age, marrying, and dying were important events, other kinds of celebrations also took place, such as the eagle-killing ceremony. Eagles were captured at an early age, reared to maturity, and then killed in a special rite. With the birds firmly grasped in their hands, the special participants (in some instances only religious leaders) danced and sang until the eagles died of suffocation. The birds were then plucked and either buried or cremated. Thought to contain magic properties, the feathers were used to decorate images of the dead or were made into special dancing skirts that were worn at the mourning ceremonies and at other occasions.[15]

While the Indians of southern California exhibited cultural uniformity, they were not politically unified. Shoshonean-speakers (even those of the same language division) were divided into many autonomous lineages—kin groups whose members considered themselves biologically related because they could trace their descent in a direct line from a founding ancestor.[16] The lineage represented the basic political unit among most of southern California's Indians,[17] for it possessed all the necessary governmental procedures for the management of its public affairs. The lineage regulated marriage, the rights of succession and inheritance, residence and kinship rules, the distribution of goods and resources, the observation of proper religious duties, and the recruitment of the necessary manpower for work or warfare.[18]

Although outsiders were sometimes adopted into a lineage, the majority of members were automatically incorporated at birth. Membership, therefore, was primarily based on descent; and since descent was reckoned through males, the lineage was patrilineal. It also served as an exogamous unit in that wives had to come from other lineages. Some Shoshonean lineages, furthermore, were grouped into clans. All lineages that shared a common founding ancestor formed a clan; and since clan members considered themselves biologically related, they could not intermarry. The clan, therefore, also served as an exogamous unit. But it also had other functions in that it temporarily brought people together for ceremonial, economic, or military purposes. The moiety concept was also present among some peoples. It separated all the lineages and clans of a language division into halves, men and women of the same half being prohibited from marrying for incest reasons.[19]

While some of the Yuman-speakers, such as the Quechan and Mohave, were the only peoples of southern California to develop centralized political systems, they too may once have been divided into politically autonomous lineages. The development of centralized organizations perhaps took place when they changed their economic orientation from hunting and gathering to agriculture. Whereas the lineage may have been the most efficient organization for exploiting natural resources, a larger aggregation was needed for an agricultural economy.[20]

Until white contact, however, most of southern California's Indians remained hunters and gatherers. One of the most favorable regions for such a people was located between the coastal plain and the Colorado Desert. Extending from the San Gabriel and San Bernardino mountains in a southeasterly direction is a corridor. Flanked on the east by the San Jacinto and Santa Rosa mountains and on the west by the Santa Ana Mountains, it funnels into the Borrego Valley and onto the Colorado Desert. Within this corridor, three language divisions of the Shoshonean subfamily converged: the Cahuilla, the Luiseño, and the Cupeño (see endpaper map).[21]

The Cahuilla were divided into several lineages and clans. Cahuilla lineages in the San Gorgonio Pass, for example, considered themselves a single entity based on genealogical relationships, a similar dialect, ceremonial cooperation, and territorial claim. They called themselves

Wanakik. This entity was clearly a clan, consisting of about ten lineages.[22] Besides the Wanakik there were other clans located in the adjacent mountains and deserts, but they were made up of fewer than ten lineages. Since they resided in areas where food resources were less abundant than in the San Gorgonio Pass, smaller clan units were needed to exploit the land. Among all the Cahuilla, there were at least seven clans and perhaps several more,[23] comprising some eighty lineages.[24]

Every Cahuilla clan had a recognized parent lineage from which all others were thought to have segmented, and the leader of this lineage was considered the nominal head of the clan. His authority, however, was limited to presiding over a council of lineage leaders when the clan acted as a unit. The clan functioned when its territory was being infiltrated by nonclan members, when large hunting activities were undertaken, when intraclan disputes developed, when a large labor force was needed, and when the participation of all the lineages was required for ceremonial purposes.[25]

Cahuilla clans were divided into exogamous moieties, the Wildcat and the Coyote. That the Cahuilla divided themselves into halves indicates that they had a concept of their "wholeness." Indeed, all Cahuilla realized that they were members of a distinct cultural and linguistic entity, even though this entity had no functions.[26] The Cahuilla comprised about six thousand persons by the middle of the eighteenth century.[27]

Even though the Cahuilla possessed definite superlineage structures and concepts, it was within the politically autonomous lineage of about seventy-five persons [28] that the individual found his identity and security. The lineage headman, called the *net*, occupied a position that theoretically passed in a direct line from father to son. With the position went important responsibilities, such as maintaining and protecting a ceremonial bundle containing sacred property. The duties of the net included adjudicating disputes between lineage members, selecting areas for hunting and food gathering, representing the lineage at clan meetings, and remembering group boundaries and individual ownership rights.[29]

The net was assisted by the *paxaa* who had ceremonial, administrative, and judicial duties. He saw to it that no lineage member behaved in a way offensive to the ceremonial bundle. He assisted the net in lineage and clan meetings and served as his messenger, communicating to the people important economic, political, and religious decisions. A ritual expert, the paxaa was responsible for organizing and directing all ceremonies. He also led community hunting parties and was responsible for the distribution of food.[30]

Individuals who possessed supernatural power made up the *puvalam* association,[31] and it was to this organization that the people turned when in want of food or assistance. By drawing the image of an acorn, for example, a member of the puvalam insured that the crop would become available. Animals would present themselves to hunters and rain would commence or terminate under the power of the puvalam. As lineage shamans, members of the organization also had the power to cure those suffering from natural or supernatural ills. Furthermore, since no important political decisions were made without first consulting the association and since the net and paxaa were usually members, the puvalam also formed a political organization that regulated many, if not most, of the lineage's important affairs. It seems to have been the main governing institution of the Cahuilla lineage.[32]

Unlike the Cahuilla, the Luiseño apparently did not have moieties,[33] and there was no name that identified all Luiseño-speakers. This indicates that they lacked a conception of themselves as one people. Yet the Luiseño formed a language division that numbered about four thousand persons by the middle of the eighteenth century.[34] As with the Cahuilla, they were divided into several lineages, each lineage having exclusive hunting and gathering rights to its own localized region. But unlike the Cahuilla, lineages from different clans tended to group themselves together, forming endogamous territorial units that had political functions. Marriage mates were found within the territory; and in times of war, all the lineages acted as a whole.[35] Along with the Juaneño, who spoke a related dialect,[36] the Luiseño may have been divided into fifty such territorial units.[37]

The lineage, however, remained the basic political group of the Luiseño. The position of the headman was hereditary, passing from father to son, although an incompetent could be bypassed. Known as the *not*, he received his authority from a ceremonial bundle. Usually he was a generous elder who knew all the traditions and ceremonial procedures of the lineage. Assisting him was the paxaa, a shaman of repute and a specialist in ritual activities.[38]

Occupying an extremely important position in the Luiseño lineage was a secret association, the *pumelum*. It consisted of a select group of men who, having achieved mastery over their social and material environments, possessed *ayelkwi* or knowledge-power.[39] Since lineage officials were always men of great ayelkwi, they were always members of the association. The pumelum seems to have been the central governing body of the Luiseño lineage, since it regulated may public affairs. For instance, upon the death of any lineage official, the association determined if the hereditary heir was fit to assume the duties of the office. In some cases, it encouraged a better qualified individual to accept the position. Perhaps its most significant role was in determining when the lineage went to war. Because its importance was enhanced during times of conflict, the pumelum had a vested interest in perpetuating interlineage hostility.[40]

Surrounded by the Luiseño to the west, the Cahuilla to the east and north, and the Diegueño to the south, were the Cupeño.[41] At one time, they may have shared a common homeland, perhaps in the desert, with the Cahuilla, or perhaps they were once a clan within a large Cahuilla-Cupeño language division.[42] But given the differences in the Cahuilla and Cupeño languages, the separation must have taken place far in the past.[43] By the middle of the eighteenth century, they had long departed from their ancestral homeland and had settled in the fertile Valle de San José.[44] The formation of this later Cupeño population, numbering only about five hundred persons,[45] may have resulted from the three "original" Cupeño lineages, all of the Coyote moiety, intermarrying with Luiseño lineages and with Diegueño and Cahuilla lineages of the Wildcat moiety.[46]

At or near the village of Kupa (Agua Caliente) resided the three "original" Cupeño lineages plus two of Cahuilla, one of Luiseño, and three of Diegueño origin. These lineages represented both the Wildcat and Coyote moieties, so the men of Kupa could marry within the village. But at the other main Cupeño village, Wilakal (San Ysidro), both lineages were of the Wildcat moiety, so the men had to look for wives elsewhere, presumably at Kupa;[47] in this respect Wilakal was clearly dependent upon Kupa. It was probably politically subordinate as well, since the most influential Cupeño lineage, *Kavalim,* was located at Kupa.[48]

The lineage headman, or *naat,* was the keeper of the ceremonial bundle, and he was responsible for food gathering activities, feasts, and ceremonies. His office, while nominally hereditary, was sometimes passed on to a younger brother or an uncle in a collateral line. The headman was supposed to be very generous, to know all ceremonial procedures, and to be a good song leader. Assisting him was the *kutvuvuc* who announced events, sang at ceremonies, and helped keep order. His duties, however, were reserved for lineages other than his own. The *paxa* was another lineage official whose duties were largely ceremonial. He was appointed by the naat and was often a member of the *pulum* association. This body consisted of individuals who had special faculties to hear and understand all sorts of natural phenomena.[49]

Residing in an extremely fertile valley, containing greatly desired hot springs, the Cupeños may have experienced more conflicts with their neighbors than most groups, and it was probably for defense that Cupeño lineages became tightly unified.[50] Their most trusted neighbors were Cahuillas from Los Coyotes Canyon. Located a few miles to the northeast of Cupeño territory, the canyon was the home of the *Wiwiistam* clan, consisting of five mountain Cahuilla lineages residing in as many settlements. Their principal village was called Wiliya.[51] Oral tradition, stating that people from the canyon were responsible for reviving Cupeño society after it had been decimated by enemies, indicates a long and very close relationship between the Cupeño and Los Coyotes Cahuillas.[52]

In all of southern California, interlineage conflicts may have been frequent, but they were not prolonged affairs and the loss of life was usually insignificant. They developed mainly over territorial infractions and usually took place when food was scarce.[53] For those whose territory was penetrated, there was reason for enmity. But retaliation rather than a desire for plunder or a need to achieve distinction was the goal when a lineage took up arms.[54] Since many of the lineage peoples of southern California were linked by reciprocity arrangements, however, there was much peaceful interaction. In the southern portion of the region, there was a regular exchange of gifts. Shell money, eagle-feather skirts, and various other items passed between mountain Cahuilla, Cupeño, Luiseño, and Diegueño lineages.[55] Similarly, to the north, all the people from the San Gorgonio Pass west to the Pacific Ocean, including the Wanakik Cahuilla, Serrano, Luiseño, and Gabrielino, were bound together in a loose ceremonial union.[56]

Many lineages were also joined in an economic network. Extending from the Colorado and Gila rivers to the Pacific Ocean, this network allowed for the transfer of any number of goods. Plain barter was the most prevalent way in which items were exchanged, although shell money, the origins of which seem to have been Santa Catalina Island, sometimes was used. While none of the lineage-organized peoples of southern California engaged in extensive trading, some, if fortunate enough to be situated along trade routes, acted as middlemen. It was, however, only after the "purchased" items had been incorporated into the general body of the lineage's trading goods that they were "resold." [57] Long-distance overland trading seems to have been limited to the Mohave who periodically sent expeditions from their homeland on the Colorado River to the Pacific Coast. They traded for olivella shells and beads which often found their way to the Pueblo Indians along the Rio Grande.[58] There was also a considerable traffic between the Shoshonean-speakers along the coast and those on the nearby islands. From Santa Catalina came goods made of steatite, such as cooking pots, ceremonial bowls, pipes, and small animal sculptures. Sea otter skins were also supplied to the mainland.[59]

Most trading activity in southern California was more localized. The Cahuilla supplied the Diegueño with roots, bulbs, cattail sprouts, yucca leaves, mescal, pine nuts, manzanita berries, chokecherries, and mesquite beans.[60] The Cahuilla received gourd rattles from the Quechan and basketry caps and conical burden baskets from the Chemehuevi.[61] The Gabrielino traded to the Serrano shell beads, dried fish, sea otter pelts, steatite vessels in exchange for acorns, deer hides, and seed foods.[62] The Diegueño supplied acorns to the Mohave; tobacco, acorns, baked mescal roots, yucca fiber, sandals, baskets, carrying nets, and eagle feathers to the Kamia; acorns to the Quechan; and eagle feathers to the Cocopa. In turn, the Diegueño received salt from the Cocopa; gourd seeds from the Mohave; vegetal foods and salt from the Kamia.[63] The Mohave delivered gourds and eagle feathers to the Quechan and received eagle and chicken hawk down from the Chemehuevi.[64] The Kamia got tobacco from the Quechan and shells from the Cocopa.[65] And the Cupeño and Los Coyotes Cahuillas regularly exchanged goods through the use of shell money.[66]

It seems, then, that the political fragmentation of the Indian peoples of southern California did not prevent them from establishing a wide range of contacts. Indeed, by the middle of the eighteenth century, marriage, ceremonial, and trade ties had extended their physical horizons far beyond their own immediate, localized territories. And in a few decades, their mental horizons would also be greatly expanded as white strangers began to arrive and settle in their territories.

Foreign Influence

From the time Juan Rodríguez Cabrillo sailed into San Diego Bay in 1542, more than two centuries elapsed before Spanish colonization was undertaken. During this time, Spanish and other European vessels dropped anchor or were wrecked in southern California waters, thus bringing Indians and whites into brief face-to-face encounters. The Europeans, however, were probably not an impressive lot, being limited in numbers, suffering from scurvy and other diseases, and having little to offer in the way of trade goods. But in the two hundred years, the Indians of southern California acquired a certain amount of knowledge about Europeans, and it is unlikely that local Diegueño-speakers expressed shock or fear when four Spanish contingents, two by land and two by water, joined forces at San Diego in the summer of 1769. Of the hundred or so foreigners who arrived, half were unfit for service owing to the hardships they had suffered in reaching Alta California.[1]

In July the Spanish established Mission San Diego de Alcalá (see map 1), the first to be founded in Alta California. A month later, when a group of Diegueños entered the grounds, apparently intent on stealing whatever they could find, the Spanish guards opened fire, killing three and forcing the rest to flee. Thereafter, the Indians kept their distance, and five months later the padres had yet to perform their first baptism.[2] Four years later only eighty-three Indians had been baptized and only twelve marriage ceremonies conducted. The converts, or neophytes as the Spaniards called them, along with those undergoing the catechism, lived in a village constructed near the

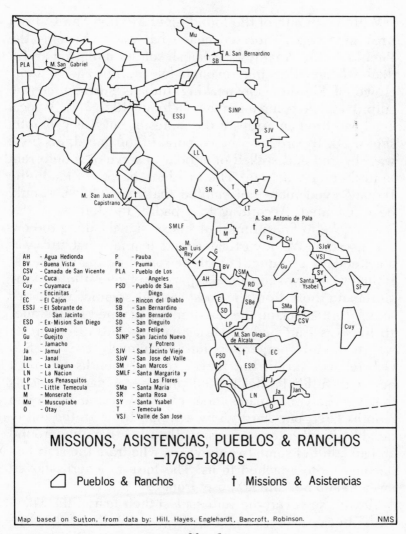

MISSIONS, ASISTENCIAS, PUEBLOS & RANCHOS
— 1769–1840 s —

◻ Pueblos & Ranchos   † Missions & Asistencias

AH - Agua Hedionda
BV - Buena Vista
CSV - Canada de San Vicente
Cu - Cuca
Cuy - Cuyamaca
E   - Encinitas
EC - El Cajon
ESSJ - El Sobrante de
      San Jacinto
ESD - Ex-Mision San Diego
G   - Guajome
Gu - Guejito
J   - Jamacho
Ja - Jamul
Jan - Janal
LL - La Laguna
LN - La Nacion
LP - Los Penasquitos
LT - Little Temecula
M   - Monserate
Mu - Muscupiabe
O   - Otay

P   - Pauba
Pa - Pauma
PLA - Pueblo de Los
      Angeles
PSD - Pueblo de San
      Diego
RD - Rincon del Diablo
SB - San Bernardino
SBe - San Bernardo
SD - San Dieguito
SF - San Felipe
SJNP - San Jacinto Nuevo
       y Potrero
SJV - San Jacinto Viejo
SJoV - San Jose del Valle
SM - San Marcos
SMLF - Santa Margarita y
       Las Flores
SMa - Santa Maria
SR - Santa Rosa
SY - Santa Ysabel
T   - Temecula
VSJ - Valle de San Jose

Map based on Sutton, from data by: Hill, Hayes, Englehardt, Bancroft, Robinson.   NMS

Map 1

mission.[3] In August 1774 the mission was moved farther inland,[4] its original location being agriculturally unproductive (see pl. 1). It fared little better at its new site; and for economic reasons, the neophytes were allowed to live in their own villages with the obligation of attending mass on Sundays.[5]

Within a month of the founding of Mission San Gabriel Arcángel (map 1), located near what was to become the Pueblo de Los Angeles, a Spanish soldier molested an Indian woman. Seeking revenge for the outrage, a large crowd of Shoshonean-speaking Indians surrounded the culprit and a companion on October 10, 1771. A local headman fired an arrow at the molester but was promptly shot dead. By order of the corporal of the guard, his head was severed and spiked on a pole to serve as a deterrent to further such action.[6] The incident, however, made the Indians even more determined that the Spanish should be eliminated. According to a padre, the following day "we awoke to find plumes of smoke signals along the entire horizon. We investigated and learned that this was a general . . . [council] of all the sourrounding rancherías [villages], convoked to make peace between those of the sierra and those from the coast, mortal enemies up to this time." [7] An attack on the mission was planned for October 16 but was canceled when a Spanish contingent, on its way to found another mission, fortuitously arrived. San Gabriel was saved, but it was several months before it began to fulfill its designated purpose. A padre laments that the Indians "made themselves so scarce that even months later, one hardly saw a single Indio in the entire neighborhood, except occasionally a boy hanging around and an adult of some twenty years, who from the start had become quite attached to us. The local ranchería moved away to another site far away from us." [8]

Slowly, however, the Indians lost their fear of the Spaniards. Because those residing in the vicinity of the mission were sometimes in short supply of seed and game and because they were often prevented by other groups from traveling to the coast to fish, they turned to the mission for food.[9] Apparently, *pozole*, a porridge made of barley, beans, and other ingredients, which the Spaniards served to the neophytes, became greatly desired by the unconverted Indians. As one Franciscan put it, "these Indians are usually caught by the mouth." [10] By October

1773 sixty-three had been baptized at San Gabriel.[11] The neophytes were required to live near the mission; but when an individual sought to visit his kinsmen or to hunt for acorns, he was usually given a specified number of days in which to do so. As a rule, at least in the early years of the mission, most neophytes returned, and some even brought back kinsmen.[12] San Gabriel eventually became one of the most prosperous of all California's twenty-one missions, incorporating Indians from at least four language divisions,[13] including some Cahuillas (see pl. 2).[14]

The region between San Gabriel and San Diego remained under Indian control for some time. Reporting in 1775, a Spanish soldier states that "the Indians of the numerous villages in the intervening territory are habitually restless, and commit hostile acts . . . when parties pass near them without an escort large enough to be formidable to these savages." [15] This discontent was most acute in the San Diego area. Shortly after the feast of Our Seraphic Father San Francisco, held at Mission San Diego on October 3, 1775, in which sixty Indians were baptized, two neophytes fled into the mountains to the east. Traveling from village to village, they mustered support for an assault on the mission and the nearby military presidio. The neophytes had come to the conclusion that Christianity was detrimental to Indian interests and sought to rid the region of its propagators.[16]

About one o'clock in the morning of November 4, perhaps as many as eight hundred Diegueño Indians,[17] representing some forty villages, quietly surrounded the mission and the presidio. The attack on the presidio was called off, but the Indians entered the mission grounds undetected. They looted the church, set it and other buildings afire, and captured one of the missionaries. They took him to an arroyo, stripped him of his clothes, shot him some twenty times with arrows, and then smashed in his head with large stones. Two Spanish artisans were also killed, and two soldiers were wounded. The fighting continued until daybreak when the Indians withdrew, fearing the soldiers from the presidio would soon arrive.[18]

Shortly after the attack, the Spanish apprehended seven Indians, including two neophytes. Both were whipped and one died from the punishment. In January 1776 the Spanish struck at least twice at the village of San Luis, capturing a few Indians, including neophytes, and recovering some of the stolen property. The principal Indian leaders of the attack, however, were never seen again.[19]

Mission San Juan Capistrano (see map 1), located about halfway between San Gabriel and San Diego, was founded in October 1775 but was abandoned for a year because of the Indian troubles at San Diego. Three weeks after mission work resumed, a soldier assaulted the wife of a local headman, but Father Junípero Serra had the culprit removed and no serious complications developed from the incident.[20] In fact, the Shoshonean-speaking Indians in the vicinity of the mission proved to be extremely peaceful and very curious. Because the arts and crafts introduced by the Spaniards were regarded as new manifestations of ayelkwi or knowledge power, many Indians were attracted to the missionaries.[21] By December 1777 the padres had baptized forty.[22]

While the primary plan for the colonization of Alta California called for a string of coastal missions and presidios, inland settlement was also planned. From the time Father Francisco Garcés first visited the Yuma-speaking Indians (see pl. 3) along the Río Gila in 1768, he had urged Spanish authorities to establish missions in the region. In fact, a Quechan chief, Palma, had asked Garcés to send him missionaries.[23] Settlement on the Colorado, however, did not begin until 1780 when four padres, twenty settlers, twelve laborers, twenty-one soldiers, along with wives and children, arrived from Mexico. Two pueblos were constructed on the west side of the Colorado, and house lots and fields were distributed to the settlers. Those Indians converted to Christianity were also to receive land

and were to become full-fledged members of the pueblo communities. While the padres were to engage in missionary work, their duties were limited to spiritual matters. Unlike their coastal colleagues, they possessed no political control over the neophytes.[24]

It was not long before the Quechans came to question the wisdom of allowing foreigners to settle in their territory, especially since they lost some of their best agricultural land. On July 17, 1781, the Quechans struck, killing more than thirty Spaniards, including the four priests. The rest of the colonists were made prisoners but were eventually recovered by two military expeditions from Mexico. The leaders of the attack, however, were never apprehended, and Indian societies on the Colorado remained free from Spanish control. Neither mission nor pueblo was ever again founded by the Spanish in the area, and, most significant, the route into California from Sonora was closed.[25]

Mission San Gabriel continued to have its share of difficulties. During the month of October 1785 a neophyte, Nicolás José, convinced a young woman shaman named Toypurina that the Spanish should be eliminated. Toypurina gained the support of six villages, and during the night of the twenty-fifth, a party of Indians entered the mission grounds. Because Toypurina was to have killed the missionaries by her special powers before the attack, the Indians would only have to contend with the soldiers. The plot, however, was discovered, and eleven Indians were arrested, including Toypurina, Nicolás José, and two local headmen. At the trial of the ringleaders, Nicolás José stated that he had planned the attack because the padres were preventing him from practicing his old traditions and ceremonies. Toypurina told her inquisitors that "I hate the padres and all of you for living here on my native soil . . . for trespassing upon the land of my forefathers and despoiling our tribal domains." Nicolás José and the two headmen were sent in irons to the presidio at San

Diego, while the rest of the male prisoners were released with twenty lashes each. Toypurina was sentenced to exile at Mission San Carlos in northern California.[26]

Of the five missions founded in the extreme southern end of Alta California, San Luis Rey de Francia (see pl. 4), established in June 1798 and located about halfway between San Diego and San Juan Capistrano, had the most auspicious beginning (see map 1). In six months the two resident priests baptized more than two hundred Indians of all ages and blessed thirty-four marriages. And by the close of 1802 the Indian population associated with the mission had passed the five-hundred mark.[27] Much of the mission's success must be attributed to Father Antonio Peyri whose personal qualities apparently endeared him to many of the local Indians.[28] Also contributing to his success was the hostility that existed between many of the Luiseño lineages, making it virtually impossible for them to unite in opposition to mission pressure.[29]

Although most of southern California's missions were not as initially successful as San Luis Rey, eventually all began to grow and prosper. Because the Spanish government made few land grants to private individuals, the missionaries could make use of practically all the land they wanted. Titles were held by the Spanish crown since the missions were regarded as temporary establishments. Fixed boundaries were not deemed necessary, and the general area controlled by each mission was arranged by agreement between church and civil authorities. The missionaries sought as much land as they thought they could administer.[30]

Most of the territory controlled by the missions was organized into ranchos. San Gabriel, for example, came to support seventeen *ranchos* for raising cattle and horses, while fifteen were established for sheep, goats, and pigs.[31] Among the ranchos were San Pasqual, Santa Anita, Azusa, San Francisquito, Cucamonga, San Antonio, San Gorgonio, Yucaipa, Jurupa, Guapa, Rincon, Chino, and San José.[32]

In May 1810 a party of missionaries, soldiers, and neophytes from San Gabriel established a rancho in the San
Bernardino Valley. The local Shoshonean-speaking Indians called the area Guachama and were scattered about
in numerous villages.[33] Structures were erected, and the
party returned to San Gabriel, leaving a neophyte called
Hipolito in charge. The settlement, taking its name from
this Indian, became known as Apolitano or Politana. The
beginning of Politana, however, was fraught with difficulties; just two years after its founding, it was destroyed
by hostile Indians. The attack came in *el año de los tem-
blores* (the year of the earthquakes), and perhaps was undertaken to appease the responsible spirits. Most of the
resident neophytes were killed, but a few survived and
remained at Politana.[34] In 1819 they invited the padres at
San Gabriel to come again to the valley, and soon a mission station, or *asistencia,* was constructed about eight
miles from the original site (see map 1).[35]

Mission San Luis Rey also established an asistencia.
Called San Antonio de Pala, it was founded in 1816 on the
San Luis Rey River, some twenty miles from the mission
(see map 1).[36] In 1818 it was reported that about three
hundred adults and a large number of children had been
baptized at the station.[37] Writing in 1827, Father Peyri
mentions that "at a distance of seven leagues, toward the
northeast, at the entry of the Sierra Madre, the Mission
has a station called San Antonio de Pala, with a church
dwelling, and granaries with a few fields where wheat,
corn, beans, garbanzos and other leguminous plants are
grown." [38]

While most of the inland possessions of Mission San
Luis Rey were located within the linguistic boundaries of
the Luiseño, such as the rancho of Temeco or Temecula,
located northwest of Pala,[39] a rancho was also established
in Cupeño territory. Peyri notes that "to the east . . .
there is another district reserved for the sheep, which is
famed for its warm spring." [40] The spring was at the village of Kupa, and sick neophytes from the mission were

often taken there for treatment.[41] A few miles to the southeast of Kupa, Mission San Diego established an asistencia called Santa Isabel (see map 1). In 1822 it had a chapel, granary, and several houses. Under its jurisdiction were 450 Indians, mostly Diegueño-speakers, who lived within a few miles of the station (see pl. 5).[42]

The Spanish mission and the territory it controlled formed a self-supporting economic community. Its main occupation was agriculture, which included the growing and processing of wheat, barley, corn, peas, beans, and various other crops. The necessary equipment for keeping the mission operational was produced in the shops where neophytes made bricks, tiles, pottery, shoes, saddles, hats, clothes, candles, and soap. Neophytes also did tanning, shearing, spinning, and blacksmithing tasks. Theoretically, all members of the mission community, Indian and Spaniard alike, shared in what was produced. There were no wages; and when goods were sold, the money was used to purchase items that the mission could not produce itself, such as dry goods.[43]

At sunrise a bell called all those over nine years old to mass. Instruction in Spanish often followed, and then breakfast was served, consisting of *atole*, a kind of gruel made of corn or grain that had been roasted before it was ground. After breakfast, the men went about their various tasks either in the fields, among the livestock, or in the shops, while the girls and women did the domestic chores. For lunch there was pozole. After a two-hour rest period, work was resumed until five o'clock when the entire neophyte community went to church for the recitation of the *Doctrina* and religious devotions. Supper, again consisting of atole, was served at six, and the remainder of the evening was free time so long as it was not spent in activities offensive to the padres.[44]

A self-supporting, economic unit, the mission also formed a political community that was separate from and semi-independent of the Spanish civil government.[45] For

example, although the governor of California issued a
special decree in 1779 stating that the Indians at every
mission had the annual privilege of electing from their
own ranks two *alcaldes* or magistrates and two *regidores*
or councilmen,[46] the Franciscans saw to it that only the
most acculturated and favored neophytes became mission
officers. This point is emphasized by a neophyte, Pablo
Tac, in his personal account of life at Mission San Luis
Rey.

The Fernandino Father, as he was alone and very accustomed
to the usages of the Spanish soldiers, seeing that it would be
very difficult for him alone to give orders to that people, and,
moreover, people that had left the woods just a few years before, therefore appointed alcaldes from the people themselves
that knew how to speak Spanish more than the others and were
better than the others in their customs. There were seven of
these alcaldes, with rods as a symbol that they could judge the
others. The captain like the Spanish, always remaining captain,
but not ordering his people about as of old, when they were still
gentiles. The chief of the alcaldes was called the general. He
knew the names of each one, and when he took something he
then named each person by his name. In the afternoon, the alcaldes gather at the house of the missionary. They bring the
news of that day. . . .

With the laborers goes a Spanish majordomo and others, neophyte alcaldes, to see how the work is done, to hurry them if
they are lazy, so that they will soon finish what was ordered,
and to punish the guilty or lazy one who leaves his plow and
quits the field keeping on with his laziness.[47]

Foreign visitors were often very critical of the alcaldes.
One notes that "the priests appoint officers to superintend
the natives, while they are at work. . . . They are called
alcaides [*sic*], and are very rigid in exacting the perfor-
mance of the allotted tasks, applying the rod to those who
fall short of the portion of labor assigned them." [48] Another observer claims that the alcaldes were chosen from
the most lazy, the padres being of the opinion that they
took great pleasure in making the others work. "They carried a wand to denote their authority, and what was more

terrible, an immense scourge of raw hide, about ten feet in length, plaited to the thickness of an ordinary man's waist! They did a great deal of chastisement, both by and without orders." [49] Still another visitor to California reports that while the majority of the neophytes attend mass on their own, "it was not unusual to see numbers of them driven along by alcaldes, and under the whip's lash forced to the very doors of the sanctuary." [50]

The alcalde occupied an intermediate position in a highly stratified social system. Pablo Tac recalls:

In the mission of San Luis Rey de Francia the Fernandino Father is like a king. He has his pages, alcaldes, majordomos, musicians, soldiers. . . . The pages are for him and for the Spanish and Mexican, English and Anglo-American travelers. The alcaldes to help him govern all the people. . . . The majordomos are in the distant districts, almost all Spaniards. The musicians of the mission for the holy days and all the Sundays and holidays of the year, with them the singers, all Indian neophytes. Soldiers so that nobody does injury to Spaniards or to Indians; there are ten of them and they go on horseback.[51]

"Thus every one had his particular vocation," reports an American visitor to San Luis Rey, "and each department its official superintendent, or alcalde; these were subject to the supervision of one or more Spanish *mayordomos*, who were appointed by the missionary-father, and consequently under his immediate direction." [52] In the interior, the missionaries also appointed Indians to positions of authority by selecting prominent lineage headmen to serve as *capitanes* of mission districts. The duties of the capitanes consisted in keeping order and protecting mission property.[53]

Reports issued by the Franciscans in 1814 indicate that resistance to Spanish acculturation efforts was prevalent at all the southern missions. At San Diego, for example, the neophytes exhibited little interest in learning the Spanish language. "To get them to talk Spanish," admits a padre, "we exhort and threaten them with punishment, and in the case of the young, we punish them from time to time." [54] At San Luis Rey the Indians continued to make intoxicating drinks from the jimsonweed,[55] while "idolatry" was still being practiced at San Gabriel.[56] The padres at San Juan Capistrano note that "these Indians retain all the customs of their ancestors." [57] And at San Diego the neophytes were still conducting the eagle-killing ceremony.[58]

That Christianity was often only superficially adopted by many neophytes is quite apparent. For instance, at Mission San Juan Capistrano in 1817, a dying thirty-five-year-old neophyte refused to confess and partake of the holy sacrament. When asked the reason for his refusal, he replied in anger "because I will not. . . . If I have been deceived whilst living, I do not wish to die in the delusion!" According to a witness, Father Gerónimo Boscana, this kind of defiance was not a rare occurrence, for "these accounts generally conform to each other in substance. . . . As all their operations are accompanied by stratagems and dissimulation, they easily gain our confidence, and at every pass we are deluded." [59]

Since the neophytes either lived in their own villages or in villages constructed near the missions, the padres faced enormous problems of control. And it seems evident that lineage officials were able to maintain a certain amount of authority over the neophytes. A padre recalls:

A missionary, of the mission of San Luis Rey, who had baptized several adults, the youngest of whom had reached his fiftieth year, attempted to explain, after the ceremony was concluded, the sort of life which they were to observe for the future; and he told them what they were to do to avoid the influence of Satan. By invoking the sweet names of Jesus and Mary, he said, and by the sign of the Holy Cross, well performed, we destroy the power of the devil, and drive out all unholy thoughts. A *satrap*, or governor, of one of the rancherías, smilingly observed to the others, "See how this Padre cheats us! Who believes that the devil will leave us, by the sign of the cross? If it were to be done by dancing, as authorized by Chinigchinich, he would depart; but that he will do so, by the means which *he* says, I do not believe!" The others united with him in laughter, and appeared unimpressed with the efficacy of such ceremony.[60]

Discontent with mission life was expressed in other ways, fugitivism being the most prevalent. Dislike for mission work and discipline, resentment at forced incorporation and conversion, and frustration caused by overcrowding forced many Indians to flee the missions.[61] Some returned on their own accord while others were brought in by force, so the mission population was never static. But as time went on more neophytes came to leave the missions than returned.[62] Those who were recovered by force were usually subjected to punishment. Explains one Franciscan:

A man, boy, or a woman, runs away or does not return from the excursion, so that other neophytes must be sent after them. When such a one is brought back to the Mission, he is reproached for not having heard holy Mass on a day of obligation. He is made to see that he has of his own free will taken upon himself this and other Christian duties, and he is warned that he will be chastized if he repeats the transgression. He runs away again, and again he is brought back. This time he is chastized with the lash or with the stocks. If this is not sufficient, as is the case with some who disregard a warning, he is made to feel the shackles, which he must wear three days while at work.[63]

For many padres, the prime concern was not that they had lost Christians but that the ex-neophytes would encourage interior groups to assume an anti-Spanish stance. Writing in 1819, Father Marino Payeras exclaims:

The spirit of insubordination, which is rampant in the world at large, has reached the Christian Indians. A considerable number have withdrawn from the mild rule of the friars, and have become one body with the savages with whom they carry out whatever evil their heart and malevolent soul dictates. . . . The spirit of insolence and idleness is spreading and affecting even the more staid of the neophytes. . . . From day to day the danger of an attack from united apostates and gentiles is growing.[64]

It became apparent to many missionaries that if they were ever successfully to colonize and Christianize southern California, a string of missions and presidios, paralleling those on the coast, must be established in the interior. The new settlements would serve as outposts for further colonization and for apprehending runaways. In 1821 Father Payeras recommended to his superiors that four sites in the south be the nucleus of a chain of inland missions that would eventually extend the length of California. The asistencia of Santa Isabel, where 450 Indians were already in residence, could easily be converted into a mission. A new site was to be founded north of Santa Isabel and named Guadalupe. The asistencia at Pala lacked nothing except a full-time resident priest. The fourth mission was to be established at the San Bernardino asistencia where two hundred baptized Indians were already living.[65]

Of the four sites, San Bernardino was the most important because of its location near the San Gorgonio Pass. "If the natives would settle down in this region," writes Father Payeras, "it would be much better for all concerned; for them, because they would have a fixed abode, and for us, because it would give us a means of approach to other more distant tribes, especially if we should desire later to establish a route to the Colorado." [66] The Spanish, however, lacked the men and resources to follow through with these plans.

The padres needed an inland string of missions to tap new population centers, for by the beginning of the nineteenth century, the mission population was beginning to decline, in part owing to the high death rate caused by European-introduced diseases. In 1798, for example, diarrhea infected the majority of the neophytes at Mission San Diego.[67] At missions San Juan Capistrano and San Gabriel an unidentified contagious fever killed large numbers in 1801.[68] Five years later San Juan Capistrano was struck with an epidemic of measles that killed more than one hundred Indians.[69] By 1810 what amounted to an epidemic of venereal disease had swept through Mission San Gabriel. Because the mission was located near the Pueblo de Los Angeles and privately owned ranchos, its neo- phytes came into close contact with the *gente de razón* (people of reason), as the Spanish-speaking population of California designated themselves. Between three and four hundred neophytes became infected with the disease.[70] As a result, states a report issued in 1814, "of every four children born, three die in their first or second year while those who survive do not reach the age of twenty-five. If the government does not supply doctors and medicine, Upper California will be without Indians at all." [71]

This was not an exaggeration. In 1817 San Gabriel claimed a total of 1,701 neophytes, but in 1825 the number was down to 1,594. By 1832 it had dropped to 1,320.[72] At San Juan Capistrano, 1,361 neophytes were linked to the mission in 1812. By 1820, however, the fig- ure was 1,064, and in 1830 it had declined to 926.[73] Simi- larly, the highest number of neophytes associated with Mission San Diego was 1,829 in the year 1824. But in 1830 the total had dropped to 1,544.[74] Of all the southern missions, only San Luis Rey was able to keep its Indian population from drastically declining during the 1820s. Reaching a peak of 2,869 neophytes in the year 1826, it still counted 2,819 five years later.[75]

Writing in 1835, an English visitor to California, Dr. Thomas Coulter, speculates on the declining mission pop- ulations.

It is a very extraordinary fact that their decrease is greatly has- tened by the failure of female offspring,—or the much greater number of deaths amongst the females in early youth than among the males . . . the fact, however, of there being a much smaller number of women living than of men, is certain. Infan- ticide, properly so called, is not common, though very frequent recourse is had to the means of producing abortion, chiefly me- chanically . . . and in Upper California, in almost all the mis- sions, a great many of the men cannot find wives. The mission of San Luis Rey is the only remarkable exception. In it the In- dians are stated to be upon the increase, and the women in numbers equal to the men; but my acquaintance with this mission is too limited to enable me to speak of the causes of their momentary escape from what appears to be the inevitable fate of their race in the neighbourhood of white men—a fate from which I fear the Luiseños are not likely to escape.[76]

Political developments in Mexico greatly accelerated the process of mission decline. The Mexican war for independence began in 1810, and immediately the viceroy of New Spain suspended each padre's annual stipend of four hundred pesos. Moreover, the governor of California levied taxes and made forced requisitions upon the missions. The conclusion of the war in 1821 did not improve the situation, for the new government of Mexico was greatly troubled by economic problems and could send only minimum assistance.[77]

Each mission was thrown back on its own resources, and many sustained themselves by selling hides and tallow to American and English sea merchants. Since the Indians did most of the manual and skilled labor in California, they were the economic mainstay of the province.[78] Writes a padre in 1826:

It seems to me that no other person in the nation has shouldered so much of the burden of supporting the government as the Indians have done in supporting this province. . . . This is the situation the Indian is in, for he has ceased to eat and clothe himself so that the province might subsist, and it could not continue in any other way.[79]

Expressing a similar view, another Franciscan asserts that "if there is anything to be done, the Indian has to do it; if he fails to do it nothing will be done. Is anything to be planted? The Indian must do it. Is the wheat to be harvested? Let the Indian come." [80]

It was not, however, the economic importance of the Indian but his servile condition that became the concern of the new revolutionary government in Mexico. Infused with the egalitarian and humanitarian beliefs of the early nineteenth century, the government sought to improve the lot of all Indians within its vast territory.[81] Citizenship and the rights of man were immediately granted, for it was thought that only when the Indian was released from missionary control would he become a useful citizen of Mexico. It was also thought that the Indian would be truly free only when he possessed his own land.[82]

Accordingly, the first Mexican governor of California, issued a Proclamation of Emancipation on July 25, 1826, which stated that certain Indians within the military districts of San Diego, Santa Barbara, and Monterey should be released from mission supervision. To be set free, however, were only those neophytes whom the missionaries thought capable of supporting themselves.[83] Indian response to the proclamation varied from mission to mission, but it is certain that many neophytes took immediate advantage of their new freedom. Writing in October 1827, an Englishman, F. W. Beechey, observes:

In my former visit to this country I remarked that the padres were must mortified at being desired to liberate from the missions all the Indians who bore good characters, and who were acquainted with the art of tilling the ground. In consequence of their remonstrances, the government modified the order, and consented to make the experiment upon a few only at first, and desired that a certain number might be settled in the proposed manner. After a few months' trial, much to his surprise, he found that these people who had been always accustomed to the care and discipline of schoolboys, finding themselves their own masters, indulged freely in all those excesses which it had been the endeavour of their tutors to repress, and that many having gambled away their clothes, implements, and even their lands, were compelled to beg or to plunder in order to support life. They at length became so obnoxious to the peaceable inhabitants, that the padres were requested to take some of them back to the mission, while others who had been guilty of misdemeanor, were loaded with shackles and put to work.[84]

On August 17, 1833, shortly after the government of President Santa Anna and Vice-President Gómez Farías came to power in Mexico, a law secularizing all the missions of Alta and Baja California was created.[85] The governor of California delayed implementing the law until a year later when he produced his own secularization decree. It stated that the padres were to relinquish all secular control over the neophytes and were to perform only religious functions until replaced by parish priests. The missions were to be converted into pueblos and their lands distributed among the neophytes. Each head of a family or adult male over twenty years of age would receive thirty-three acres of land. Half the missions' livestock, tools, and seeds were also to be distributed among the neophytes, but all surplus lands, cattle, and other property would become the responsibility of the administrators of the missions who would be appointed by the governor. Furthermore, the government possessed the right to force the neophytes to work in the vineyards, orchards, and fields that remained undistributed. Indians could not sell or otherwise dispose of their newly acquired property. If an owner died without an heir, his lands would revert to the state.[86]

Secularization ushered in a period of great confusion. At San Luis Rey, for example, Captain Pablo de la Portilla reported only a month after taking charge that "these Indians will do absolutely no work nor obey my orders. In consequence, though the season for sowing the wheat is at hand, and the necessary plows have been prepared, I must suffer the pain of being obliged to suspend work for the want of hands." Portilla complains that "nothing would suit them, nothing would change their ideas. . . . All with one voice would shout, 'We are free! We do not want to obey! We do not want to work!'" [87]

In November 1835 a group of neophytes from Mission San Luis Rey traveled to San Diego and complained to officials that the new civil administrator of the mission, Pío Pico, had mistreated them. In June of the following year, a neophyte leader, Pablo Apis, was imprisoned by Pico, evidently because Apis had sent a petition to officials in San Diego seeking a redress of Indian grievances. When followers of Apis secured his release, they journeyed to

San Diego and made charges against the administrator. There Apis and four others were detained until sent back to San Luis Rey under guard.[88]

Two years later, Apis and his followers petitioned directly to the governor of California.

The neophytes of this Mission come before Your Honor with the greatest respect and obedience, and represent that we have experienced all the evils which have visited us for many years. We have suffered incalculable losses, for some of which we are in part to be blamed because many of us have abandoned the Mission; but this could be remedied, Your Honor, by imposing some penalty or punishment on those who absent themselves at their own pleasure, and upon those who admit them into their houses for work. We implore this of your merciful heart. Meanwhile we hope Your Honor will listen to our supplication. We plead and we beseech you to deign to attend to this earnest supplication, if it seems just and right, to grant us a Rev. Father for this place. We have been accustomed to the Rev. Fathers and to their manner of managing the duties. We labored under their intelligent directions, and we are obedient to the Fathers according to the regulations, because we considered it was good for us all. Your Honor, we promise you who has the power that, if our petition is granted, we will work as before with more energy. We hope from the kind disposition of Your Honor that we shall receive this grace and favor.[89]

In July 1840 José Antonio Estudillo replaced Pío Pico as administrator of Mission San Luis Rey. Pico and his brother, Andrés, however, provisionally received from the government the Temecula rancho which was claimed by some of the mission's neophytes (see map 1). Opposed to the transaction, Estudillo and eleven neophytes went to Los Angeles and protested to the authorities. While not completely successful in their mission, the neophytes did retain partial control over some of the mission's ranchos, including Pala, Temecula, and San Jacinto.[90]

The neophytes associated with the asistencia of Santa Isabel were not so fortunate, however. In 1839, when the administrator of Mission San Diego, José Joaquin Ortega, first petitioned for the station, Santa Isabel was prospering. According to Father Vicente Pascual Olivas, the locality of Santa Ysabel is not vacant land as the petitioner says in his representation; it is now a Mission with church, cemetery and other requisites of a civilized Pueblo, and the Priest does not reside in it only because of the scarcity of priests. The Indians of the said Mission have their plantings of wheat, barely, corn, beans, peas and other plants for their sustenance, and two vineyards, with their gardens, their horse stock; and in summer their lands occupied with sheep. And if the government should grant this land to the petitioner to what point will it banish the Indians, now 580 souls? The law says the native possessors of the soil are its true owners.[91]

Five years later, however, the asistencia was in ruins and was granted to Ortega and his father-in-law, Eduardo Stokes. Olivas recalls:

In consequence of their not being any possibility of improvement of the ranch at Sta. Isabel belonging to the Mission, all right of the Mission thereto is ceded: there does not exist on the said premises more than a few crumbling walls and two small vineyards with a small number of vines in good condition which are also ceded in consideration of 150 cows killed by Ortega for the neophytes of this Mission.[92]

Ortega also got control over the nearby rancho of Pamó or Santa María (see map 1).[93]

By the time Richard Henry Dana visited California in the mid-1830s, the effects of secularization were already quite visible. In his *Two Years before the Mast* he writes:

Ever since the independence of Mexico, the missions had been going down; until, at last, a law was passed, stripping them of all their possessions, and confining the priests to their spiritual duties, at the same time declaring all the Indians free and independent rancheros. The change in the condition of the Indians was, as may be supposed, only nominal; they are virtually serfs, as much as they ever were. But in the missions the change was complete. The priests have now no power, except in their religious character, and the great possessions of the missions are given over to be preyed upon by the harpies of the civil power, who are sent there in the capacity of *administradores,* to settle up the concerns; and who usually end, in a few years, by making themselves fortunes, and leaving their stewardships worse than they found them.[94]

In 1842 the neophytes at Mission San Luis Rey discussed their problems with a visitor, Duflot de Mofras.

You see captain . . . how miserable we now are; the Fathers cannot protect us, and those in power rob us. To stand by and watch these men take over the missions which we have built; the herds we have tended, and to be exposed incessantly, together with our families, to the worst possible treatment and even death itself, is a tragedy! Would we be blamed if we defend ourselves, and returned to our tribes in the Tulares, taking with us all the live stock that could be led away?[95]

This was no idle threat, for with secularization thousands left the missions. Many trekked east to join interior groups, while others drifted into the towns, especially Los Angeles, to work intermittently and to drink and gamble. Still others found work on the old mission ranchos (map 1) that had become the possessions of prominent Californios as the gente de razón called themselves.

Unlike the Spanish padres and soldiers before them, who had ventured inland on temporary religious and military expeditions, the *rancheros* moved into the interior to stay. Life, however, was often very insecure, especially in the San Diego area. During the 1830s the ranchos were repeatedly harassed by hostile Indians, and there is evidence to suggest that conspiracies were formed between ex-neophytes and nonmission Indians. For example, in 1833 a leader by the name of Tajochi was apparently attempting to unite Quechans from the Colorado River with ex-neophytes from the missions in southern California. An attack on white settlements was to be launched from El Cajon; but before the plan could be executed, Californios from San Diego apprehended, without resistance, Tajochi and other ringleaders. Tried and convicted, Tajochi was assigned to public works activity for two years, while three of his associates received shorter terms of punishment.[96]

Indians from the Cuyamaca Mountains, the Colorado River, and Baja California continued to strike at the ranchos. For example, in 1837 Indians attacked Rancho Jamul (see map 1), located about twenty-two miles southeast of the old mission in which four men were killed and two young girls taken captive. A military command was hastily organized and gave pursuit. Years later a Californio recalls that the

force consisted of 18 regular soldiers, with 30 friendly Lower California Indians, under the noted chief Jatañil: the whole commanded by Alferez Macedonio, who in those days had great repute as a fighter of Indians. We started from Descanso, about 50 miles below the town of San Diego, passing through Tecate, las Juntas, Milquatai, Jacum, Matacawat, Guatay, Cuyamaca valley, round to Valle de las Viejas; being out four months. During this time, we had several encounters with the wild Indians and killed many of them: but finally, at a place known as "Matadero," in the Jacum mountain, . . . our munitions, having fallen into the hands of the Indians, in consequence of the guard of four men in charge of them being overcome, we abandoned our horses at night, after a fight through the whole day, and returned to the Presidio at San Diego. Yumas as well as Cuillamaca Indians were in the battle.

The Indians then living among the Cuyamaca mountains, were still "gentiles": the missions never were able to convert more than one and another, here and there,—could do nothing permanently with them. They were cut up into hostile (several distinct) rancherias, fighting often with each other; were numerous (at Guatay and Cuyamaca Valley), and, in every sense of the word, savage. Little or nothing was known of them at the Presidio or the mission of San Diego; they kept apart from the Indians of San Felipe, Santa Ysabel, and other points, then (more or less) Christianized; and they had little or no intercourse with the white people. Even in going only as far as the Valle de las Viejas, about 33 miles N.E. of the Presidio it was considered dangerous; and the greatest caution was used by soldiers.[97]

In July or August 1839 a party of some three hundred Indians occupied the Otay Rancho, located southeast of San Diego (see map 1). A visitor to California, Don Augustín Janssens, who was at the rancho, claims that these and other Indians were conspiring to recover all the territory lost to the whites.

The Indians of Jacum had made a plan for recovering California, which they claimed belonged to them. I had heard this sev-

eral times by the chiefs, Cartueho and Pedro Pablo. The latter
was more expressive, as he spoke better Spanish, and served as a
spokesman for the others. I told them that they were crazy to
think about things that could never come to pass. But the Indian
replied that I didn't know the connections they had made. He
said they were not alone, but that there were many others
throughout California and in places where they would be least
expected. It seems that this was not mere bragging, because a
warning was received from the north which corroborated what
Pedro Pablo had said.[98]

The Indians remained at Otay for two weeks, finally departing toward the Colorado River. Californios of the area,
instead of organizing a force to challenge the Indians,
withdrew from their ranchos to the relative security of
San Diego.[99]

During the 1830s Indian raiders were also active in the
San Bernardino Valley. Indians from the desert burned
down the asistencia of Mission San Gabriel in 1831.[100]
Rebuilt at once, three years later it was again attacked,
this time by a band of Paiutes under the command of an
ex-neophyte called Perfecto. The raiders were driven off
by the resident neophytes,[101] but in the same year a large
party of Cahuillas stole some horses from the station. A
contingent of twenty Californios gave chase and apparently inflicted casualties in a brief skirmish. But three
years later, Cahuillas again struck at the asistencia, killing
a few neophytes but also losing some of their own men.[102]
As a result of this latest attack, most of the neophytes felt
it expedient to move to San Gabriel. Thus in 1834 the
asistencia of San Bernardino was abandoned.[103]

By the late 1830s, however, rancheros were moving into
the area. Their herds, in turn, became the targets of the
Indian raiders. The extent of the rancheros' vulnerability
can be perhaps most clearly seen in the great horse-
stealing raid of 1839. Walkara, a Ute chief of great skill
and audacity, arrived that summer in the Cajon Pass. With
him were a half a dozen mountain men, including Jim
Beckwourth and Pegleg Smith. Walkara sent Beckwourth
to Rancho del Chino to gain the confidence of the ran-

cheros. Upon returning to the Cajon Pass, he issued information as to the whereabouts and numbers of the great
herds. Divided into small groups, the Indians and their
white allies struck simultaneously at several ranchos, ren-
dezvoused at the Cajon Pass with, according to Pegleg
Smith, five thousand horses, and fled into the Mohave
Desert. And while they were vigorously pursued by a
party of rancheros who were able to kill several of the
raiders, Walkara and his followers supposedly still got
away with about three thousand horses.[104] It seems the
chief's boast that the rancheros were only allowed to remain in the valley by and for his pleasure was not a total
exaggeration.[105]

Chasing Indian horse raiders through the Cajon Pass in
July or August 1845 was an early American resident of
southern California, B. D. Wilson, and a force of eighty
well-mounted and armed Californios. They proceeded
through the pass, up the San Bernardino River, over to
Bear Lake, and then down the Mohave River. Finally,
they came across four Indians, one being a famous
marauder called Joaquin who, according to Wilson,

had been raised as a page of the Church in San Gabriel Mission,
and for his depredations and outlawing, bore on his person the
marks of the Mission, that is, one of his ears cropped off, and
the iron brand on his lip. This is the only instance I ever heard
or saw of this kind; that marking had not been done at the Mission, but at one of its ranches (El Chino) by the Majordomo.
. . . Immediately that he discovered the true nature of things,
he whipped from his quiver an arrow, strung it on his bow, and
left nothing for me to do but shoot him in self defense. We both
discharged our weapons at the same time. . . . His shot took effect in my right shoulder, and mine in his breast.[106]

After pursuing and killing the other three Indians, most
of the Californios proceeded on down the Mohave River,
while Wilson remained in camp with five men to allow
his wound to heal. Two days later the force returned to
camp, having been unable to dislodge a group of Indians
from their fortified positions and having suffered several
casualties. The command then returned to Wilson's ran-

cho at Jurupa, but in a few days, minus some twenty men, set out again.

Our march this time was through the San Gorgonia [*sic*] Pass, our object being this time to capture two renegade San Gabriel neophytes, who had taken up residence among the Cahuillas, and corrupted many of the young men of that tribe, with whom they carried on a constant depredation on the ranchmen of this district. Nothing of note occured on our journey, till arriving at the head of the desert, in the place called Agua Caliente (Hot Springs). We were there met by the Chief of the Cahuillas, whose name was Cabezon (Big Head) with about twenty of his picked followers, to remonstrate against our going upon a campaign against his people, for he had ever been good, and friendly to the whites. I made known to him that I had no desire to wage war on the Cahuillas, as I knew them to be what he said of them, but that I had come with the determination of seizing the two renegade Christians, who were continually depredating on our people. He then tried to frighten me out of the notion of going into his country, alleging that it was sterile, and devoid of grass and water, and then ourselves, and our horses would perish there. I replied, that I had a long experience in that sort of life, and was satisfied that a white man could go wherever an Indian went. I cut the argument short by placing the Chief and his party under arrest, and taking away their arms. He became very much alarmed, cried and begged me not to arrest him, as he had always been a good man.[107]

Cabezon, however, was able to convince Wilson that if he released his brother Adan and twelve men, they would bring in the Indians. A day or two later the severed heads of the renegades were delivered to Wilson. The Californios gave Cabezon and his men all their spare rations and then departed for home.[108]

The individual arrested by Wilson represents a new kind of Indian leader who was then emerging in southern California. Cabezon, while a lineage headman and the dominant figure in the *Kauwicpameauitcem* clan, was, by the mid-1840s, asserting his control over previously ununited desert Cahuilla settlements. He had been encouraged by Californian officials to assume this control and had been issued special papers to legitimize it.[109]

To the west, where the white impact was much greater, this process of political centralization was even more intense. With the incorporation of thousands of Indians into the missions and with the reduction of the aboriginal population as a result of European diseases, many lineages ceased to exist. Those that survived remained as descent groups, but only the most isolated continued to function as independent political units. As on the desert, clusters of lineages were coming under the personal control of powerful, self-made leaders. It seems that most of these leaders, even those who were ex-neophytes, had traditional political positions from which to expand their power. That is, they were either headmen or at least were members of important lineages. The core of their followers, therefore, were probably lineage or clan kinsmen; but they also attracted to their banners ex-neophytes and nonkinsmen from shattered lineages. Thus, they developed personal followings that were not necessarily based on kinship considerations. And although they could not command the allegiance of every member of their language division, some came to control widely scattered settlements.

No longer governing as traditional headmen, these leaders ruled as powerful territorial chiefs. While the religious, judicial, political, and economic duties of the headman were largely undifferentiated, limited, and localized, the functions of the chief consisted in regulating all the society's public affairs. These included negotiating with the whites and neighboring Indian groups, convening council meetings, appointing and dismissing subordinate officials, adjudicating disputes between individuals and villages, and issuing summary punishment that included death. In short, the change from headmanship to chieftainship can be seen as a shift from the *right* to govern based on consensus to the *ability* to rule based on power.[110]

As might be expected, the rise of territorial chiefs profoundly affected inter-Indian and Indian-white relations in southern California. The Spaniards had to deal with relatively powerless headmen who were usually inexperienced in white ways; the Californios and later the Americans had to interact with powerful chiefs who often had years of experience in dealing with white men.

3

Chiefs and Californios

In 1842 the three sons of Antonio María Lugo, the patriarch of a very influential Californian family, were granted Rancho San Bernardino (see map 1). Comprising over 37,000 acres, it had ample room for the establishment of several settlements. José María Lugo erected his dwellings, known as Homolla, near what was to become the town of San Bernardino. José del Carmen Lugo settled close to where the old asistencia was located. And Vincente Lugo built his home near Politana. Also settling on the rancho, at the request of the owners, were several families from New Mexico, under the leadership of one Lorenzo Trujillo.[1] They were given land in the vicinity of Politana and were to protect the rancho against hostile Indians. The following year, however, they moved several miles to the south and took up residence on the domain of another ranchero, Juan Bandini.[2]

Their departure left the rancho undefended, and a few years later, local rancheros and Cahuillas held a conference. Invited, recalls one of Trujillo's followers, were "all the owners of the ranches and the old chief of the Coahuilla Mission Indians, the big president, Juan Antonio, who came with his interpreters and body guard and all together enjoyed a council . . . and established a lasting peace and friendship." [3] Accepting the Lugos' offer to settle on the rancho to protect it from hostile Indians,[4] Antonio built his principal village on a small hill at Politana.[5] Californian authorities issued the chief special papers that authorized him to kill Indian thieves and to recover stolen property.[6]

Little is known of Juan Antonio's early life, except that he was probably born somewhere in the San Jacinto Mountains, perhaps around the year 1783.[7] He was a member of the important *Kostakiktum* lineage,[8] and he may have been appointed *capitán* of the San Jacinto mission district by the padres of San Luis Rey.[9] By 1844 Antonio probably had become the leader of five mountain Cahuilla lineages—*Kostakiktum, Pauatiauitcem, Tepamokiktum, Natcutakiktum,* and *Temexwanic.*[10] Also under his control were ex-neophytes. One, for example, told an army officer in 1854 that he had been taken to Mission San Luis Rey as a boy but had joined Juan Antonio's Cahuillas when the mission was secularized.[11] Furthermore, because large numbers of Cahuillas had been incorporated into Mission San Gabriel, it is likely that many joined Antonio after its collapse. Some remained true to the Christian faith,[12] women often traveling great distances to have their children baptized.[13]

Exactly when Juan Antonio moved to Rancho San Bernardino is not known, but in February 1844 Antonio María Lugo mentioned in a letter that Cahuillas were battling other Indians who had come to run off livestock.[14] Certainly by late 1846 Antonio was providing the Lugos with valuable service, as can be seen in an incident that took place shortly after the Battle of San Pasqual during the Mexican-American War. Early in December 1846, when Stephen W. Kearny and his dragoons crossed the desert from the Colorado River, they were confronted by a force of Californios under the command of Andrés Pico. The ensuing battle left nearly twenty Americans dead and as many wounded, while the Californios suffered only one fatality.[15] After the battle, eleven Californios hid on the Pauma Rancho, an isolated tract of mountain land on the San Luis Rey River (map 1).[16] Several had brought their cattle, sheep, and horses to Pauma to conceal them from the Americans.[17] The rancho had been granted to José Antonio Serrano in 1844,[18] but Indian residential rights had been recognized.[19]

Located on the rancho were two villages, Pauma and
Potrero, of the Luiseño-speaking Paumas. Less than seventy-five strong, they were led by Manuelito Cota, an individual who was on good terms with the nearby Cupeños.[20] Probably of mixed Spanish and Indian
ancestry,[21] Cota was soon to buy part of the Pala Rancho,
which in May 1845 had been granted to an Indian called
Fortunato.[22] Assisting him was Pablo Apis, whose stepfa-
ther, also called Pablo Apis, was the leader of the Indians
at Temecula and a former neophyte of Mission San Luis
Rey.[23]

Shortly after the Californios arrived at the rancho, an
Indian informed Serrano that the lives of the eleven men
were in danger. Serrano warned but apparently did not
convince the men of the impending trouble, and the
officer in charge of a Californian military detachment at
Mission San Luis Rey also refused to take Serrano's fears
seriously.[24] On a night between December 8 and 12,[25]
Manuelito Cota sought permission to enter the house
where the men were staying. Against the protestations of
the rest, one of the Californios opened the door. Indians
rushed in, seized the men, and took them to a place somewhere between Potrero and Kupa where they were murdered.[26] The reason for the killings is not known, but it
may have been in retaliation for the recent deaths of five
or six Indians, supposedly the work of some Californios.[27]

Upon hearing that the Californios had been captured,
an Indian contingent from a nearby village set out to secure their release but arrived too late.[28] Pablo Apis, the
elder, offered his protection to the whites in the area and
probably prevented the conflict from spreading.[29] The
Paumas confiscated several hundred head of cattle [30] and
occupied Serrano's fields, while Indians from Las Flores,
Pala, and Temecula settled on some of the rancho's remaining tracts.[31]

As soon as word reached Los Angeles that eleven Californios had been murdered by Pauma Indians, the commander of the region, General José María Flores, ordered

José del Carmen Lugo to apprehend those responsible. According to Lugo,

I left that same hour for Jurupa where I could enlist . . . Juan Antonio. . . . We arranged our plan of attack. . . . In one of the canyons from which we could reach the enemy, I placed an ambuscade of fifty Indians and fifteen white men, with strict orders to not show themselves until the last of the Indian enemies passed.

We lured them on about a league until they passed the ambuscade. Then the men rushed out from the ambush upon them from the back at the same time that we fought them from in front.

We made a great slaughter and falling upon them from the rear killed many of them. Before reaching Aguanga in their flight, eighteen or twenty of them turned back and gave up their arms. They were made prisoners and placed in charge of Chief Juan Antonio, who told me to care for my men and he would care for the prisoners.

On reaching Aguanga, we amused ourselves killing some three Indians who continued fighting. After terminating the affair . . . we went back to Juan Antonio and found that he had killed all the prisoners. I reproached him for these acts of cruelty, and he answered me very cooly that he had gone to hunt and fight and kill Indians who would kill him; that he was sure that if they had caught him they would not have spared his life but would have burned him alive.

The booty that was collected amounted to no more than a few sarapes, arrows, lances and other trifles, all of which I gave to Juan Antonio and his people.[32]

Thirty-eight Luiseños and Cupeños were killed at Aguanga.[33]

As this incident clearly indicates, Juan Antonio's Cahuillas served as important military allies to the Lugos. Their principal duty was defending Rancho San Bernardino against Indian cattle and horse raiders, a task that took up much of their time. José del Carmen Lugo, writing to his father in February 1848, states that "we set out for the mountains of the Agua Caliente in pursuit of the Indians who stole the horses, and Juan Antonio and his people fought with them and killed six Indians—two of them captains. The number of Indians seen was fifty, but more may have been in the mountains." [34] On another occasion, in the winter of 1850–1851, when Walkara was very active and drove off a large herd belonging to José María Lugo, a party went in pursuit, including Juan Antonio and his fighting men. They followed Walkara across the Cajon Pass but were ambushed on the Mohave River, and one white man was killed.[35] In mid-August 1851 it was reported that Cahuillas had recently clashed with some thirty-six well-armed Ute Indians, most likely Walkara's; in the fight a Cahuilla officer, Manuel Largo, was severely wounded.[36]

During his stay on the Lugos' rancho, Juan Antonio greatly expanded his influence and authority, becoming in effect the titular head of the Cahuilla.[37] "Juan Antonio is not a hereditary chief," claims the *Los Angeles Star* of January 24, 1852, "but acquired his position at the head of the 'Cahuilla Nation' by his own efforts." [38] The degree of his authority, however, diminished the farther villages were located from his main settlement. Cabezon, for instance, remained the head of the desert Cahuilla, although he acknowledged the supreme position of Antonio. And Chapuli, chief of the Los Coyotes Cahuillas, kept his people outside Antonio's political orbit. But according to the B. D. Wilson Report, written in 1852 on the condition of the Indians of southern California, so powerful was Antonio that he could summon to his village all his followers, excluding the old and the sick, at any one time.[39] To a white admirer, Antonio "was accorded more absolute respect and deference by his people than we show to the president of the United States. The word of such chiefs as Juan Antonio and Manuelo [Cota] of the Luiseños was law. . . . And they were grand men! Natural leaders! Juan Antonio kept absolute order among his people." [40]

By the 1850s the Cahuilla numbered about three thousand persons and resided in twenty villages (see map 4).

Each village was governed by a capitán who had judicial as well as political authority. When disputes occurred or when crimes were committed, the parties were brought before the capitán by the alcalde. Witnesses were summoned, testimony taken, judgments issued, and if necessary, punishment inflicted. The case was then reported to Juan Antonio who if disapproving would reprimand the capitán. Disputes arising between members of different villages were personally investigated by Antonio.[41]

A Los Angeles judge, Benjamin Hayes, describes Antonio as being "very stout, scarcely five feet four inches tall—short and thick—wirey even in old age, and with an aspect about the eyes, nose and brow, that came nearer to that of the African Lion, than I ever have seen in another human face." Hayes recalls that "in his earlier days he never appeared in public without an escort of from ten to twenty men. When he wished to stop, an Indian of his body guard took off his spurs and replaced them at leaving, bending down so that resting one foot upon his back, the supreme chief could easily mount into the saddle." [42]

That Antonio ruled his people with strict authority is well known. In late 1850 or early 1851, when one of his men was taken to jail in San Bernardino for killing an Indian, Antonio and his men appeared before the hall of justice. He demanded and was given the prisoner who was taken back to Politana and buried alive with the man he had killed. Says Benjamin Hayes, "this is one of the many undoubted circumstances told of him, shewing his fierce character and his firmness of will, in all matters concerning the management of his people." [43] Other accounts support this view. An early resident of San Bernardino claims that "Juan Antonio once hung three of his men on a hill in Yucaipa Valley for stealing our horses." [44] For taking a calf from a white rancher, two Indians received fifty lashes each on their bare backs and were forced to give a horse, saddle, and bridle to the settler. On another occasion, Antonio supposedly cut off the ears of two boys who had been caught stealing. And Antonio ordered 150 lashes applied to an individual convicted of murdering a woman. The culprit was then hung from a tree, finally to be lowered into his grave and buried alive. Because of his reputation as an impatient administrator of justice, the Serrano supposedly called him *yámpooche* or "quick mad." [45]

On at least one occasion, Antonio's application of punishment brought him into conflict with the white authorities. When one of his followers killed another in a drunken brawl, Antonio, the day after the incident, forced the culprit to dig a grave where he was buried alive with the man he had killed. A white man issued an affidavit against Juan Antonio for murder, but the sheriff, not wishing to execute the warrant, sent word to Antonio that the authorities in Los Angeles wished to speak with him. At the hearing, one of the judges explained to Antonio that the court had heard about the incident and sought more information. With great frankness, Antonio described the entire affair. When the county attorney asked what right he had in executing the individual, Antonio calmly replied because "he had killed the other man." Joseph Lancaster Brent and another lawyer volunteered as friends of the court and suggested that it was an internal Indian affair and that the court had no right to intervene. While the county attorney disagreed, the court accepted the advice and dismissed the entire matter. Brent, who pictured Antonio as "a taciturn man, saying little, and seemingly having a capacity to talk but little," felt that when the chief left the courthouse he did not realize that his right to administer punishment to his own people had been questioned by the white authorities.[46]

Causing the authorities even more concern was Antonio's involvement in what was essentially a dispute between Californios and Americans. In 1851 an Irishman and a Creek Indian were killed in the Cajon Pass about the time a party led by José del Carmen Lugo was in the area chasing Indian horse raiders. A Sonoran in the

group subsequently confessed that he and Lugo's sons,
Chico and Benito, had killed the men because they be-
lieved the two had been in league with the horse raiders.
The county attorney brought charges against the Lugo
brothers, but acting in their defense was Joseph Lancaster
Brent who felt that he would have little difficulty in prov-
ing their innocence.[47] Complicating the situation was
John "Red" Irving and his gang, recently arrived from
Mexico where they had been fighting Indians. Irving told
José del Carmen Lugo that he would break into the jail
and rescue the boys for the price of $10,000. Lugo's re-
fusal infuriated Irving who threatened to kill the brothers.
When released on bail, they had to be escorted out of
town by fifty Californios.[48]

In late May 1851 Irving and twelve men left Los
Angeles for Rancho San Bernardino. When José del Carmen Lugo, who was rounding up stock, heard the news,
he immediately sought assistance from the American military detachment that was stationed on his rancho. Its captain, however, was away, and the lieutenant in charge had
no authority to take troops from the camp.[49] Lugo, therefore, dispatched an assistant, Ricardo Uribe, to Juan Antonio who was told to proceed with haste to Lugo's house.
Upon arrival, Uribe, Antonio, and about twenty of his followers found Irving and his men about to depart with
many of Lugo's possessions. After firing on Uribe who
approached to speak with them, the outlaws fled toward
the village of Yucaipa. The Indians, numbering around
sixty when joined by a contingent from the village of
María Armenta, gave chase in a running fight, dismount-
ing from time to time to launch volleys of arrows that
usually fell far short of their mark. Irving and party also
stopped now and again to fire on the Indians but inflicted
no casualties. At Yucaipa, however, the Irving gang entered the cañada of Santa María, formed on the south side,
and fired on the Indians, killing an alcalde, José Antonio.
It was then about five o'clock in the evening.[50]

Irving and gang were trapped, and soon two of the outlaws were dead. Forced to dismount, they fought on, but the Indians, firing their arrows from the sides of the brush-covered ravine, had the advantage. Ricardo Uribe, who with six other Californios had accompanied the Indians on the chase, repeatedly called on Irving to surrender. Irving refused, the fight continued for an hour, and eleven of the twelve outlaws were killed. When found, Irving had five arrow wounds in the region of his heart,[51] and all the outlaws had their heads smashed in. They were also stripped of their clothes which, together with their arms, horses, and stolen goods, were carried off by the Indians as spoils of war.[52] José del Carmen Lugo recovered only a pair of pantaloons, and estimated that he lost between $1,500 and $2,000 worth of property.[53]

Shortly after the fight a posse composed of Californios and Americans arrived at the site. Understandably, the Californios were delighted that Irving's gang had been eliminated. The Americans, in contrast, resented the gloating of the Californios over the dead and mutilated bodies of countrymen with whom they now sympathized. Insults were bandied about, and the two factions formed on either side of the slain. Before a shot could be fired, however, one of the leaders stepped in, preventing what could have been a bloodier encounter than the one that had just taken place. Sullenly, the posse returned to Los Angeles and was disbanded.[54]

A day or two later, Juan Antonio learned from a Sonoran that two hundred men were on their way from Los Angeles, with artillery, to take vengeance on the Indians for having killed white men. Antonio and his people immediately fled into the mountains, in such haste that they left behind two children whom they were unable to locate for several days.[55] The rumor, although untrue, reflected the mood of many Americans, and a company of militiamen was only restrained by its officer from attacking Antonio.[56] Concerning this affair, the B. D. Wilson Report states that "doubtless, the Indians thought they were only acting in obedience to the authorities it having been the custom, in the Mexican times, to employ them in services of this kind. . . . The necessity for correcting their ideas on this subject is evident. I mean, of course, that they ought never to be allowed to meddle with the punishment of whites for public offenses." [57]

When the county coroner went to Politana to interview Antonio about the deaths of the eleven Americans, the chief and his people were still hiding in the mountains.[58] The coroner's inquest absolved Juan Antonio of all guilt in the affair. On June 14, 1851, the *Los Angeles Star* published the statement made at the inquest.

Whereas Juan Antonio, Chief of the Cahuillas, and friend of the inhabitants of this county, as well as of all good and peaceable men, has withdrawn from his residence in Politana, in consequence of a report that harm was meditated against him—which report is false—since he has always been considered in peace with all, and a friend of order, he is hereby notified that he can return with his people to their homes, to live as before they left; take care of their property; work as they have always done; and associate with his white neighbors; with a guaranty that no harm shall be done him, either by individuals or by county authorities, because all consider him as a good friend, and will not consent to let him be injured, but will cooperate with force if necessary to punish any person who may disturb the peace.[59]

When Antonio returned to Politana, he was given $100 worth of cloth, hats, and handkerchiefs out of the county treasury, in recognition of his valuable service in eliminating the Irving gang.[60]

Evidently, Antonio harbored no ill feelings against the white authorities, for early in August, accompanied by fifty of his men, he marched into Los Angeles to offer the town his assistance, having heard that it was about to be invaded by outlaws. All his men were armed with bows and arrows and caused quite a stir as they proceeded down Main Street to the mayor's office. After a brief interview, the Indians retired to their camp.[61] Antonio and his men remained in town for three days, acted with great propriety, and conducted some rather unusual business. In the office of the county judge, with great solemnity,

Juan Antonio was deposed as chief of the Cahuillas, evidently because he was considered too headstrong. A successor, recommended by Antonio, was chosen.[62]

By this time Los Angeles (see pl. 6) was crowded with Indians. A member of the Mormon Battalion had seen between three and four hundred lining the streets when the command entered the pueblo on March 16, 1847, during the Mexican-American War.[63] In April 1852 a visitor notes that he

saw more Indians about this place than in any part of California I had yet visited. They were chiefly "Mission Indians," i.e. those who had been connected with the missions, and derived their support from them until the suppression of those establishments. They are a miserable squalid-looking set, squatting or lying about the corners of the streets, without occupation. They have now no means of obtaining a living, as their lands are all taken from them; and the missions for which they labored, and which provided after a sort for many thousands of them, are abolished.[64]

It was also reported in 1852 that "in some streets of this little city, almost every other house is a grog-shop for Indians. They have, indeed, become sadly deteriorated, within the last two years; and it may be long, very long, before a sound public opinion will speak like the potent voice of the Mission Fathers." [65]

Some Indians found steady employment in the town and earned a maximum of one dollar per day. Most, however, worked intermittently, usually for nearby ranchers and winegrowers. When paid in cash, the Indian farmhand earned from eight to ten dollars per month.[66] But the winegrowers often paid their help in an alcoholic drink called *aguardiente*. Since "payday" was usually on a Saturday evening, the Indians would meet in great numbers in Los Angeles to drink and to gamble at peon. On Sundays the streets were often crowded with drunken Indians, usually yelling and fighting. About sundown the marshall with his special Indian deputies, who had been locked in jail all day to keep them sober, would herd the

Indians into a big corral where they would sleep away their intoxication. The following morning they would be "sold," usually to the winegrowers, for a week's work. At the end of the week they would again be paid in aguardiente and the cycle would begin once more.[67]

All this was quite legal after August 16, 1850, when the pueblo passed an ordinance stating:

When the city has no work in which to employ the chain gangs, the Recorder shall by means of notices conspicuously posted notify the public that such a number of prisoners will be auctioned off to the highest bidder for private service, and in that manner they shall be disposed of for a sum which shall not be less than the amount of their fine for double the time they were to serve at hard labor.[68]

As an early resident put it, "Los Angeles had its slave mart, as well as New Orleans and Constantinople." [69]

Games of peon often resulted in violence that led to many Indian arrests. Producing enormous excitement and extravagant betting—not only for the players but for the bystanders as well—the games were hotly contested, especially if opposing teams were members of different language divisions or political groups. For example, a widely advertised game between local Luiseños and Cahuillas from San Bernardino was attended by large crowds from both groups. During the night a fight erupted, and the "next morning," writes one observer, "dead Indians were found in every direction. . . . These all had their heads smashed beyond recognition. . . . It was a moderate estimate that fifty lost their lives." Shortly after this fight, the playing of peon in Los Angeles was prohibited by city ordinance.[70]

In late October 1851, when refused permission by the marshal to play peon within the city limits, a group of Cahuillas moved out near the cemetery and started a game in front of the house of a Californio named Ivarra. During the evening, an argument erupted between an Indian called Coyote and Ivarra's wife. When the Californio attempted to take Coyote to jail, five or six Indians secured his release. A patrol of Californios arrived, but the Indians drove it off and then set fire to Ivarra's house. Several Americans soon joined the Californios; and of the hundred or so Indians who were engaged in the fight, eight were killed and twenty were taken to jail.[71]

Shortly after the incident, Juan Antonio, who had resumed his duties as chief, rode into town with a large party to secure the release of his followers. Described by the *Los Angeles Star* as being "rigged out in epaulets, and other paraphernalia of military chieftains, and altogether has quite a martial bearing," Antonio was successful in his mission and immediately departed for Politana.[72]

Antonio continued to serve the Lugos until they sold Rancho San Bernardino to a Mormon colony at the end of 1851.[73] He then moved his people into the San Timoteo Canyon where he established the village of Sahatapa.[74] Nearby was the rancho of Paulino Weaver who claimed but could not prove he had a Mexican grant.[75]

In the meantime, to the south in the Valle de San José, the interaction of Indians and Californios proceeded along different lines. In 1844, a naturalized Mexican citizen, originally from Connecticut, Juan Jose Warner (see pl. 7), was granted the valley by the Californian authorities.[76] He built his first house near the village of Kupa and the hot springs and by 1847 had ten or fifteen acres under cultivation, including a small vineyard (see map 2). His grazing land was some three miles distant.[77] Warner lived comfortably and raised large herds of cattle, horses, and sheep.[78] Local Cupeños worked for him as herdsmen and servants.[79]

Located on the southern route into California, Warner's rancho became a halfway station between the Colorado River and Los Angeles. During the last half of the 1840s, the rancho and the village of Kupa were visited by numerous immigrant parties and by American military commands entering California during the Mexican-American War. General Stephen Watts Kearny and his dragoons ar-

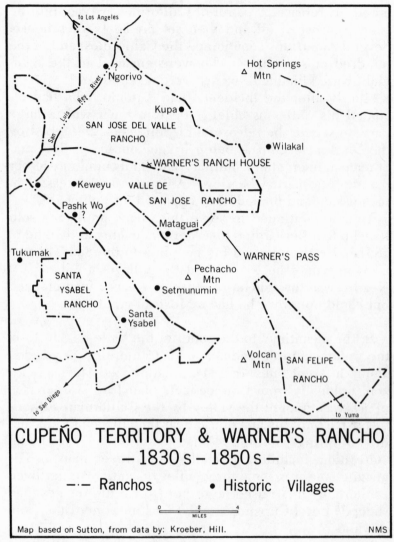

Map 2

rived at the rancho on December 2, 1846, exhausted from
their trek across the desert.[80] They asked the Indians for
flour, and many women immediately set about preparing
it.[81] According to a Cupeño account, recorded years later,

the general gave his jacket to an old woman who ground more flour than all the rest.[82]

When the command arrived, Warner, suspected of having Californian sympathies, was a prisoner of the American occupying forces in San Diego.[83] In charge of the rancho was Bill Marshall who in 1844 had jumped ship in San Diego.[84] Described as "a small man with regular and rather agreeable features and a head indicating . . . great determination," [85] Marshall had moved into the valley in 1846 and married the daughter of José Noca, a Cupeño Indian.[86] He set up a store at Kupa and kept it well stocked with goods from San Francisco.[87]

On the evening of December 3, Antonio Garra, the chief of the Cupeños, spoke with Kearny. He declared that his intention was to keep the peace and not to engage in the war between the Californios and Americans. He said that he and his people intended to go about their work. The general replied that if the Indians kept the peace and worked hard they would be well treated by the Americans.[88] Little is known of Garra's early life, but San Francisco's *Daily Alta California* of December 18, 1851, reported he was a Quechan by birth. At an early age he had been taken to Mission San Luis Rey where he learned to read and write Spanish, married a mission woman, and became an official.[89] In a statement issued in mid-December 1851 Garra makes no mention of his supposed Quechan birth, but he does assert that he "was baptized in Mission St. Louis Rey, and from my earliest recollection have been connected with the St. Louis Indians." [90] The B. D. Wilson Report claimed that Garra did not have the appearance of a Quechan but acknowledged that it would not be unusual for one to be a man of power among the Indians of southern California.[91]

The details of Garra's rise to power remain a mystery. On one occasion he claimed that General Kearny had appointed him chief,[92] but as naat, or headman, of the important Kavalim lineage, he had a traditional base of authority.[93] By the late 1840s, Garra had emerged as a powerful territorial chief who ruled all the inhabitants, including ex-neophytes, of the villages of Kupa and Wilakal (see map 2). It is known, for example, that in 1851 the capitán of Wilakal, Francisco Mocate, was appointed to his position by Antonio Garra.[94] The *San Diego Herald* of November 27, 1851, reports that Garra "is regarded by all who know him as a man of energy, determination, and bravery. As one of the most outstanding chiefs, his power and influence among the Indians is almost unbounded." [95]

Following Kearny and his dragoons into California was George Cooke and his Mormon Battalion. They arrived at Warner's rancho on January 21, 1847, about three weeks after Juan Antonio and José del Carmen Lugo had clashed with Manuelito Cota and young Pablo Apis at nearby Aguanga. In his journal, Cooke mentioned that the chief of the Indians was called Antonio and indicated that Cupeños had been among those ambushed by Juan Antonio's Cahuillas. "Lately these Indians," he writes, "attacking a few Californians in the valley of Temecula, were drawn by them into an ambush of Indians of a connected tribe and thirty-eight slain." Furthermore, Cooke found at Kupa about thirty head of cattle that had been taken from the Pauma Rancho.[96]

When Garra and Cooke met, the chief requested that the battalion accompany his Indians to Aguanga, where they would be able to bury their dead under its protection. Cooke agreed if Garra and some of his men would scout and herd for the battalion.[97] Cooke also spoke with Juan Bautista, capitán of the Cahuillas at the nearby village of Pauki (Powky) and a subordinate of Juan Antonio's.[98] Cooke was disturbed that Cahuillas had given assistance to the Californios by participating with them in an ambush of Indians friendly to the Americans.

I told him that I regretted that any part of his nation should have taken so unwise a course in favor of the Californians, who would now abandon them. . . . I advised him to settle his people to their usual pursuits for a regular livelihood; that the Americans were pouring in from every quarter and would forever govern the country. . . . I told him to tell his people to settle down and be more quiet, and to drive in all the captured horses, etc., to Warner who I had commanded to take care of them until disposed of by the general.[99]

On January 25, 1847, Garra and ten of his men led the Mormon Battalion into the upper part of the Temecula valley, "very pretty," according to Cooke, "with green meadows of great extent, and snowy and green mountains to be seen in every direction." By sundown they were near where the ambush had taken place, and already present were some 150 Indians. "As I approached the ground," writes Cooke, "I saw them marching in regular single file and form a line across the road. We could see the glitter of arms, and the galloping of men about the array. A drum was also beating. Few but believed we were about to have an action." [100] Evidently, the Indians were preparing to attack, having mistaken the battalion for a force of Californios. Soon, however, Indians and Mormons were heartily shaking hands.[101] The following morning, as the Indians were burying their dead, the battalion departed, Cooke having refused Garra's request to stay until noon. "I reluctantly told him that I could not possibly do so. They fear, he said, an attack from the heathen Indians." [102]

Two years later in January 1849 Cave J. Couts, soon to play a prominent role in southern California affairs, visited Kupa (see pl. 8) while on his way to Los Angeles. In his journal, Couts notes that the village is "in the hands of a fine old Indian, Captain Antonio, who came over some distance with us, telling of his whipping the Mexicans during the war, his great regard, friendship, etc. for the Americans. The old man lives very comfortably, indeed, dressed well and his whole family the same, all talk Spanish, and has everything he wants." [103] The following January Benjamin Hayes arrived at Kupa and noticed that a large house, formerly the property of Mission San Luis

Rey, was occupied by Antonio Garra.[104] An Indian told him that their chief had many books.[105] Hayes identifies Garra "as their chief or General—a man of some note. I saw him but once—a cursory glance; he made little impression on me, by his features, as he was seated talking and laughing with another Indian, on his porch." [106] While at Kupa, Hayes saw many Indians arrive to attend a meeting called by Garra.[107]

That large numbers of ex-neophytes resided at Kupa is evident from the accounts of the white visitors. W. H. Emory, a member of Kearny's Dragoons, states that the Indians told him "that when they were under the charge of the missions they were all comfortable and happy, but since the good priests had been removed, and the missions placed in the hands of the people of the country, they had been ill treated." [108] A Cupeño told Hayes that the "people are *todos Christianos*"; another complained that "they have no padre . . . but want one." [109]

Many of the visitors also discussed the physical and moral condition of the Indians. Emory writes:

Around, were the thatched huts of the more than half naked Indians. . . . I visited one or two of these huts, and found the inmates living in great poverty. The thermometer was at 30°, they had no fires, and no coverings but sheepskins. . . . The Indians have made pools for bathing. They huddle around the basin of the spring to catch the genial warmth of its vapors and in cold nights immerse themselves in the pools to keep warm.[110]

A white man told Hayes that "four years ago, in these mountains, it was impossible to find a woman otherwise than virtuous. Now, such has been the force of temptation set before them by the traders, it is almost impossible to find one who is virtuous." [111]

On one occasion, while at Bill Marshall's store, Hayes saw some twenty Indians ride up briskly on their ponies. They were dressed in various attire, one "in a really fine blue coat, having a naked sword dangling at his belt." Hayes found them good looking, pleasant, and "polite enough" and recalls that "amongst them they bought a handkerchief, a pack of playing cards . . . and started a game of monte before I left. I observed one come out with a small jug of *aguardiente*." [112]

At another time, Hayes found a large number of Cupeños intoxicated from liquor purchased at Marshall's store. Gambling had been going on for several days, and a capitán of a neighboring village had pawned his horse, worth $100 in Los Angeles, for $15 and had borrowed the same on another mount.[113] Marshall eventually got possession of both animals.[114]

Much of village life was quite normal and routine, however, especially for the women and children (see pls. 9, 10). Hayes observes:

Women brought down their young children, apparently only a few months old; one or two undressed themselves modestly enough and washed themselves; the rest were washing clothes or softening the acorn, or wild plum seed, in the boiling spring, chatting freely; others attending to a small quantity in another little sulphur spring; others filtering the nut flour in little furnaces.[115]

Visitors to Warner's ranch and the village of Kupa also discussed the relationship between the ranchero and the Indians who worked for him. One mentions that on Warner's rancho "the labor is performed by California Indians, who are stimulated to work by three dollars per month and repeated floggings." [116] Another states that all the rancheros "seem to live in feudal style . . . each man has his band of Indian dependents. . . . They are certainly in a most miserable condition, worse by far than worst treated slaves in the United States." [117] Still another claims that Warner held the Indians "in a sort of serfdom." [118]

Warner often had serious problems with the Cupeños. George Cooke mentioned that Warner wanted to rid the Indians from the valley because they had nearly ruined him.[119] Benjamin Hayes reported that on one occasion Indians had stolen nearly all the ranchero's horses.[120] Furthermore, Warner's claim to the vineyard, clearly located within the confines of Kupa, was a source of friction with the Indians.[121]

Even after an American military government was established in California early in 1847, Cupeño and Luiseño relations with the Californios remained strained. Some time in late May or early June 1847, about fifty ex-neophytes raided Mission San Luis Rey. They removed or destroyed church furniture, threatened the life of an Indian, Samuel, who worked at the mission, and drove off a herd of cattle.[122] On June 27, prominent San Diego Californios, including José Antonio Estudillo, José Antonio Serrano, and J. J. Warner, sent a petition to the military authorities in Los Angeles. They requested that local Indians be prevented from roaming through the countryside in armed parties and that no Indian ranch worker be allowed to carry arms unless granted written permission by his employer.[123]

In late June, Lieutenant J. D. Stevenson met a party of Garra's followers at Santa Margarita. They had come from Mission San Luis Rey in pursuit of the neophyte Samuel. Stevenson informed the Indians that Samuel was under the protection of the U.S. Army and was not to be harmed. He also warned them that further destruction of mission property would be followed by prompt retaliation. In his report Stevenson mentioned that he was temporarily placing Samuel in charge of the mission and was searching for a qualified person to assume the duties of Indian agent and thereby take control of all the Indians between Mission San Luis Rey and Warner's rancho.[124]

On July 6 Antonio Garra and about eighty followers rode into Los Angeles to speak with the American military authorities. The resident Californios were stunned by such boldness and feared that the Indians had large numbers of lances, pistols, knives, and rifles at their camp on the far side of the river. The party that Lieutenant Stevenson sent to search the camp returned with only a few bows and arrows, one lance, and two pistols. At 10

A.M. the Indians assembled in front of the dragoons's barracks. While admitting to cattle stealing, they convinced Stevenson that others were responsible for the recent robbery of Mission San Luis Rey. They requested that an Indian agent be appointed over them but insisted that he be an American as the Californios were their sworn enemies. Stevenson assured them that the agent would be an American and would be named within six weeks.[125]

On August 1 Stevenson chose J. D. Hunter, formerly of the Mormon Battalion, as Indian subagent for the lower district of Alta California. Specifically, he was to take charge of all the Indians in the neighborhood of Mission San Luis Rey and was paid a salary of $750.00 per year.[126] Hunter, however, lacked the men and resources to effectively assist and control the Indians under his jurisdiction. American Indian policy, in fact, intensified rather than alleviated the problems faced by the Indians.

Considered "Mission Indians" by the local American authorities, Cupeños, Luiseños, and Diegueños were classified as residents of San Diego County and thus were liable to pay county taxes. Accordingly, in 1850 the "Mission Indians" were assessed for about $600, the money being collected by the county treasurer. The following year, by instruction of the court of sessions and following state law, they were assessed again. According to the sheriff of San Diego County, Agostin Haraszthy, the Indians issued no complaint. But when General Joshua Bean, commander of the California militia for the southern section of the state, arrived in San Diego in July or August 1851, he, for reasons not understood, forbade the Indians to pay the taxes. He informed Haraszthy of his order, challenging the sheriff to sue him for the sum owed by the Indians. The sheriff postponed collection until he had heard from the attorney general's office. He was informed that the taxes must be collected and immediately sent word to various Indian leaders that they must pay.[127]

Several capitanes refused because of General Bean's

order, and the sheriff's first reaction was to take a posse and force collection. Reconsidering, he visited the Indians only in the company of his servant, but he told them that he would be forced to confiscate their herds if the tax money was not forthcoming. Many offered cattle, but Haraszthy was not authorized to receive property in lieu of money. He suggested that they sell their cattle in San Diego, and the capitanes of Temecula, Pala, Potrero, La Joya, and Pauma, all possessing large herds, sent in a total of nineteen head. The money was turned over to the authorities, but it did not equal the amount owed. Antonio Garra sent his son (also known as Antonio Garra) to San Diego with cash, but it too was short of the assessment. Apparently, the sheriff did not seek the balance. Cahuillas living in San Diego County were not taxed because they were identified as "wild" Indians and therefore outside of local jurisdiction.[128]

Few Americans or Californios in San Diego County realized how deeply the Indians of the region resented being taxed. One who did was José Joaquin Ortega, who on October 11, 1851, was host to a large number of Diegueños who had come to his rancho Santa María (map 1) to hold an eagle-killing ceremony.[129] Led by an Indian called Tomás, these Indians were economically well off at this time, having an abundance of chickens, eggs, melons, grapes, pears, and corn.[130] Ortega provided them with four calves to butcher, and they commenced their dancing about four in the afternoon, continuing on through the next day. The following morning, before Ortega departed to attend a state political convention in Santa Barbara, he told the Indians that he was going to petition the government to divide California so as to reduce the heavy tax burden suffered by all the people in the south. Ortega knew the Indians were aggravated over the taxes and therefore cautioned them to remain peaceful so as not to antagonize the government and ruin the chance for success.[131]

Taxation, however, was not the only reason the Indians of southern California were becoming discontented. Many had heard that Indians in the San Joaquin Valley to the north were making treaties with American authorities, were receiving land exclusively for their own use, and were being supplied with food and agricultural implements.[132] Part of what they understood was true, for on September 20, 1850, the United States Congress had appointed three commissioners to negotiate treaties with all the California Indian societies that were still intact. Commissioned were Redrick McGee, O. M. Wozencraft, and George W. Barbour, each of whom was designated a section of the state. The first treaty was negotiated with six Indian societies near the Mariposa River on March 19, 1851.[133]

In June, Barbour, who had been designated the southern section of the state, sent word to the Indians in San Bernardino and San Diego counties that he would soon be in the south to enter into negotiations. But on the day he was to arrive, Barbour failed to appear. He had received word that the Indians in the Tulare Valley were about to begin hostilities and concluded "that I would best advance the object of my mission . . . more by returning to the Tulare Valley than by remaining to treat with the Indians who were entirely friendly with the whites." When Barbour arrived in San Francisco at the end of July, he was informed that the Indians in the south were expressing dissatisfaction that he had not come to negotiate the promised treaties. Because of lack of funds, Barbour did not return to the south and instead left for Washington, D.C., in early October.[134]

The meeting place was to have been Rancho del Chino, owned by an American, Isaac Williams. Large numbers of Indians congregated at his rancho, and Williams provided them with two cows a day for food.[135] On hearing that the commissioner was not coming, many leaders expressed great annoyance, some of them refusing with disdain the presents offered by Williams.[136] After waiting five days, Juan Antonio and his capitanes returned home, feeling they had been slighted. A few days later Williams journeyed to Politana, where he was received with much courtesy, to discuss the situation with Juan Antonio. The ranchero distributed farm utensils and blankets and assured the Indians that a commissioner would soon pay them a visit. The Indians appeared satisfied but still could not understand why they had been overlooked. They expressed a strong desire to see the commissioner.[137]

Late in 1851, Indian Commissioner O. M. Wozencraft finally arrived in southern California. An Indian uprising, however, had already begun.

The Uprising

With the discovery of gold in 1848, thousands of immigrants, both Anglo-American and Mexican, began trekking into California by the southern route. Fording the Colorado River near its junction with the Gila, they proceeded across the desert to the Valle de San José and continued on to San Diego, Los Angeles, or the mines far to the north. At the Colorado, local Quechans went into the ferry business, charging the immigrants one fee when they left the east bank, another when they were in midstream, and still another when they arrived at the west bank. That they were prospering from the traffic seems evident. According to an army officer who crossed in late 1849, they were "well mounted and in good circumstances, whereas when the command under Bvt. Major S. P. Graham passed in November 48 they were in a most deplorable state of barbarity. This is sufficient evidence of their having committed many robberies and outrages." [1]

It was not long before white men entered into the ferry business. The first important company was established by Dr. A. L. Lincoln in January 1850. Initially employing six men, Lincoln augmented his staff by nine the following month, when a party of Texans and Missourians, under the command of Jack Glanton, arrived at the crossing.[2] According to Lincoln, the profits of his ferry business were enormous. In a letter to his parents he mentions that "I have been here some three months, during which time I have crossed over 20,000 Mexicans, all bound for the mines and I am still carrying some 100 per day. . . . I have taken in over $60,000. My price, $1 per man, horse or mule $2, the pack $1, pack saddle 50 cents, saddle 25 cents." [3]

Some of the immigrants refused to pay Lincoln's price and crossed by their own means. In April 1850 one such individual crossed the river in his own boat and then turned it over to a Creek Indian who had accompanied him from Tuscon. With the boat went a certificate stipulating that the Indian had rightful possession and would cross all Americans for one dollar per person. Horses and packs would also cost a dollar each. The Indian was to use the lower crossing called the Algondones.[4] Evidently, the Creek went into business with the local Quechans and soon the Indians were cutting into the profits of Lincoln's company. Outraged at this, Jack Glanton had their boat destroyed and personally murdered an Irishman who was in their employ. When a Quechan chief, probably Cavello en Pelo, called upon Glanton, proposing that the Indians ferry only the immigrants' animals while the Americans cross all men and baggage, the ferryman struck the chief with a club and threw him out of his house. The chief held a council, and it was agreed that the Americans should be eliminated.[5]

When a party of the ferrymen returned from a trip to San Diego, the Indians struck, killing Lincoln, Glanton, and nine others.[6] According to the *Daily Alta California*, Cavello en Pelo beat Glanton's head in as he slept, and the bodies of the slain were piled together and burned.[7] Only three ferrymen made their escape, eventually reaching San Diego more dead than alive.[8] After the killings, the Indians held another council and unanimously agreed that all Americans passing through the region should be killed. Sonorans and other Mexicans, however, were not to be harmed.[9] While the Quechans were unable to halt American immigration, they did implement a policy of continuous harassment.[10]

The possibility of making big money brought another company to the river a month or so later. About two hundred Quechans soon made their appearance, armed with clubs, bows and arrows, and knives. George A. Johnson, the leader of the company, allowed only five chiefs, including Council Chief Santiago and War Chief Cavello en Pelo, to enter his camp. Through his interpreter, Santiago asked "Why are you going no farther? . . . The white man and the Indian cannot live together. This is Indian country; white men can go through, rest and feed his horses; if he has anything to sell the Indian wants, we will buy, but he can't live here." Johnson told Santiago that he and his men were going to build a ferry, but they would not interfere with the Indians. At that moment, Santiago signaled to his men who brought their bows to the ready; but when Johnson leveled his rifle at the chief, the Indians departed. The Americans immediately commenced digging a trench and constructing a picket. During the days that followed, they remained continually on guard and kept their howitzer loaded.[11]

In response to the murders of Lincoln, Glanton, and the others, Governor Peter Burnett ordered Major General Joshua Bean of the state militia to march against the Quechans. Bean sent a force under his Quartermaster General, Joseph C. Morehead, to the Colorado in the summer of 1850.[12] Upon arrival, Morehead sent for the chiefs and demanded that they deliver to him eleven hostages and the money they took from Glanton and Lincoln. The chiefs refused and fighting broke out. Only by falling back to the ferrymen was Morehead's command saved from annihilation.[13] A short time later, the force was ordered back to Los Angeles and disbanded. The Morehead Expedition, as it came to be called, cost the new state of California (admitted to the union in September 1850) $120,000.[14]

It had now become apparent to the United States government that a permanent military garrison should be established on the Colorado River. On July 4, 1850, Captain Samuel P. Heintzelman was ordered to the region, although it was not until late October that his three companies of the Second Infantry were ready to depart. About half a mile below the Colorado's junction with the Gila,

Heintzelman established Camp Yuma. In March 1851 the camp was moved to a hilltop near the mouth of the Gila and the traditional crossing point.[15]

Because of the great expense of transporting provisions east across the desert, especially during the summer months, it was decided to reduce the number of men on the Colorado, and in early June 1851 Heintzelman withdrew the greater part of his command to Santa Isabel. Left behind to protect public property and the numerous immigrants was Lieutenant Thomas W. Sweeny and a contingent of ten men.[16] Sweeny built a stockade six miles below the junction of the two rivers and named it Camp Independence.[17] Nearby was the ferryboat company run by the new owners W. J. Ankrim and J. E. Iaeger.[18]

Shortly after the departure of Heintzelman's force, a delegation of chiefs, accompanied by some forty warriors, paid Sweeny a visit, seeking to know why he was left behind. In his journal, Sweeny recounts his meeting with the chiefs telling them that he would

remain here to protect his children—the red man as well as the pale-face. . . . That so long as they submitted to the will of their great Father at Washington, I would prevent the pale-face from injuring them and afford them all the protection and assistance in my power; but the moment they disobeyed his commands; I would punish them with the utmost severity, destroy their planting-grounds, and drive them beyond the Colorado towards the rising sun! Big talk, this, from an officer in command of a detachment consisting of a noncommissioned officer and nine men.[19]

The following month Sweeny records in his journal that "the Indians are beginning to steal, which is a dangerous sign. This is the first time I have detected them in the crime since I have been here—it is a sure omen of their hostility." [20]

On the tenth of November 1851 seven men on their way to Los Angeles with some fifteen hundred head of sheep arrived on the east side of the Colorado. James Quay, a German named Neagle, and two Sonorans took

the sheep across that day and left early the next morning
for the coast. Washington Morgan, Charles Hines, and a
Mr. Wilson crossed the river later that morning and soon
caught up with the others. About four miles west of the
river, Indians surrounded the sheepmen and demanded
their blankets and provisions.[21] In the fight that ensued,
five sheepmen [22] and twelve Indians lost their lives.[23]
Neagle escaped into the brush, remained hidden until
dark, and finally reached Sweeny's camp about eleven
o'clock at night.[24]

About two hours after Morgan, Hines, and Wilson had
crossed the river, Indians identified as Quechans and Cocopas gathered around Camp Independence. Claiming
they had come to trade, the Indians offered one horse for
every American blanket, terms the soldiers thought too
good to be sincere. Lieutenant Sweeny, suspecting they
were seeking entrance into the stockade for other than
commercial purposes, ordered them to disperse. When
they refused, he placed his twelve-pound howitzer in position to rake the only possible point of attack. The Indians then retired, envincing great shock and disappointment.[25] From Neagle's description of the Indians who had
attacked him, Sweeny had no doubt that they were the
same who had visited his camp.[26]

Arriving the following evening at Camp Independence
was Lieutenant E. Murray who had been ordered from
San Diego to relieve Sweeny. Murray, who had left his
small detachment of sixteen men and six wagons at the
Algondones, had gone on ahead to the camp. Hearing
what had happened the previous day, he returned immediately to his command. The next morning, on his way to
Camp Independence, he discovered the bodies of four
men, thought to be Quay, Morgan, and the two Sonorans.
Hines and Wilson were not accounted for.[27] One of the
Sonorans, however, was not killed. Although wounded,
he somehow crossed the desert to San Gorgonio where he
was given treatment by a ranchero, Paulino Weaver. He
reported that all the members of the party were dead, but

that his life had been spared because the leader of the Indians did not wish to kill Sonorans or Californios. He identified the leader as Antonio Garra.[28]

For the previous few months, Garra, greatly disturbed about the taxes his people were being forced to pay and probably terribly concerned over the number of immigrants passing through his territory, had been sending couriers over much of southern California in an attempt to enlist as many chiefs and capitanes as possible in a coordinated and massive uprising against the Americans. Garra was in communication with the leaders of San Pasqual, Santa Isabel, San Luis Rey, and Temecula.[29] He sent word to Indians in Baja California, inviting them to join in the outbreak.[30] He gave a feast for Cahuilla leaders Juan Antonio, Cabezon, and others, at which time he encouraged them to participate.[31] That Juan Antonio considered joining in the hostilities is indicated by the probability that he, rather than Garra, sent a delegation north to the Tulareños to see if they were interested in challenging the Americans.[32] The Tulareños refused the invitation because on June 10, 1851, they had negotiated a treaty with Indian Commissioner George W. Barbour and intended to abide by it.[33]

Garra also sought the support of Indian societies to the east, for it is likely that on different occasions he visited the Quechans, Cocopas, and Diegueño-speaking Kamias. Garra's main agent among the river Indians may have been the Kamia leader Gerónimo, whose village, located on the Colorado Desert, was at the extreme northern limits of New River near a mud volcano and salt lake.[34] Since he had worked for Sweeny as guide and interpreter when Camp Yuma was first established,[35] Gerónimo probably passed on to Garra important information concerning Sweeny's garrison.

The first step in Garra's strategy was the destruction of Camp Independence. Once it had been taken, a coordinated descent upon all American settlements in southern

California would follow.[36] The Tulareños were to fall upon Santa Barbara; the Cahuillas and Cupeños were to attack Los Angeles; and the Quechans would strike at San Diego. Only Americans, however, were to be killed.[37]

Probably in the company of Gerónimo, Garra departed for the Colorado River sometime in late October or early November 1851.[38] He failed, however, in his mission to destroy Camp Independence. Sweeny's howitzer and constant vigilance made a direct assault on the garrison impossible. And a quarrel over the distribution of the stolen sheep severed whatever unity Garra had been able to forge with the river Indians.[39] The Quechans and Cocopas, however, continued their harassment of the camp. They burned the defense around the stockade and on succeeding nights sent volley after volley of arrows into the compound. A new site, more easily defended, was selected by Sweeny, but the harassment continued. On November 23, the ferryboat owner, J. E. Iaeger took shelter with the soldiers. He had been attacked and wounded by some two hundred Indians about a mile and a half below Camp Independence while on his way from San Diego with supplies. He recognized two Quechan chiefs—Cavello en Pelo and Pasqual.[40]

Garra, in the meantime, had left the Colorado River on November 12, the day after the sheepmen had been killed. Arriving at Los Coyotes Canyon five days later, Garra learned that an attack on Warner's rancho was imminent. Apparently, he argued against such a move but was overruled. He accompanied the war party only as far as Wilakal where he remained because of illness.[41] Asked why he was backing out, Garra retorts, "you do this to have the blame laid on me, but I have nothing to do with it." [42] Garra, however, realized that war with the Americans could not be averted, and on November 21 he wrote a letter to the prominent Californio, José Antonio Estudillo. "Now the blow is struck," he states, "if I have life I will go and help you, because all the Indians are invited in all parts, and it is possible that the San Bernardinos [Cahuil-

las] are now rising—and here a man by the name of Juan
Berro [Verdugo] told me that the white people [Califor-
nios] waited for me . . . and you will arrange with the
white people . . . and send me your word." [43]

Shortly after midnight, November 21, 1851, probably
after a meeting to coordinate their movements, the Indians departed from Wilakal in two groups. Chapuli, chief
of Los Coyotes Cahuillas, and some other officials led
one contingent to Warner's rancho. Garra's son, who went
by his father's name, commanded the other and set out for
Kupa. Rendezvousing at the house of Luis, the alcalde of
Kupa, were young Garra and several other Indians, including Bonifacio, José (son of Dominga), José Luis, José
(son of Julian), Juan Bautista (Coton), Carlos, and Cosme.
They proceeded to the house of José Noca's daughter,
Dominga, the wife of Bill Marshall, where three American invalids, Fiddler, Ridgeley, and Slack, were sleeping.
Young Garra and his party stormed into the house, seized
the three Americans, stripped them of their clothes, took
them to the burial ground, and murdered them. Bill Marshall was present when the Indians arrived but remained
in the house and did not see the murders take place.
Later, Marshall may have ridden to Wilakal, probably to
consult with Antonio Garra, but if so, he had returned by
morning.[44]

The party then went to the house of José Noca where
another American, Joe Manning, and a Sonoran called
Juan Verdugo were staying. Entering first was Luis, the
alcalde, who informed José Noca that they had come to
kill Manning. Noca replies "well—let them take him."
The American was led outside and struck on the head
with a club probably wielded by Cosme. It seems that
Carlos finished the job with his lance.[45] Verdugo was perhaps spared the same fate as Manning by the intercession
of José Noca.[46] In Noca's house, the Indians divided up
Manning's possessions. Juan Bautista and a relative of
Garra struggled over Manning's money until the alcalde
intervened and forced them to give it all to him. Of the

three large and three small gold pieces, he gave a $50 coin to young Garra, probably to appease him for not getting part of the spoils, and a smaller piece to José Luis. The alcalde took Manning's jacket while Bautista got his pantaloons, José Luis his saddle and boots, Cosme his mango, and Bonifacio his rifle.[47]

Meanwhile, the other party, led by Chapuli, Panito, and Francisco Mocate, who was capitán of Wilakal by appointment of Antonio Garra, proceeded to Warner's rancho and attacked at sunrise.[48] Warner had been warned on November 19 by Lázaro, one of the leaders of the Santa Isabel Indians, that an attack was imminent, and had sent his family to San Diego. He was to follow shortly.[49] Alone except for his young Indian servant, Santos, and another boy, Warner was awakened by the yells of the attacking Indians. Rifle in hand, he ran to the doorway and discovered that the two horses he had tied near the house had been cut loose. Seeing Warner, some twenty Indians took cover, but the ranchero shot two as he dashed to his barn to saddle another horse. Warner then sent Santos to talk with the Indians. But when he failed to return, Warner and the other boy made a daring escape.[50]

Later that day, on his way back to his rancho, Warner came across an Indian straggler who had some of his belongings. When ordered to return the goods, the Indian attempted to draw an arrow and Warner shot him. At his rancho, he found his house stripped of everything; and while the Indians had left his work horses and breeding mares,[51] they had driven off all his cattle.[52] Warner estimated that his losses amounted to nearly $59,000.[53]

After the killing of the four Americans, the Cupeños abandoned their villages and along with Juan Verdugo and Bill Marshall fled to the Cahuillas in Los Coyotes Canyon. From a mountaintop where they stopped to rest, they could see the fires from Warner's rancho. In two days they were in the canyon, probably at the village of Wiliya. The following day about forty Indians rode in, presumably the party that had attacked Warner's rancho. By this time, the village was in a great state of excitement, Indians arriving and departing daily. Most were armed with bows and arrows, but a few had guns and lances. There may have been two hundred at the village.[54]

Garra's son wrote to Manuelito Cota of the Luiseños, requesting that he bring his people to the canyon and join in the struggle against the Americans. Cota replied that he would have no part in the uprising, and most Luiseño leaders immediately expressed their loyalty to the Americans.[55] For example, in a letter to officials in San Diego, Pablo Apis, leader of the Indians at Temecula, states that "we will mix in nothing; always obedient to the laws of the government." [56] Domingo, capitán of the Luiseños at San Luis Rey, received word from the San Diego authorities to remain where he was until called upon for assistance.[57] Domingo wrote to Cota stating that he was ready to take the field with all his people and those from Las Flores and Santa Margarita in support of the Americans.[58]

Antonio Garra left Wilakal two days after the murders and the attack on Warner's rancho, arriving at Los Coyotes Canyon in four days.[59] There he attempted to convince Juan Verdugo to join with him, but the Sonoran refused even on threat of being killed. He did, however, accept Garra's request to deliver a letter in San Diego. But Bill Marshall intervened and convinced Garra that Verdugo would offer his services to the Americans and would guide them to the canyon.[60] The letter Garra wanted delivered more than likely was the one he wrote on November 28 to José Joaquin Ortega, the Californio on whose rancho an Indian feast had been held in October. He asks Ortega to "animate the captains, before many Americans can arrive," and to "arrange quickly, because it is for all that the damage has been done. They do not rise for anything but the taxes—not for the mere wish of revolting." [61]

Crucial to Garra was the support of Juan Antonio, whose Cahuillas were probably the most powerful Indian society in San Bernardino and San Diego counties. On

December 2 Garra wrote to the Cahuilla chief, explaining that he had invited Indians in Baja California and those of the Colorado River to join with him. To Garra this was the last chance for the Indians. "If we lose this war, all will be lost—the world. If we gain this war, then it is forever; never will it stop; this war is for a whole life." [62]

Juan Antonio, in the meantime, had denied any connection with Garra and had professed his friendship with all whites. On November 26, just a few days after the attack on Warner's rancho, Antonio, accompanied by Paulino Weaver, rode into San Bernardino. On being told that the Mormons were convinced that he was in league with Garra, the Cahuilla chief indignantly denied it. He claimed that the thought he could conspire against the whites was a slander upon his former course of conduct. He stated that he had always been a friend of the Mormons and that he stood ready at all times to prove this by any means in his power. [63]

About this time, Juan Antonio received a letter from Augustín Olvera, a Los Angeles county judge. Olvera sought from Antonio information as to why the Indians were in such a state of unrest. He asked him to contact Antonio Garra and report to the white authorities the reasons for the uprising. If Garra would explain his grievances, the problem could be settled without further violence. Olvera warned Juan Antonio not to get embroiled with the rising Indians, that if he had any thoughts along these lines he should get rid of them at once. The Cahuilla chief was told to work hard and be content. [64]

Olvera's letter was written on November 25. On December 8, Juan Antonio replied, stating that his people were peace-loving and that none desired war. He claimed he had visited all the nearby villages and had spoken with his capitanes. All sought peace, especially Cabezon, who evidently was not on good terms with the white authorities. Antonio mentioned in his letter that what men were saying about Cabezon was false. In fact, Cabezon was to take the letter to Los Angeles and present himself to the judge and other authorities as an act of good will. Because of his advanced age, however, Cabezon canceled his trip, and the letter was delivered by a messenger instead.[65]

It is not known what effect Olvera's letter had on Juan Antonio; but shortly after receiving it, he wrote to Antonio Garra suggesting that they meet at the village of Razón,[66] located on the desert about fifteen miles from Los Coyotes Canyon.[67] While Garra did not want to go, he was urged on by the leaders of Los Coyotes Cahuillas. Accompanied by Juan Bautista and Cosme and herding eight head of cattle, Garra arrived at Razón's village very late at night.[68] The following day Juan Antonio rode in, the mules and provisions being supplied by Paulino Weaver,[69] who probably accompanied the chief on the journey. Also at Razón's village were capitanes Cabezon and Toro.[70]

When they met, Juan Antonio had Garra and Cosme seized and stripped of their clothes. Antonio accused his captive of being the devil that was always playing tricks and was about to have him murdered. Juan Bautista, however, intervened and convinced Antonio that Garra would soon meet his fate anyway. Antonio confiscated the cattle Garra had bought, declared that peace was restored, and sent word to the people in Los Coyotes Canyon that they should return to their respective villages.[71] With Garra in his custody, Antonio departed for home, the journey taking three days.[72] As soon as word reached Los Coyotes Canyon that Garra had been captured, the Cupeños dispersed. Bill Marshall, Juan Verdugo, José Noca, and Santos, departed for San Diego.[73]

When the white residents of southern California learned that Sweeny's command and Warner's rancho had been attacked, their primary concern was how ill prepared they were to meet the emergency. According to a citizen of Los Angeles,

the great cause of alarm and apprehension here is, that we have not adequate means of defense against a powerful foe. . . . We are also nearly destitute of arms. There is not a cannon in this county, and as for muskets, there are not more than eight good, bad and indifferent, in the county, except with the twenty U.S. soldiers at the Rancho del Chino.[74]

Being an infantry unit, the soldiers at Chino could offer only limited assistance. An early resident of Los Angeles, Horace Bell, has little to say that is complimentary about the detachment, claiming that its commander, Captain Lovell, is

a sedate, methodical, sober kind of an officer, who seemed perfectly content to sit in his elegant quarters, issue orders to his little army of a dozen or so of well-fed, clean-shaved, white-cotton-gloved, nicely dressed, lazy, fat fellows, who were seemingly happy and content on their $8 per month. . . . They all, from Captain to Corporal, seemed resigned to a life of well-fed indolence.[75]

In a letter to the governor of California, General Bean of the state militia is clearly worried about the lack of arms and military support.

An examination of our means of defense exhibits an alarming state of weakness—This proceeds, not, from a want of men, but of arms. We are without guns, pistols, or any of the proper arms for cavalry, which alone can conduct effective war upon the hostile Tribes of savages that are devastating our country.

The United States have a company of infantry consisting of about twenty men at Chino about thirty miles from this place. They are unable to render any assistance, as they are not mounted nor have they suitable arms and are short of ammunition.[76]

Even the capture of Antonio Garra in early December had little effect in quelling white fears. A report from Los Angeles, published in the *Daily Alta California* of December 13, states that "the disaffection is much too widespread, and the preparations on the part of the Indians much too systematic and extensive, to be entirely overwhelmed by the capture of a single chief, though he may be the leader." [77] In San Diego the capture of Garra convinced few that the hostilities were to end shortly. In a letter written on December 17, Thomas Whaley, a San Diego businessman, laments that "the war is lulled but not at an end by the capture of Antonio." [78]

Realizing their own weakness but exaggerating Indian strength, the whites of San Bernardino, Los Angeles, and San Diego made preparations for a prolonged Indian war. The day following the attack on Warner's rancho, the Mormons rounded up all their horses and cattle and dispatched a party to the military post at Rancho del Chino to procure much-needed arms. It returned with only six muskets and five hundred rounds of ammunition.[79] Before evening nearly all the families of the Mormon colony had moved to San Bernardino and the construction of a fort had commenced. By November 30, the structure had begun to assume the appearance of a regular fortification (see pl. 11) and a party sent to Los Angeles had returned with some arms and ammunition. There were at least 150 men capable of bearing arms in case of attack. The Mormons organized themselves into three companies, under the overall command of Jefferson Hunt. A black man called Uncle Grief used his six-foot-long tin horn as a bugle, sounding different calls for different commands.[80]

On November 23, the Los Angeles Court of Sessions met and authorized Sheriff Barton to take a force into Indian country to gather information. Four days later he returned and confirmed the rumors that an uprising had commenced. He failed to locate Juan Antonio who was then at San Gorgonio with large numbers of followers. On November 27, another court of sessions was convened and it was agreed to appoint five commissioners to procure arms, ammunition, horses, and other equipment to outfit a force that would proceed at once against the Indians. The commission consisted of Pío Pico, Augustín Olvera, Francis Mellus, General Bean, and Abel Sterns.[81]

A proclamation was issued to the residents of Los Angeles and letters were sent to the justices of the peace in the various precincts, calling upon all able-bodied men to rendezvous at Rancho del Chino on December 1. A

company of fifty Californios, all well mounted, was raised
by Andrés Pico, which was to operate in conjunction with
the group formed by the commissioners. In a few days
Los Angeles organized and armed a force of some two
hundred men.[82] Benjamin Wilson was placed in command
of a city guard that patrolled every night, keeping order
and quiet in the town.[83] The citizenry felt some relief
when José Zapatero, a principal capitán of the Tulareños, visited the pueblo on December 4 to declare the
peaceful intentions of his people.[84]

In San Diego, meanwhile, Captain S. P. Heintzelman,
commander of the United States Army detachment, upon
receiving word of Indian troubles on the Colorado, dispatched a contingent of sixteen men, under Captain D.
Davidson, to the river. The small force with seventeen
pack mules set out on November 24 for a journey that was
to take a week or ten days at the most. At the Colorado,
Captain Davidson was to make all necessary inquiries
into the circumstances concerning the killing of the
sheepmen and to apprehend the responsible Indians. The
wagon train and pack mules were to be escorted back to
San Diego by Lieutenant Sweeny's detachment and by a
few men that Davidson could spare from his own command.[85]

Captain Davidson experienced great difficulties in
reaching the Colorado. On the third day Indians surrounded but did not attack his camp. Seven days were
required to reach the desert, and according to Davidson,
only by destroying some nine bags of oats and mounting
his men on the pack mules was he able to cut his time by
two days. They arrived at Camp Independence on the afternoon of December 3. There, Davidson found a Major
Kendrick in charge of a detachment of the Second Artillery, the escort for a topographical party that had been
doing surveying work along the Colorado River. Both the
escort and the party, numbering between fifty and sixty
men, were in a destitute condition, having existed for the
past three weeks only on mule meat. They complained

that all the Indian groups they had encountered on the
Colorado had either been hostile or exceedingly troublesome.[86]

On examination of the provisions at Camp Independence, Davidson calculated there were only enough to
see the entire group to San Diego, and all the officers
present unanimously agreed that the camp should be
abandoned. Consequently, on December 6, 1851, the
United States Army withdrew from the Colorado River.
All equipment that could not be transported was destroyed to prevent it from falling into the hands of the Indians.[87] Moreover, by command of Davidson, all the possessions of the ferryboat owner, J. E. Iaeger, which had
not been requisitioned, were also destroyed, including
his wagons, farm implements, and ferryboats.[88]

On its way to San Diego, the army command, now numbering about one hundred men, expected to be attacked
and kept its twelve-pound howitzer loaded during the
first two days.[89] At Vallecitos the soldiers found a recently
deserted village, the Indians having departed so hurriedly
that they left behind many of their possessions. The Indians of Vallecitos, San Felipe, and other villages along
the route may have considered attacking the detachment
but changed their tactics when they discovered how numerically strong it was. The soldiers, however, could only
interpret ominously the numerous smoke signals they saw
between Carriso Creek and Santa Isabel. In the Valle de
San José they rested for a day and received an Indian delegation, headed by the alcalde of Santa Isabel, which offered hospitality and friendship. The following day they
pushed on; but at San Pasqual, they received orders from
Captain Heintzelman to join him at Santa Isabel.[90]

When Lieutenant Murray took his small detachment to
the Colorado River in late November, San Diego (see pl.
12) was left virtually defenseless. On November 26, martial law was proclaimed, and the town soon took on the
appearance of a fortified camp. There were sentinels on

duty at every approach to the city, and no Indian was permitted to pass without giving a good account of himself.[91] According to one citizen, "the whole number of men now in the county will not amount to *one-hundred*, so we are utterly unable to do more than protect ourselves and families." [92] Thomas Whaley writes that "every man is enrolled a Soldier. . . . As it is necessary to keep a good night patrol, my turn to stand guard comes rather frequently." [93]

Shortly after the attack on Warner's rancho, Deputy Sheriff Ryner was sent to Santa Isabel to collect information on the whereabouts of the hostile Indians. Returning to San Diego on November 26, he reported that Garra had established himself at the head of a strong force at Kupa.[94] While Ryner was collecting information that proved to be incorrect, the citizens of San Diego held a public meeting to consider how best to meet the emergency. Attending were J. J. Warner, General Bean, Captain S. P. Heintzelman, Sheriff Agostin Haraszthy, Cave Couts, Bvt. Major E. H. Fitzgerald, and others of the town and vicinity. Captain Heintzelman promised to lend fifty muskets and ammunition to a volunteer force, and Sheriff Haraszthy offered to join such a force as a private or in any other capacity. Numerous other individuals expressed their willingness to do the same, and unanimously it was decided that a command should be created and led by Bvt. Major Fitzgerald, who would have the right to nominate his officers.[95]

General Bean addressed the meeting and expressed his thanks to the citizens of San Diego for their prompt and enthusiastic response. He gave the volunteer company the right to purchase upon the credit of the state the necessary equipment and provisions for two months' service. By virtue of his rank in the California militia, he took command over all the forces raised in the southern part of the state and ordered the volunteers to proceed at once to Kupa where he would join them with a company he was going to raise in Los Angeles.[96]

On Thursday, November 27, Fitzgerald's Volunteers, as they came to be called, trekked out of San Diego,[97] leaving the town to be defended by only thirty-five men.[98] Arriving at Warner's rancho on Tuesday, December 1,[99] they found much of the ranch property either burned or smashed to pieces. Before Warner's door lay the body of an Indian the ranchero had shot, and a wounded, half-charred dog was howling amid the smoldering debris. All Warner's cattle had been driven off except three which the volunteers ate. They found the village of Kupa deserted, the property of its inhabitants scattered about in much confusion. The bodies of the invalids were discovered with their hands tied, all having been murdered with knives and clubs. After burying the victims, Fitzgerald set fire to the village, creating what he called a funeral pyre for the slain.[100]

Before leaving Kupa, Fitzgerald sent three Indian messengers to contact Garra. They were to try to convince the Cupeño chief to meet Fitzgerald halfway between the sierra and the volunteer's camp. Each would arrive with only four to six men, and they would discuss the cause of the outbreak. One of the messengers returned and reported that Garra could not be located but that there were several hundred warriors with Warner's cattle in Los Coyotes Canyon. Fitzgerald realized that since the canyon was on the opposite face of the mountain his men would be forced to attack on foot. Because it would be necessary to leave part of his small command with the horses and baggage, he deemed it unwise to advance against the Indians without reinforcements. Consequently, he decided to return to San Diego. On December 6, the other two messengers caught up with the volunteers, relaying the news that Garra had been captured by Juan Antonio. They claimed Antonio took such action because Garra had been endeavoring, without Antonio's consent or knowledge, to bring Cahuillas into the conflict. The command also learned that the Indians at Los Coyotes Canyon had dispersed after receiving the news of Garra's capture.[101]

Joining Fitzgerald's Volunteers in the Valle de San José
was a force of some thirty Californios, and together the
two groups proceeded homeward, camping the first night
at Santa Isabel. The following day they pushed on to
Santa María where word was received that Bill Marshall,
Juan Verdugo, and José Noca had arrived at Santa Isabel.[102] Fitzgerald suspected the three of being implicated
in the outbreak [103] and sent Agostin Haraszthy and a small
party of Americans and Californios back to Santa Isabel
where the three men and Santos, Warner's servant, were
arrested without incident.[104] The prisoners were locked
in the city jail to await trial when the volunteers returned
to San Diego on December 9, 1851.[105]

By this time the seriousness of the uprising was realized by the governor of California who ordered two volunteer companies be sent to San Diego. They were to set
sail on December 10. But General Hitchcock, commander
of the United States Army in California, upon receiving
the news of Garra's capture, advised the governor that San
Diego was in no immediate danger, and the companies
were disbanded.[106] To reassure the citizens of San Diego,
however, another volunteer company, consisting of forty
men, was raised and sent south by steamer.[107] According
to Thomas Whaley, by the middle of December "volunteers and regulars are coming to our aid from all parts of
the state. We shall soon number some four or five-
hundred strong, more than a match for all the Indians in
California." [108]

On December 23, the forty-man company of volunteers
arrived in San Diego on the brig *North Bend*. Under the
command of Captain Haig, the unit was initially described by the *San Diego Herald* "as fine a looking set of
men as ever shouldered arms." [109] By the time they arrived, however, their services were no longer needed,
and soon the citizens of San Diego were sorry they had
ever come. On Wednesday evening, January 3, Haig and
one of his lieutenants engaged in a knife fight in which
Haig was slashed about his head. The following day they
dueled with large Colt revolvers at a distance of twenty

yards. After an exchange of two shots, however, their seconds intervened, and the dispute was settled without further violence.[110]

To prevent the trouble from spreading, the civic authorities called upon the assistance of Lieutenant Sweeny, now commander of the military detachment at San Diego. The day Sweeny and nineteen men took up quarters in Old Town another fight took place, this one between a San Diego citizen, Philip Crosthwaite, and Lieutenant Watkins of Haig's Volunteers. In the shooting both were hit, Crosthwaite in the abdomen, Watkins in the thigh.[111] Although seriously wounded, Crosthwaite recovered,[112] but Watkins's leg had to be amputated. According to Sweeny, "it was the general opinion that if my men had not been present that day . . . the streets of San Diego would have been drenched with blood." [113]

In the meantime, on December 4, General Bean's Los Angeles volunteers of about thirty-five men left town for Kupa, expecting to be reinforced at Rancho del Chino by twenty-five Mormons and a force of Californios under Andrés Pico.[114] General Bean, accompanied by Major Myron Norton, followed the next day and joined the command at Chino. There, Bean received word that Garra had been captured and was being held at Juan Antonio's village of Sahatapa in the San Timoteo Canyon. Because most of the command's horses had given out, Bean and a Lieutenant Caleb Smith proceeded alone to Sahatapa where they found the chief with 250 men keeping a close watch on Garra. Bean spoke with Garra and was able to convince him to write to his son, instructing young Garra to deliver himself, his family, and the important capitanes to Juan Antonio. After three days of negotiating and only after promising to send Antonio and his people various presents, Bean finally took custody of Garra.[115]

Back at Chino, with his prisoner safely locked up, Bean sent a company of the volunteers to Kupa where it was to link up with the command from San Diego.[116] Fitzgerald's

Volunteers, however, had already destroyed the village
and had returned to San Diego.[117] On December 18,
Bean, accompanied by Major Norton, Lieutenant Smith,
and five or six men, again departed for Sahatapa, this time
to pick up young Garra who, in obedience to his father,
had delivered himself and ten other Indians to Juan Antonio. Shortly before Bean arrived at the village, Juan Antonio had gone in among the prisoners and in conversation with young Garra, had made some insulting remarks.
"I am your prisoner," retorts Garra, "but I will not permit
you to insult me." He then pulled a knife and stabbed Antonio, the blade passing through the flesh in the chief's
left side and into his arm. As Antonio's men were about to
take revenge, they sighted General Bean and his party
galloping toward them. Antonio's wound was only super-
ficial and things soon quieted down.[118]

While at Antonio's village, General Bean, representing
the people of the state of California, negotiated a treaty
with Juan Antonio, representing the Cahuilla nation. The
treaty stipulated that there was to be everlasting peace
between the two contracting parties. As long as Juan Antonio continued to act in a friendly manner toward the
American people and the citizens of the state of California, he would be protected and would be maintained in
possession of his lands and property and in his authority
and command over his people. The treaty also acknowledged the donation of presents to Antonio in appreciation
for capturing Antonio Garra and for delivering his important capitanes to the American authorities. Antonio agreed
that in case of any outbreak of Indian violence, he would
give warning and assistance if he could, and for such action he could expect remuneration from the state of California.[119] The treaty was signed on December 20, 1851.
The Indians were quite pleased with the presents distributed by General Bean, and a feast was held that night.
The following morning Bean and his small group left for
Chino.[120] In custody were eleven Indians—five men and
six women and children.[121]

In San Diego, meanwhile, Captain Heintzelman had received orders on December 13 from General Hitchcock to proceed at once against the hostile Indians. The next day the command left San Diego, arriving at Santa Isabel on the seventeenth. Accompanying Heintzelman was United States Indian Commissioner, O. M. Wozencraft, who spoke to a gathering of chiefs and capitanes the following day, presumably to inform them that he would shortly negotiate treaties with all the Indians in the region.[122] Joining Heintzelman on the seventeenth was Captain Davidson and his detachment that had abandoned Camp Independence on December 6. While at San Pasqual, Davidson had received orders from Heintzelman to meet him at Santa Isabel.[123]

Heintzelman divided his command, placing Bvt. Major J. B. Magruder in charge of some fifty men who were to proceed directly from Santa Isabel across the mountains to Los Coyotes Canyon. Captain Heintzelman, with a force of forty-six men, left on a circuitous route so as to enter the canyon by way of the desert. Before dawn on the morning of December 20, Heintzelman's unit left its desert camp and was in the canyon by daybreak. After moving about a half a mile, the soldiers sighted a party of between thirty and forty Indians advancing to attack. Leaving a small detachment to guard his rear, Heintzelman led his men across a small stream to meet the Indians.[124]

Leading the attacking Indians was Chapuli, chief of Los Coyotes Cahuillas. Some twenty-five or thirty of his followers were armed with rifles.[125] After a short exchange of shots, the Indians cut off the engagement and fled through a dense swamp of willows and tules, up the canyon about half a mile to a village.[126] According to one soldier, the Americans were more frightened than the Indians, and had the Indians held their ground fifteen minutes longer, they might have remained in possession of the field.[127]

Be that as it may, Heintzelman pursued the Indians to

the village but found it deserted, his foe having moved on up the side of the mountain and around a point.[128] Under orders from Heintzelman, the village was set on fire and a party was sent out after the retreating Indians. Soon, a woman with a child in her arms appeared, seeking permission to speak with the commander of the soldiers. She identified herself as the wife of Bill Marshall and convinced Heintzelman that if he would call off the pursuit, the Indians would come in on their own accord. The fire was immediately extinguished and the pursuing party called back. Shortly, ten Indians appeared on the side of the mountain and were induced to come down by Heintzelman. Their leader was Juan Bautista, capitán of Pauki, a Cahuilla village located a few miles to the northwest. Bautista claimed that he and his people had been invited to join in the fighting but had refused because of their friendship for the Americans. To prove his point, Bautista agreed to send runners to the capitanes of nearby villages with orders that they report at once to Heintzelman.[129] The runners also told the leaders that they were soon to assemble at Temecula where they would meet with the United States Indian Commissioner, O. M. Wozencraft.[130]

The following day a few Los Coyotes Cahuillas came in, seeking permission to look for the body of their chief, Chapuli, one of the eight Indians killed in the engagement. Most of the Indians, however, failed to report. Some Cahuilla leaders sent back friendly messages stating why they could not come. One claimed that he had to conduct a burial feast for his recently departed father, while another excused himself on account of illness.[131] When most of the Cupeños failed to arrive at the specified time, Heintzelman sent Bvt. Major Magruder with two companies to search for them by way of the desert, and a detachment under a Lieutenant Hendershot was ordered to cut off their possible line of retreat. Magruder, however, met the Indians, including women and children, on the desert.[132] Taken into custody were those who were thought to have directly participated in the murder of the invalids at Kupa.[133] Two days later Heintzelman's command departed for Temecula by way of Juan Bautista's territory.[134] Even though it would take longer, Heintzelman felt that by following the direct route across the mountains his force would be displayed and would demonstrate to the Indians that United States soldiers could traverse the country in any direction.[135]

For his swift and successful action, Heintzelman received the heartfelt congratulations from his superior, General Hitchcock. Writing to Heintzelman, Hitchcock's aid states that it is the opinion of the general

that no more important service has been rendered by the troops on the Pacific Coast than that just accomplished under your directions. He is persuaded that not only a vast expenditure of both blood and treasure has been spared the country, but that the peace of the Southern part of the state of California has been effectually secured by it.[136]

Heintzelman's career as an Indian fighter, however, was not yet over. At the head of several companies, he reoccupied the region around the junction of the Gila and Colorado rivers. Arriving there on February 29, 1852, he promises his superiors to "scour the country and punish the Indians if they or their villages can be found." [137] This is precisely what he did, attacking the Quechans and their neighbors in a series of military campaigns.[138]

The short engagement at Los Coyotes Canyon saw the end of Indian resistance. By late December 1851 most of the principal participants, except for Antonio Garra, had been either killed in action or had been tried and sentenced. Garra's trial took place in early January 1852 the last in a series of military tribunals. It was the United States Army and the state militia, not the civil authorities, who assumed the responsibility for seeing that justice was carried out.

Military Justice

Once Fitzgerald's Volunteers had captured Bill Marshall, Juan Verdugo, José Noca, and Santos, they returned to San Diego, arriving on December 9, 1851.[1] The following day, in the presence of Major McKinstry of the U.S. Army, Marshall issued a declaration. He claimed that he had not known the intention of the Indians until the night of the murders. About twelve o'clock he and Verdugo had received a message (probably from young Garra) which stated that the Indians were about to commence a war against the Americans and that the two of them would be killed if they refused to join. Marshall admitted not warning the invalids of the impending danger. He also stated that while he was in Los Coyotes Canyon Garra had told him that various Californios, including the Lugos of San Bernardino, were to join the Indians and that José Joaquin Ortega had promised Californian support and had encouraged the Indians to rise when they had gathered at his rancho in October.[2]

The following day, December 11, Marshall made further disclosures. He stated that before he left the canyon, Panito had told him that even if Garra were killed the Indians were determined to fight on until exterminated. Marshall asserted that the war was not over, that six thousand Indians were ready to fight. He also stated that a Cahuilla, Juan Bautista, had told him that the Indians could rely on the Californios and the Mormons of San Bernardino. And in one last statement, Marshall linked Manuelito Cota with the uprising. Cota's role was to profess friendship with the Americans and offer to reconnoiter Los Coyotes Canyon for them. He and his men were then to lead the American force into an ambush laid by Garra.[3]

While Marshall was issuing his declarations, the proceedings to try him, Verdugo, Noca, and Santos were being arranged. After hearing the opinion of the district attorney who acknowledged the existence of martial law, E. H. Fitzgerald ordered a court-martial, under the jurisdiction of the state militia, to convene at once.[4] Agostin Harazsthy was appointed the presiding judge; I. M. Robinson, the judge advocate; and Major McKinstry consented to act as defense counsel. Most of the testimony was contradictory and court procedure was complicated because most of the witnesses were Indians whose testimony, legally, could not be used against a white man.[5]

Bill Marshall was first to be arraigned. He was charged with the crime of high treason in aiding the Indians who took up arms against the citizens of the United States and the state of California. He was further charged as being an accessory to the robbery of Warner's rancho and to the murder of the four Americans. Marshall pleaded not guilty to all the charges. He voiced no objections to the members of the court, but he did request that Santos and Tomás, a Diegueño leader from Santa Isabel, he summoned as witnesses. Marshall claimed that he had not seen any of the men killed and that he also would have been murdered had it not been for the intercession of José Noca, his father-in-law. Furthermore, he asserted that he and Juan Verdugo had been taken to Los Coyotes Canyon as prisoners.[6]

When called as a witness, José Noca stated that he had returned to Kupa four days before the murders and knew nothing about the Indians' plans until he was taken prisoner. At the canyon he saw Juan Bautista, Chapuli, Panito, and Antonio Garra but did not know if the Cupeño chief had participated in the attack on Warner's rancho. Noca said that Bill Marshall had expected to be killed along with the other Americans.[7]

Juan Verdugo was then called to the stand. He testified that he had been taken to Los Coyotes Canyon as a prisoner and that Bill Marshall had arrived the following day with a party of forty Indians and had threatened to kill him when he refused to join in the uprising. Furthermore, he asserted that Marshall had sent Antonio Garra to his ill-fated meeting with Juan Antonio. When news of Garra's capture reached Los Coyotes Canyon, he agreed to accompany Marshall to San Diego.[8]

When cross-examined, Verdugo stated that he had heard Marshall issue the order for the murder of Joe Manning but did not know who was responsible for the killing of the other three Americans. He said that José Noca had pleaded with the Indians not to injure the invalids. Again he insisted that Marshall was never a prisoner but was at the head of the forty Indians that rode into the canyon the day following his arrival. Furthermore, Verdugo claimed that Marshall was an influential officer among the Cupeños and had issued the orders that he be taken prisoner. Finally, he testified that he had engaged in no conversation with Garra concerning Californios being ready to join with the Indians.[9]

José Noca was examined again and recounted the events during the night of the murders and his personal experiences in the flight to Los Coyotes Canyon. He said that he did not know if Marshall held any office among the Indians and that he had never heard him speak ill of Warner. He stated that both Marshall and Verdugo had been taken to the canyon under guard and that only his influence with the Indians had saved the two from being murdered. He was present when Garra departed to meet Juan Antonio and insisted that the Cupeño chief had been forced to go by the leaders of Los Coyotes Cahuillas.[10]

When Noca was recalled, he prefaced his remarks with an apology for whatever false statements he may have issued in his first testimony. This time Noca said that Marshall on the night of the murders had disappeared, probably to Wilakal, but that he was seen with young

Garra the following morning at Kupa. He insisted that Verdugo had not cooperated in any way with the Indians and that the Sonoran was a free man at Los Coyotes Canyon and could have left at any time. Concerning Marshall's position within the political organization of the Cupeños, Noca felt that he may have been a capitán but had no knowledge of him occupying any office of authority, at least before the uprising began. Marshall did not command the Cupeños when Antonio Garra was away. Moreover, Noca asserted that he knew of no evidence to suggest that Marshall had participated in any way in the killing of the four Americans.[11]

When the defense counsel examined Juan Verdugo, the Sonoran stated that he had heard of no feast in which José Joaquin Ortega had encouraged the Indians to open hostilities against the Americans. Furthermore, he knew of no letters written by Garra to Ortega. Tomás, when called, insisted that Ortega had told the Indians that he would ask the government not to tax them. Neither Antonio Garra nor his son were at the feast and no encouragement to rise had been given the Indians. Lázaro of Santa Isabel also testified that Ortega had told the Indians that he was going to Santa Barbara to see if he could influence the government into reducing their taxes.[12]

Juan Verdugo was tried next, and José Noca was again called as a witness. According to Noca, Verdugo had no specific occupation at Kupa and sometimes slept at his house or in the house of his daughter. Prior to the uprising, Noca had neither witnessed Verdugo in the company of Garra nor had he seen him in possession of arms. After the murders, Verdugo and Marshall went with separate parties to the canyon. The Sonoran, however, was not a prisoner. The Indians did not take his horses, and he could have left at any time. Santos, however, presented a different story when first called to the stand. He insisted that both Verdugo and Marshall had been prisoners at Los Coyotes Canyon and had been tied up for a while. But when recalled later, Santos admitted that he had previously lied to the court. This time he claimed that Verdugo and Marshall had never been bound while at Los Coyotes Canyon. He also said that he had heard Marshall tell Verdugo that he was against what the Indians were doing and would join the Americans whenever he could. Verdugo had agreed to do the same.[13]

On Friday, December 12, 1851, the trial was concluded. On Sunday morning it was announced to the people of San Diego that Bill Marshall and Juan Verdugo would be executed at two o'clock that afternoon. Santos was given twenty-five lashes on the bare back for giving false testimony. The *San Diego Herald* reports that "the poor devil stood the flogging like a Christian, and when he had received his compliment, shrugged his shoulders, muttering 'that it hurt some,' but he was glad to get off so." [14] José Noca was severely reprimanded but was sent back to his village as designated chief of the Cupeños. He was to exert all his resources to bring in those rebel Indians still at large and in turn would receive the support of all the white authorities.[15]

A few hours before the hanging, a priest visited Marshall and Verdugo and later accompanied them to the scaffold erected near the Catholic cemetery. There the prisoners were allowed to speak. Marshall said that he was prepared to die and hoped that his friends and those present would forgive him for his many transgressions. He insisted, however, that he was innocent of the crime for which he was about to die. Verdugo, speaking in Spanish, acknowledged his guilt and admitted the justness of his sentence. He said he was ready and willing to die for his crimes and wickedness. Because the fall was only about a foot, the necks of the prisoners did not break. Marshall struggled violently but Verdugo twisted only slightly, their bodies dangling about an hour-and-a-half before being cut down. Witnessing the execution was a large assembly, including many Indians who "seemed to be impressed with becoming awe," as the *San Diego Herald* put it.[16]

The second military tribunal, this one conducted by the United States Army, was convened on December 23, 1851, in Los Coyotes Canyon.[17] Once the Indians had been defeated, messages were sent to various capitanes in the vicinity, ordering that they present themselves at once to Captain Heintzelman. Furthermore, the United States Indian Commissioner, O. M. Wozencraft, demanded that the Indian capitanes deliver all those who were instigators and active participants in the murder of the four Americans and in the attack on Warner's rancho. Some turned themselves in on orders from their leaders while others were brought in by force.[18] Captain Heintzelman decided that there was enough evidence against four Indians to convene a council of war. Brought to trial were Francisco Mocate (capitán of Wilakal), Luis (the alcalde of Kupa), Jacobo (Qui-sil), and Juan Bautista (Coton).[19]

Composed of eight commissioned officers with J. J. Warner as interpreter, the council opened at three in the afternoon on December 23. The first to be tried was Juan Bautista (Coton), who was charged with assisting in the murder of Joseph Manning. The charge was explained to Bautista and he pleaded not guilty. After being confronted with testimony from José Noca, however, who evidently had been brought up from Kupa, he confessed and recounted what had taken place on the night of the murders. The council found Juan Bautista guilty as charged and sentenced him to die.[20]

Jacobo (Qui-sil) was then arraigned on the charge of assisting in the murder of Manning and the three other Americans, to which he pleaded not guilty. José Noca was again called as a witness and insisted that he had only heard that Jacobo had been present at the killings. While José (son of Dominga) claimed that he had actually seen Jacobo in Manning's room armed with a lance, Luis, the alcalde of Kupa, insisted that Jacobo had not been present at the murders. Another witness, Bonifacio, first denied that Jacobo had been present, but changed his testimony when his father, Ramón, stated that he had seen Jacobo when Manning was taken from the room. Ramón also claimed that immediately after the murders, Jacobo had gone to Wilakal, probably to convey the news to Antonio Garra, who had sent him back to Kupa with orders that all the people should evacuate Kupa for Wilakal or other remote points. Francisco Mocate told the court that Garra (probably young Garra) had ordered Jacobo to follow Bill Marshall and Juan Verdugo, both of whom had been instructed to kill the invalids. The council of war, after examining all the evidence, declared the testimony of José (son of Dominga) to be the most valid and based its verdict on it. Jacobo was found guilty and was sentenced to be executed.[21]

The third case brought Luis, the alcalde of Kupa, before the tribunal. He also was charged with assisting in the murder of Joseph Manning and the three other Americans. Luis pleaded guilty and proceeded to recount his version of the murders. Unanimously, the court found Luis guilty and sentenced him to die.[22]

Francisco Mocate, capitán of Wilakal, was the last Indian to face the tribunal. He was charged with assisting in the attack on Warner's rancho and in destroying and despoiling the house and property, to which he pleaded not guilty. Francisco, the son-in-law of José Noca, was called as a witness and asserted that Mocate had led his own people in the attack on the rancho but that Chapuli, chief of Los Coyotes Cahuillas, had been in overall command. According to Francisco, the Indians attacked the rancho because they had been ordered to do so by Garra (probably young Garra) and because they feared to disobey. Mocate, when confronted with Francisco's statement, confessed that he had led his people to the rancho but only from fear of Garra. He said that he had had no intention of killing or hurting Warner and had arrived at the rancho after Warner's escape. Francisco, however, claimed that he had seen Mocate in Warner's house, joining in the plunder. Another witness, Augustín, stated that he had seen Mocate and his people returning from the attack but had not noticed if they possessed stolen property. J. J. Warner was then called to testify but could add no pertinent information as to Mocate's guilt or innocence. The tribunal found Francisco Mocate guilty as charged and sentenced him to die with the other convicted prisoners.[23]

The Indian Commissioner, O. M. Wozencraft, a witness to all the proceedings, agreed with the findings of the council of war. He states in his report that "being present by request in the foregoing Council of War . . . and being convinced of the urgent necessity of inflicting summary punishment in order to prevent future occurrences . . . and being fully satisfied of the guilt . . . I concur fully in the proceedings, findings, and recommendations of the Council." [24] After listening to a short speech by the commissioner and after supposedly admitting that their punishment was well deserved,[25] the four prisoners, kneeling at the head of their graves, were shot to death by a squad of twenty soldiers.[26] According to Wozencraft, "to have done less after they knew we were aware of their guilt would have been fraught with evil; as it is we may confidently anticipate a continued peace." [27] Witnessed by some eighty Indians, the execution took place at ten o'clock Christmas morning, 1851.[28]

The day before the execution at Los Coyotes Canyon, General Joshua Bean had returned to the U.S. Army post at Rancho del Chino with eleven Indian prisoners, the most important being young Garra.[29] A military court-martial was convened at once, this one again conducted by the state militia. Consisting of General Bean, Major M. Norton, Lieutenant C. Smith, Roy Bean, Diego Sepulveda, Ignacio Palomares, Luis Roubidox, and Ignacio Alvardo, the tribunal brought charges against young Garra and followers by the names of José, José Luis, Blass, and Juan. They were accused of treason, murder, and robbery—treason for levying war against the people of the United States, murder for killing the four Americans, and robbery for stealing cattle and other property from Warner's rancho.[30]

Young Garra was first called before the tribunal and stated that he was the son of Antonio Garra, that he wrote and spoke a little Spanish, that he knew nothing about the murders at Kupa, and that when his father was absent José María Moro commanded the people. He claimed that he had neither killed the invalids nor taken Warner's cattle or horses, but he admitted having been at Kupa when the murders were committed. Roy Bean, however, testified that young Garra, while a prisoner on his way to Rancho del Chino, had told him that he had been in command of the Indians that had killed the four Americans. Bill Marshall's declaration, made in San Diego, was then presented to the court as evidence. It identified young Garra as the commander of the Indians who had killed the invalids.[31]

At this time, the court retired until nine o'clock in the evening. During the adjournment, young Garra issued a confession. He admitted having been a member of the party that had murdered the three Americans in the cemetery. He also confessed that he had gone to Warner's rancho, arriving when Chapuli's Indians were dividing up the spoils. Inside the house he found a sugar tray and some wine. After rounding up some of Warner's cattle and horses, he journeyed to Los Coyotes Canyon with José and José Luis. There, his father told him that José Joaquin Ortega had pledged the help of various Californios and said that a war was beginning which would last for two or three years. When the military tribunal resumed, it found young Garra guilty of all charges and sentenced him to die. It adjourned until five o'clock the following morning, December 27, 1851, when young Garra was shot to death by a firing squad.[32]

The court then proceeded to try José and José Luis under the same charges brought against young Garra, to which they pleaded not guilty. Earlier, however, both prisoners had made declarations. In his statement, José Luis confessed that he had been a member of the party that had killed the invalids. After the murders, his group was to join the one commanded by Chapuli in attacking Warner's

rancho, but when they arrived, the rancho had already
been plundered. They then journeyed to Los Coyotes
Canyon where they remained until Garra's capture. The
other Indian, José, insisted in his statement that he had
not been a participant in the murders. He claimed that the
day following the killings he had left Kupa for Wilakal
where he met Antonio Garra, and a day later they had set
out for the canyon. When young Garra received word
from his father to proceed to Juan Antonio's village, José,
without being invited, traveled with the party and became a prisoner with the others.[33]

The statements of both prisoners were offered in evidence, Ignacio Palomares testifying that they were volun-
tary and had been dictated that morning. Young Garra's
confession was also presented to the prisoners and both
asserted that it was true. Unanimously, the court found
José Luis guilty and sentenced him to be shot. The other
Indian, José, also was found guilty but only by a majority,
Don Diego Sepulveda casting the one dissenting vote.
While two members of the court, Smith and Roubidoux,
were in favor of a death sentence, the majority decided
that because of José's youth he should receive fifty lashes
on the bare back for his punishment.[34]

The following morning at sunrise, December 28, the
sentences were carried out. The other prisoners were
turned over to Don Ignacio Palomares, a magistrate, there
not being enough evidence to bring them to trial.[35] Apparently, the prisoners were transferred to the civil authorities because Captain Lovell, already extremely concerned that a military court-martial conducted by officers
of the state militia had taken place on a U.S. Army post,
refused to take responsibility for the remaining Indians
unless they were placed entirely under his control.[36] Prisoners Juan, Blass, and a woman subsequently made their
escape.[37]

By the end of December, three military tribunals had
convicted and executed six Indians, one American, and a

Sonoran. Of all the Indian prisoners, only Antonio Garra had yet to be brought to trial. While a prisoner at Rancho del Chino, Garra issued two statements, the first being made on December 13, 1851, in the presence of Captain Lovell, General Bean, and others.

I am a St. Louis Indian; was baptized in Mission St. Louis Rey, and from my earliest recollection have been connected with the St. Louis Indians. Have had authority over only a portion of the St. Louis Indians. Never had any connection with the Cahuillas. Was appointed by General Kearny, U.S. Army, commander-in-chief of the St. Louis Indians, in the year 1847. Captain Chapulgas [Chapuli] and Captain Vincente, Cahuillas, came to my rancheria and insisted on my going immediately to take command of the people and Juan Largo (Hon. J. J. Warner) told me that the Americans would come in a few days and kill all the Indians. I excused myself to them by saying that I was sick, and the responsibility would all fall upon me. My people, in company with a party of Cahuillas, from Los Coyotes, started on Saturday, November 23rd, [sic] to rob Juan Largo's rancho of all the cattle, and killed three Americans. Three of my people were also killed by Juan Largo. The Sonoranian boy who was in the employ of Warner is now held a prisoner by my people, at Los Coyotes. The two men named Bill Marshall and Juan Verde [Verdugo], *had nothing to do with the transaction.* I concealed them on purpose to keep them from the knowledge of it. Neither have those men taken any part in the hostilities practiced towards the Americans. They were entirely ignorant of what has been done. I was advised by Joaquin Ortego [sic] and Jose Antonio Estudillo, to take up arms against the Americans. They advised me secretly, that if I could effect a juncture with the other Indian tribes of California, and commence an attack upon all the Americans wherever we could find them, that the Californians would join with us, and help in driving the Americans from the country. They advised me to this course that I might revenge myself for the payment of taxes, which has been demanded of the Indian tribes. The Indians think the collection of taxes from them a very unjust measure. This advice was given to me by Juan Ortego in his (Ortego's) rancho. No other person was present at the time. I afterwards saw Antonio Estudillo, who advised me to the same effect, assuring me of the co-operation of the Californians, throughout the country.

My men under arms have never exceeded 30 or 40 at any one time. I myself have had no communication with any other tribes than the Yumas [Quechans] and Cahuillas. The former agreed to join with me, but they subsequently refused. I only know of the readiness of the other tribes to combine and kill the Americans, from what Ortego told me. The reason that the Yuma did not stick to their contract was, because of a quarrel about the division of the sheep which we had taken conjointly from the five Americans whom we killed. In the affair with the men with the sheep, ten of my men were killed by the Americans. The party with the sheep were killed this side of the Colorado. I know of no murders committed by my people, other than those of the men with the sheep, and those at Agua Caliente [Kupa]. Know nothing about the killing of the ferrymen.[38]

On December 16, Garra made another declaration, again claiming that it was Ortega who first encouraged him to lead the Indians against the Americans. Again he insisted that Estudillo had told him that the Californios would come to the assistance of the Indians. Garra mentioned the fight with the sheepmen, but claimed that he had attempted to prevent it. He also said that he had attempted to halt the attack on Warner's rancho. He went with the war party to Wilakal because "he always went with them" but remained at the village because he was ill. Garra was still there when the party returned with the stolen cattle on its way to Los Coyotes Canyon. Two days later he departed for the canyon where he remained silent until he left for his meeting with Juan Antonio.[39]

On January 9, 1852, General Bean, with Garra in his custody, arrived in San Diego.[40] Garra was turned over to Lieutenant Thomas Sweeny of the U.S. Army, the commander whose small detachment on the Colorado River had witnessed the outbreak of hostilities. According to Sweeny, he and Garra had a long talk one night as the trial was proceeding. Garra admitted that he was one of the chiefs who had urged that Sweeny's command be surrounded. Furthermore, Garra claimed that the Quechans had attempted to enter the stockade under his orders and that only Sweeny's twelve-pound howitzer had saved the soldiers. The chief also mentioned that he had been present when the sheepmen were killed.[41]

Garra also talked with Captain Robert Israel, mentioning to him that a chief in the San Bernardino Mountains, presumably Juan Antonio, had offered him three hundred warriors and that José Antonio Estudillo and José Joaquin Ortega had promised to come to his assistance. Garra also told Israel that he had convinced his followers that he could turn the white man's bullets into water.[42] Years later, O. M. Wozencraft asserted that Garra had persuaded his people that he could charm the bullets of the white man so they would hurt no more than water.[43]

Once captured, the Cupeño chief realized that all his efforts to unify the Indians of southern California had failed and that his followers, defeated in battle, were anxious for peace. He was aware that even if released his influence among his people would now be tenuous at best. Before dying, he sought a confrontation with José Joaquin Ortega to prove that various Californios had encouraged him to lead an uprising against the Americans.[44]

On January 9, 1852, the state militia convened the fourth and final court-martial of the Indian rebels. The tribunal consisted of General Bean, Major M. Norton, Major Santiago Arguello, Captain G. B. Fitzgerald, and Lieutenants Hooper and Tilghman of Fitzgerald's Volunteers.[45] Lieutenant Sweeny refused to sit on the court because it was organized by state authorities.[46] Captain Cave Couts was appointed judge advocate, J. J. Warner interpreter, and Major McKinstry, at the request of the court, consented to act as defense counsel. The prisoner was arraigned on charges of treason, murder, and robbery. The specifications stated that Garra levied war against the state of California during the months of November and December 1851, that he abetted and ordered the attack on Warner's rancho, resulting in the killing of the four invalids at Kupa, and that he aided and abetted the stealing of cattle at Warner's rancho and sheep on the Colorado River. Garra pleaded guilty only to having participated in the stealing of the sheep.[47]

The first witness for the prosecution, J. J. Warner, testified that he had no evidence that would incriminate Antonio Garra. He then described what had happened to him the morning the Indians struck. When asked if he knew the names of the Indians who attacked his ranch, he replied that he did not. When asked who is looked upon as chief of the party that made the attack, he replied that it was Antonio Garra. "I know nothing further, of the Agua Calientes murder," states Warner, "except that I saw the dead bodies. I believe those who attacked me are of the San Louis Indians of whom the prisoner is chief." [48] The prosecution had no further questions but pointed out that the Indians who had attacked Warner's rancho were Cahuillas, not Luiseños.[49]

Garra agreed that the Indians who had attacked the rancho were Cahuillas. When probed as to why he had remained at Wilakal while his people went on to Kupa to kill the Americans, Garra replied that he had been sick. He insisted that he had not commanded the parties that had killed the Americans and attacked the rancho.[50] Garra admitted forcing Bill Marshall into joining him but claimed that no harm would have come to the American had he refused. Concerning the October feast held at José Joaquin Ortega's rancho, Garra stated that neither he nor any of his people had attended.[51]

After Garra's testimony, the court adjourned until four o'clock when it heard more from J. J. Warner.[52] Then Garra's defense counsel, Major McKinstry, challenged the court's right to issue the charge of treason, arguing that Garra, being an Indian leader, had a perfect right to make war. Moreover, having never taken the oath of allegiance to the United States, he could not properly take cognizance of the offense he had committed. The court then adjourned until the following day.[53]

At nine in the morning of January 10, the court resumed with Lieutenant Hamilton being sworn. He had acted as recorder at the council of war at Los Coyotes Canyon on December 23, 1851, and related to the court the details of the Indian testimonies at that tribunal. General Bean was then called upon to make a statement, followed by Major McKinstry who addressed the court in a long argument, again denying the right of the court to charge an Indian with treason. McKinstry insisted that Garra was a prisoner of war and was recognized as such by many citizens. In conclusion, the major demanded, in the name of an outraged community, that José Joaquin Ortega be brought before the court, for Garra was prepared to reveal incriminating evidence against the Californio.[54]

McKinstry's request was refused and the members of the court retired to deliberate. Finding the prisoner guilty of murder and theft, but not of treason, they sentenced him to die. About three o'clock the same day, January 10, Garra was informed of the verdict. A padre remained with him till half past four when the preparations were ready.[55] Lieutenant Sweeny refused General Bean's request that his men shoot Garra because he considered the trial and execution strictly an affair of the state of California.[56] Escorted to the spot of his execution by a ten-man squad, Garra seemed unconcerned. "No unbecoming levity marked his conduct," reports the San Diego Herald, "but his whole deportment evinced the brave man prepared to meet his fate." Only after the padre's repeated demands that he seek forgiveness for his sins did Garra, with a smile denoting contempt and in a voice devoid of any tremor, calmly retort: "gentlemen, I ask your pardon for all my offenses, and expect yours in return." Finally allowing a blindfold to be placed over his eyes, Garra, kneeling at the head of his grave, was shot to death.[57]

To one observer, "his obstinancy exceeded anything I ever witnessed." [58] Another exclaims that "no man could have met his fate in a more brave and dignified manner than did Antonio Garra. I could not but feel a sort of sympathy for him, notwithstanding his crimes." [59] For the San Diego Herald, the occasion produced the following rhetoric:

The sun's last rays were at this moment lingering on the hills of Point Lobos, while the bells of the neighboring church chimed vespers. In an instant, the soul of a truly "brave" winged its flight to the regions of eternity, accompanied by the melancholy howling of dogs, who seemed to be aware of the solemnity of the occasion—casting a gloom over the assembled hundreds, who, whilst acknowledging the justness of Antonio's fate, failed not a drop of tear o'er the grave of a brave man once powerful chieftain.[60]

The following week, the *Herald*, in a caustic mood, printed a brief note condemning Garra to hell. Signed by Dr. Wozencraft, Indian Agent, General Bean, and staff, it was printed in the section reserved for steamer sailings.

DEPARTURES,—*Antonio Garra*, Tierra Caliente.[61]

The Garra Uprising was now over.[62] Its repercussions, already apparent locally, were to extend far beyond the region where the events took place.

Repercussions

While Antonio Garra failed to forge a solid alliance (by his own admission he had never commanded more than thirty or forty armed men),[1] the initial response of the whites was based on the belief that the Indians had, indeed, united. Shortly after the attack on the sheepmen and on Sweeny's command, speculation was beginning to run wild. Writing to the *Los Angeles Star* on November 20, 1851, a Californio claims that a messenger from Garra had told him that his chief "had gone to the river Colorado and had killed all the Americans who were there and had thrown them into the river . . . and that already Antonio had sent to the river, to draw the cannon that belonged to the deceased . . . to enter Los Angeles." [2]

On November 23, the Mormons at San Bernardino received word from Los Angeles that the river Indians had risen and killed all the Americans in that neighborhood. It was reported that J. J. Warner was dead and that a confederacy had been formed between the Cahuilla Indians of the San Bernardino region and all the mountain Indians as far as Santa Barbara. These Indians were poised, ready to attack simultaneously all points between the two towns.[3]

In Los Angeles and San Diego rumors spread as to how many warriors were involved. General Joshua Bean, of the state militia, wrote to the governor on November 30 stating:

If the Indians of the Rivers Gila and Colorado, should destroy the United States Troops and Ferrymen, they would probably advance in order to form a junction with the Aguas Calientes

[Cupeños] and Cahuilla Indians. If this junction should be effected, it would present an Indian force of four or five thousand warriors. It would strain the energies of this country to their utmost tension, to resist so formidable a combination, if it could be resisted at all.[4]

Also writing to the governor was the sheriff of San Diego County, Agostin Haraszthy. He estimated that Antonio Garra had from four to five hundred men under his command and could muster within three days at least three thousand more. The sheriff claimed, moreover, that Garra's followers had a large number of six-shooters and rifles and were proficient in their use.[5]

The *San Diego Herald* of November 27, 1851, calculates that if all the Indians from the Colorado River west to Warner's rancho and south to Baja California took up arms, an "Indian mob numbering ten-thousand souls" would be involved.[6] In a letter to his relatives in the East, dated December 2, Thomas Whaley, exclaims that "we momentarily expect to be attacked by Indians who under their great chief Antonio Garra are swarming by the thousands in the south." [7] A report from San Diego, published in San Francisco's *Daily Alta California* on December 3, states that Garra was "in command of not less than three-thousand Indians, which he has been over twelve months organizing; is now, and has done this within *sixty miles* of this town." [8] On December 5, the *Los Angeles Star* printed a letter from Duff Weaver, brother of Paulino and resident of San Bernardino. Weaver claims that Garra sent him the following message:

Tell them that the Americans and Californians are not worth a cigar. They can't fight and are cowards. Tell them I have a good and strong hold here with 2,000 armed men, and they can't get me out of here for the three years to come. Tell them also that I have plenty of money, horses, mares, sheep &., and tell them to come on.[9]

Why Garra would contact Weaver is not known. But whether true or not, the publication of the note contributed to the speculation as to how many Indians were under arms.

When it became known that Garra had written to José Joaquin Ortega and to José Antonio Estudillo, a widespread belief emerged among the American community that various Californios were either in support of or actually in league with the rising Indians. The *San Diego Herald* of November 27 cautions its American readers "to pause and reflect, before proceeding to execute vengeance upon a people [the Californios] who, speaking a language different from our own, are not enabled to fully explain their position in the present unhappy state of affairs." One of the reasons for proclaiming martial law, claims the newspaper, is that "a portion of the native Californians were backward in volunteering to punish the Indians, and it was deemed prudent, under the circumstance, to bring them under strict military discipline." [10] Similarly, the *Los Angeles Star* of November 29 warns its readers that "there can be no doubt that the Indians have been stimulated to an insurrection at this time by some outlawed Californians, and it is not improbable that the Indians have been led to believe that they would have the assistance of all the Californians in the attack upon the Americans." [11]

A letter written in Los Angeles on November 30 states:

Almost the whole California population is disaffected with our *institutions*—or, you may change the word, and say our *tax system*. Fond of changes—use to *"revolution"* every two years, they are restive under our system. . . . There are undercurrents at work here, which I have not time to explain, but which point to but one common cause—a deep, deadly hatred in the minds of the lower order of native Californians against Americans. The smouldered fire is breaking out in a general Indian war, excited, as Indians themselves say, by Californian emissaries.[12]

The *Herald* reports in late December that at Los Coyotes Canyon, "letters were found signed by some of the native Californians, and addressed to Antonio, the contents of which prove the truth of the *confessions* we published last week." [13] And in early January the *Herald* claimed that a member of the "notorious" Lugo family was openly at work in Baja California raising a company of Mexicans to assist the Indians.[14]

Given the excitement generated by this kind of speculation, it is no wonder that Californian and American tempers easily flared. In San Diego, for example, a duel was arranged between two antagonists who were to fight on horseback with Mexican lances. The matter, however, was eventually settled over a drink or as the *Herald* caustically put it, "a 'sling'—differing from that which the valorous little Davy slew the vaunting Philistine in it being a weapon used in a more spiritual warfare." [15]

José Joaquin Ortega was not long in strongly denying any involvement in the uprising. Early in January a letter from Ortega was published in California's newspapers, countering Garra's charges that he had encouraged the Indians to rise. "Were it not that my name has been published to the world in this transaction," he writes, "I should not think it of sufficient importance to make a defense in public." Relying on a clear conscience, fidelity to the flag, and the opinion of friends, he refutes "with indignation, every and each implication of Antonio Garra, and, with the relation of one or two matters which passed under my own observation, leave an intelligent public, capable I believe of discriminating between the character of a white man and an Indian, to draw just conclusions." Ortega continued with an account of what transpired at his Santa María rancho in October 1851, when a large group of Indians, all of whom he identified as Diegueños, had gathered for a feast. According to Ortega, he advised the Indians to remain quiet and not to cause any trouble.[16]

Ortega and José Antonio Estudillo had both supporters and critics. In a letter to the *Los Angeles Star*, one individual questions "how any man in his senses could have done as they are charged with doing. . . . They are both men having large interests in the country; have families and positions in society." While acknowledging that "in conversations with Indians, they may have made some inconsiderate remarks upon the condition of affairs with reference to the enormous taxes which were levied in the county of San Diego," the writer does not believe they were guilty of encouraging the Indians to rise.[17] Another supporter suggests that if Estudillo "had ever made any promises of that kind, it must have been when old Antonio had him scared. . . . He was trying to find out what the Indians were up to and . . . never promised them any help." [18] Expressing the opposite view—that the Californios were indeed implicated—a citizen writes:

I understand that Estudillo was one of the jury which sentenced Marshall to be hung. For consistency's sake they should have added Joaquin Ortega. San Diego is immortalized and unless I am very much mistaken her immortality will be of a kind not to be coveted. These men, (Estudillo and Ortega), are suspected, and not without strong grounds, of being the real leaders of the insurrections and yet one of them is put upon a jury to try a man who is probably the least guilty of the three. I believe that the innocent are oftener punished than the guilty. Influence of family, and money, will shield them under any circumstances, but woe to the innocent man, if he be but friendless and poor. The whole organization for the dispensing of justice—judges, officers, and other paraphernalia—is not worth a fig, and promises no very speedy improvement. God befriend the innocent.[19]

On January 17, 1852, the *San Diego Herald* published an opinion of the members of the court-martial that had tried and convicted Antonio Garra.

Everything that has come before the Court shows conclusively, that Antonio Garra is himself the author of this slander; that no papers were found in the Coyotes confirmatory of the connection of any Californians with the Indians, (as published in the San Diego *Herald*); and that these gentlemen now stand in our community as they have always, in our highest estimation.[20]

A week later, the *Los Angeles Star* printed a letter in which the author, calling himself "Justicia," refused to ac-

cept the opinion of General Bean and his staff without
further evidence. He questions if

Ortega and Estudillo think the unsupported certificate of that
court has the authority of law? It may have with the Californians, but it has not with Americans. The people demand some
legal evidence to be published exonerating these two Senores
before they can arrest their present convictions, that there was a
deep laid, damnable plot with the Indians, in which those two
men are supposed to have had some agency, against law, civilization and the fraternization of Californians and Americans in a
lasting common brotherhood. Let us have the evidence! The
shade of Marshall calls for evidence! [21]

In response, General Bean composed his own letter to
the *Star*.

I know Antonio Garra well; I was with him constantly for thirty
days, and had frequent conversations with him, relative to his
revolt, and a more prevaricating old scamp, I never knew; he
would tell me that all the Californians were implicated with
him, and then he would say that none of them were concerned
except Messers. Ortega and Estudillo, and he so frequently con-
tradicted himself as to establish in my mind the belief that he
was indebted entirely to his imagination for everything that he
related. I have known Messers. Ortega and Estudillo, for several years, and with the latter I have been officially associated
during the administration of Gen. Riley, when that esteemed
and popular veteran appointed Mr. Estudillo, on account of his
unblemished reputation, Prefect of San Diego, and I always
found him in my intercourse, whether public or private, an
upright and honest man, and I speak only the individual opinion of the entire population of San Diego, Americans as well as
Californians, when I say that I believe those two gentlemen to
be totally innocent of the charges made by Garra.

Justicia speaks of the shade of Marshall calling for evidence. I
cannot but condemn the stoical morality of violating the memory of the dead to blast the reputation of the living.[22]

Also causing much controversy was Bill Marshall's
statement that the Lugos and the Mormons of San Bernardino had been in league with Garra.[23] Writing to the *Star*
in early January 1852, Benjamin Wilson stated that Garra,
in the presence of General Bean, himself, and others, had

Plate 1. Mission San Diego

Plate 2. Mission San Gabriel de Arcangel

Plate 3. Quechan (Yuma) Indians

Plate 5. *Asistencia* of Santa Isabel

Plate 4. Mission San Luis Rey de Francia

Plate 6. Los Angeles in 1850

Plate 7. J. J. Warner (Courtesy of Security Pacific National Bank, Los Angeles)

Plate 8. The village of Kupa (Agua Caliente) in 1898 (Courtesy of Title Insurance and Trust Company, Los Angeles)

Plate 9. Cupeño women about 1890 (Courtesy of Title Insurance and Trust Company, San Diego)

Plate 10. Hot springs at the village of Kupa (Agua Caliente) (Courtesy of Title Insurance and Trust Company, San Diego)

Plate 11. San Bernardino fortified during the Garra Uprising (Courtesy of Security Pacific National Bank, Los Angeles)

Plate 12. San Diego in 1850

Plate 13. Edward Fitzgerald Beale, California's first superintendent of Indian affairs (Courtesy of Title Insurance and Trust Company, San Diego)

Plate 14. Indian Agent B. D. Wilson (Courtesy of Title Insurance and Trust Company, Los Angeles)

Plate 15. Indian Subagent Cave J. Couts about 1850 (Courtesy of Title Insurance and Trust Company, San Diego)

Plate 16. Manuelito Cota about 1873 (Courtesy of Title Insurance and Trust Company, San Diego)

Plate 17. (above and below) Luiseño Indians at a celebration in San Diego about 1892 (Courtesy of Title Insurance and Trust Company, San Diego)

Plate 18. (below) Luiseño Women at a celebration in San Diego (Courtesy of Title Insurance and Trust Company, San Diego)

insisted that he knew nothing about any such charge made by Marshall and had never said anything to implicate the Lugos in the uprising.[24] Marshall's claim that Juan Bautista had told him that the Mormons would give aid to the rising Indians was emphatically denied by Charles Rich, one of the Mormon elders. Rich wrote to the *Star* suggesting that if the story had not emanated from Marshall then someone who was against the Mormons must have told it to Bautista. According to Rich, Bautista had been to the Mormon rancho only once, seeking work for his people and claiming friendship to all Americans.[25]

The causes of the outbreak were also debated. To some it was a result of governmental neglect. According to O. M. Wozencraft, the Indians rose because General Kearny had failed to keep the promises made to the Indians when he passed through their territory in late 1846 and because Commissioner George Barbour had failed to meet with them to conduct a treaty.[26] Indian subagent Adam Johnston declares that the Indians "became dissatisfied in consequence of treaties having been made with other Indians in the valley, who have to some extent, been furnished with substance." [27] In a similar vein, the *Daily Alta California* editorializes "that the present warlike movement of the southern savages may have been promoted by jealous and indignant feelings arising from the fact that the northern Indians have been treated with so much more consideration than they, by the agents of the United States government." [28]

To others, the taxing of the Indians was thought to be the major cause of the uprising. A Los Angeles resident claims that

there is nothing new in their being troubles with the Indians at Warner's. He has been driven off his rancho before by the Indians. There is a quarrel of long standing between Warner and the Indians, on account of some land which both claim. The old trouble has received fresh aggravation this season, in consequence of the Sheriff of San Diego having seized the property of the Indians for taxes; and as Warner is the Senator from that county, it is natural that the Indians should charge the business to him.[29]

The *Los Angeles Star* of December 20 reports that "upon inquiry we are informed that the laws of the State sustain the taxing of Indians. If so, the law should be changed, for certainly the Indians receive no protection from the government and there can be no good reasons why they should be compelled to bear its burdens. . . . Rebellions have grown out of slighter causes than this." [30]

An explanation as to why the uprising failed was presented in an editorial in the *San Diego Herald* on February 3, 1852.

Many of their leaders were men of information, and of such a degree of education as is ordinarily met with among the self-styled *gente de razon,* or civilized people of old California. Their endeavors to combine the tribes, so as to commence a course of hostilities that should end in the complete extinction of the white inhabitants, were characterized by a degree of system and military skill that would be credible to many persons occupying a higher degree of social consideration. That they failed, is principally owing to the difficulties of subduing the hatred existing between different tribes; to the jealousy of the principal chiefs; to the difficulty of effecting a simultaneous rising over so large an extent of country; to their neglecting to direct their first movement upon the most important position; and to the natural caprice of Indian characters, so averse to the constant pursuit of one object.[31]

Juan Antonio's role in the uprising was also discussed. The *Los Angeles Star* of December 20 states that "Juan Antonio has proved himself a useful friend to the whites, although in his capture of Garra, his treachery requires no very strong commendation. His course was influenced beyond a doubt by the hope of gain, and he had made a pretty nice calculation as to which side would pay the best." [32] The *Star* of January 24 is also very uncomplimentary, declaring that Antonio "is a remarkable cunning and sagacious Indian, and his enemies are not a little slow to charge him with being at the same time a very dishonest one, and attribute the part he has played in the late disturbances, to his judgment in choosing between two enemies rather than from any good feeling towards the Americans." [33] According to O. M. Wozencraft, only when the northern Indians refused his request to join in the war did Antonio become a good friend of the Americans.[34]

In the meantime, as the debate continued, the long-promised treaties with the Indians of southern California were finally negotiated. While in Los Coyotes Canyon, Captain Heintzelman had sent word to Indian leaders in nearby villages to meet Commissioner O. M. Wozencraft at Temecula. Heintzelman and his command, along with Wozencraft, arrived at the village on December 30, 1851, and found assembled nearly all the important Luiseño capitanes.[35] Those who had fled to Mission San Luis Rey for protection had returned by this time.[36] Juan Antonio and other Cahuilla officials, however, were not present, the chief having sent word to Wozencraft that he was a good Indian and therefore did not need to come.[37] J. J. Warner and Lieutenant Patterson immediately departed for Saha-tapa to speak with Antonio. Arriving on the morning of January 1, 1852,[38] Warner told a hesitant Antonio that troops would be sent against him if he refused to meet with the Indian commissioner.[39] Antonio was reluctant to journey south because Temecula was in enemy territory. It was near there in January 1847 that Antonio and his followers had slaughtered thirty-eight Luiseños and Cupeños.

Antonio, however, had little choice in the matter. With twelve of his capitanes,[40] and accompanied by Warner, Patterson, and Paulino Weaver, he journeyed to Teme-cula, arriving on January 2. According to one observer, Antonio's men "had a very warlike appearance as they rode up to Apis' Rancho, and there could be seen the deep hatred and distrust existing between the San Lui-seños and the Cahuiyas. For some time there appeared to be nobody in existence except Juan Antonio." [41] Arriving the same day was L. D. Vinsonhaler whom Wozencraft had sent into the region between Merced and the Tejon Pass to ascertain if the Indians there had been in contact with Cahuillas. He reported that runners from the southern portion of the state had been sent into the area, inviting the Tulareños to join with them in a war against the Americans.[42]

That evening Antonio and Wozencraft met alone in the house of the Luiseño leader Pablo Apis, the Cahuilla chief not wanting any of his capitanes present. Antonio was very indignant that he, a good Indian, had been compelled to come to Temecula.[43] He explained to the commissioner all he had done for the Americans and stated that he had taken charge of all Indian affairs in the region. Wozencraft, deeming it bad policy to have any one Indian exercise too much authority and desiring to put Antonio in his place, informed the chief that he was aware that Cahuilla emissaries had been sent north, seeking the support of the Tulareños.[44] According to Wozencraft, "when I charged him with this treachery, all his boasting arrogance departed, and he thought I was going to kill him. I told him . . . that I was not going to kill him, but was going to make him behave himself, and be a good Indian, as he boasted he was." Because Antonio had insisted on meeting without the presence of his capitanes, the commissioner held him directly responsible for all the actions of his people.[45]

On January 5, 1852, Wozencraft conducted a treaty with the chiefs and capitanes of the Cahuilla, Luiseño, and Serrano. The treaty stated that the Indians must acknowledge the United States to be the sole and absolute sovereign of all the territory ceded to it by the treaty of peace with Mexico. The Indians agreed to accept the exclusive jurisdiction, authority, and protection of the United States government and to refrain from all acts of hostility and aggression against its citizens. Furthermore, the Indians were to live at peace among themselves and with all other Indian societies under the protection of the United States.

They were to conform to and be governed by the laws and regulations of the Indian Bureau.[46]

The territory set aside for the Indians was to be for their sole use and occupancy, although the government of the United States claimed all mineral rights. The United States also claimed the right-of-way over any portion of the territory and the right to establish and maintain military posts, public buildings, schoolhouses, and houses for agents, teachers, and other individuals who may be needed. The Indians, in turn, were never to claim any other lands within the boundaries of the United States.[47]

To aid the Indians in their subsistence while making their settlements on the reservation, the United States government promised them, free of charge and within two years, 2,500 head of beef cattle and 350 sacks of flour. Moreover, after the ratification of the treaty by the president and senate of the United States, the government, to help the Indians acquire the arts and habits of "civilized" life, also promised the following: one pair of pantaloons and one red flannel shirt for each man and boy, one linsey gown for each woman over fifteen years of age, 7,000 yards of calico, 1,700 yards of brown sheeting, 70 pounds of scotch thread, 4 dozen pairs of scissors, 14 dozen thimbles, 5,000 needles, 7,000 pounds of iron, and 6,000 pounds of steel. During the first year after ratification, the Indians were to receive for their permanent use 130 brood mares and 7 stallions, 600 young cows and 36 bulls, 20 head of working oxen with yokes and chains, 20 work mules or horses, 42 plows of assorted sizes, 340 corn hoes, 140 spades, and 20 grindstones.[48]

The government was to employ and settle among or near the Indians one practical farmer and two assistants to supervise all agricultural operations, one wheelwright, one blacksmith, one principal school teacher and as many assistant teachers as needed. All the workmen and teachers were to be maintained and paid by the government for a period of five years and as long after as the president thought advisable. The United States would

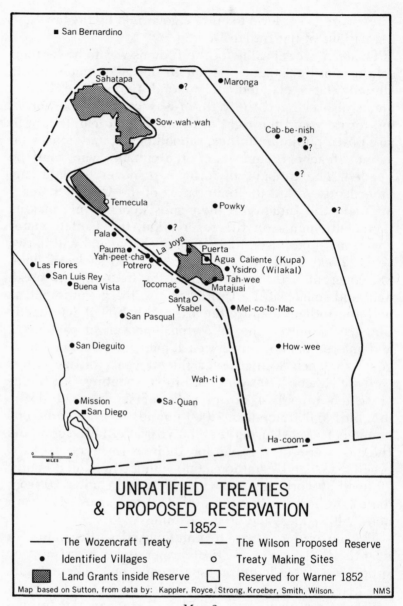

■ San Bernardino

●Sahatapa

●? ●Maronga

●Sow-wah-wah

Cab-be-nish
●
●?
●?

●?

○Temecula ●Powky

●?

Pala● ●?

La Joya

Pauma● Puerta
Yah-peet-cha● ☐ Agua Caliente (Kupa)
Potrero ● Ysidro (Wilakal)
●Las Flores Tah-wee
●San Luis Rey Tocomac● Matajuai
●Buena Vista
Santa○
Ysabel ●Mel-co-to-Mac
●San Pasqual

●San Dieguito ●How-wee

Wah-ti●

●Mission ●Sa-Quan
■San Diego

Ha-coom●

0 5 10
MILES

UNRATIFIED TREATIES
& PROPOSED RESERVATION
−1852−

—— The Wozencraft Treaty — — The Wilson Proposed Reserve
● Identified Villages ○ Treaty Making Sites
▨ Land Grants inside Reserve ☐ Reserved for Warner 1852

Map based on Sutton, from data by: Kappler, Royce, Strong, Kroeber, Smith, Wilson.   NMS

Map 3

also erect suitable schoolhouses, shops, and dwellings for the accommodation of these people.[49]

The territory set aside for the Cahuillas, Luiseños, and Serranos was bounded on the north by the San Jacinto and San Gorgonio mountains, on the east by the desert, on the south by San José del Valle, and on the west by a line running from Pauma to beyond Temecula (see map 3).[50] Wozencraft estimated that included within this region would be fifteen to twenty thousand Indians, but the land was rich enough to support all.[51] An addendum to the treaty stated that in case the United States and the proprietor of the Temecula grant could not agree upon terms for its purchase, the government would provide the Indians with another reservation of equal extent. While thirteen Luiseño leaders signed the treaty, Pablo Apis and Manuelito Cota, two of the most important, did not. Because there was no specific treaty negotiated with the Cupeños, José Noca of Kupa signed as a Luiseño. Signing for the Cahuillas were Juan Antonio, Juan Bautista, and twelve other officials.[52]

Shortly after concluding the treaty, Wozencraft, accompanied by J. J. Warner and Lieutenant Hamilton, departed for Santa Isabel, arriving on January 6.[53] The following day a treaty was negotiated with the Diegueños. Tomás and Lázaro of Santa Isabel were two of the twenty-two leaders who signed the document. The territory set aside for the Diegueños was bounded on the north by the Cahuilla and Luiseño grant, on the east by the desert, on the south by the border with Mexico, and on the west by a line running north from the boundary to San Felipe and then northwest to San José del Valle. An addendum to the treaty set aside for J. J. Warner one square league in the vicinity of Kupa for the purpose of improving the hot springs (see map 3).[54] Wozencraft felt that the region was capable of providing the Indian inhabitants with sufficient food.[55]

The two treaties along with sixteen others conducted by the United States Indian Commissioners in California

were debated in the state legislature. The Senate Standing Committee on Indian Affairs issued a majority report
that objected to any recognition of Indian rights to California land. J. J. Warner, whose property had only recently been destroyed by Indians, was the only member
of the legislature to oppose the majority report. He asked
his peers "if the Indians are to be told that those Commissioners had no power to make treaties or that the President or Government can falsify itself, will you expect
them, hereafter, to enter into any treaty or keep one in-
violate after having entered into it?" [56] Presenting the mi-
nority report, Warner questions:

Will it be said that the land is not broad enough for them and us
or that while our doors are open to the stranger from the utter-
most parts of the earth, we have not spare room for the residence of the once sole inhabitants of our magnificent empire?
Shall future generations seek in vain for one remaining descen-
dant of the sons of the forest? Has the love of gold blotted from
our minds all feelings of compassion or justice? [57]

The state legislators, nevertheless, remained adamant
and instructed California's senators in Washington to oppose confirmation. They also felt that the federal government should relinquish all its control over the Indians
residing within the boundaries of the state. Their main
objection to the treaties was that Indians were receiving
valuable land.[58] By February 18, 1852, when the last of
the treaties arrived in Washington, officials in the Department of the Interior and the Bureau of Indian Affairs were
aware that in California there was much opposition to
confirmation. Submitted to the Senate in early June, the
treaties were rejected and remained unratified.[59]

Meanwhile, in March, Congress had established an independent Indian superintendency for California and had
appointed Edward Fitzgerald Beale (see pl. 13) as its first
superintendent. A supporter of ratification, Beale departed for California after the treaties were rejected, arriving in San Francisco in mid-September. He immediately

began to search for a workable Indian policy,[60] and one of his first acts was to offer B. D. Wilson (see pl. 14) a salaried commission as Indian Agent for the state of California.[61] Concerning the appointment, the *Los Angeles Star* comments that the

universal expression of satisfaction at the appointment of Mr. Benj. D. Wilson to the office of Indian Commissioner is the surest evidence that the appointment is a good and proper one. Mr. Wilson is thoroughly acquainted with the Indian character, and has visited most, if not all, the tribes within one hundred miles of this point. In occasions of difficulty between themselves he is always looked to as a mediator, and scarcely a week passes that does not bring some of the chiefs to his residence, invoking his aid and protection. Mr. Wilson accepts the office as much from a desire to secure peace and justice to the Indians, as from a disposition to render the government of the United States whatsoever service may be in his power. We regard the appointment as securing permanent peace with all those tribes which have in times past, been so troublesome to this country.[62]

Wilson's first major assignment was to submit a report on the Indians of southern California. Prepared by Benjamin Hayes from his own vast knowledge and from that contributed by Don Juan Bandini, J. J. Warner, and Hugo Reid, it contains much valuable information on the history, culture, and condition of the southern Indians and offers suggestions as to where they should reside and how they should be controlled.[63]

The B. D. Wilson Report, as it came to be called, recommends that the land set aside for specific Indian occupancy should correspond to where the Indians of southern California were then residing (see map 3).

They are the only places where the different nations could be colonized and established in large numbers, with sufficient land for cultivation. San Gorgonio and San Jacinto each has more than 2000 acres capable of raising barley and wheat, without irrigation; and sufficient water, husbanded as the Missions taught Indians to manage this matter, to supply in abundance beans, pumpkins, and the other crops Indians are familiar with, or can soon be made so. The beautiful valley of Temecula—the granary of San Luis Rey Mission—presents an agriculture area of three times this capacity; and Agua Caliente [Kupa] and the Tejon are not inferior, perhaps superior to Temecula. In the direction of the Tejon, but rather out of the line proposed, there are other good selections that can be made. The Cahuillas can raise 100,000 bushels of wheat or barley annually, at San Jacinto or San Gorgonio. Temecula and Agua Caliente would yield $300,000 worth of like produce every year for the San Luiseños and Diegueños. Equal resources would reward the Tulareños at the Tejon. They do not need annuities. Nature has these in ample store, with their mere rights of property secured, and a judicious management. At Agua Caliente, Coyote, and other places, they still have producing vineyards; and at others, orchards; all planted by themselves for the Missions. At Coyote the grape ripens two months sooner than nearer the coast—at Los Angeles, for instance. All these valleys are fine for every species of fruit, as well as for vegetables and small grain.[64]

According to the report, not a thousand acres of all the proposed territory was then being used by whites, and only three white men were actually residing within the region. The report also requests that three military posts be established: one at the Four Creeks or its neighborhood, a second on the Mohave River, and a third at the junction of the Gila and Colorado rivers. With troops on the Mohave and near the Cajon Pass, Los Angeles County and San Bernardino Valley would be spared the incursions of desert Indians.[65]

The report suggests that on each reserve there should be at least one principal town or pueblo [66] where a subagent, farmer, blacksmith, and carpenter would reside.[67] The land of each town would be held in common until such time as it would be expedient to dispose of it. The land would be cultivated by all the people who were not assigned other tasks. In the beginning, the Indians would need a small supply of clothing, blankets, farm implements, and a few work animals. One thousand head of cattle would amply support them for the first six months.[68]

The Indians should not be allowed to live in dispersed settlements on the reserves because it would interfere with practical education and religious instruction and would make them more difficult to observe. The report also states that the Indians would require a vigilance for their own protection. Because of their wastefulness, all their food products should be kept in common stock and distributed in daily or triweekly rations. Moreover, there should be a fixed number of working hours for every day of the week except Sunday. Although the report does not favor an oppressive reserve system, it does stress that "two rules—a common-stock and compulsory labor—are absolutely indispensable." [69]

The chief was to have no place in the new order. His "desire of power and place may be as well gratified by the substitution of other analogous offers of more civilized life, such as justices of the peace and sheriff." The super-intendent or agent would have the power to make such appointments and all advancements would be contingent upon good behavior. According to the report, the Indians were accustomed to this method of filling the office of chief, it having been the regular practice of Californian of-ficials to appoint Indians to positions of authority.[70]

The report concludes by presenting economic as well as moral reasons why the recommendations should be ac-cepted.

It is not strange that the State government, driven in its in-fancy to expenditures on the scale of an old empire almost, and busy the three years past with the perplexed affairs of its white population—and having very narrow sources of revenue withal—should not have impressed the salutary influence of a wise legislation upon the southern Indians, at a distance of six hundred miles from its capital, whose members were unknown and character completely misconceived. Nor can it be imagined that the people of this State have ever desired, or will desire to put upon its treasury the burden of governing these Indians, and a hundred thousand more within its borders.

Still less will they covet the greater burden and cost of an at-tempt to exterminate such a multitude of tribes, many of them savage and warlike, whose means and mode of life, though very meagre and very miserable, enable them to sustain an almost endless resistance. After all, the experiment of extermination inevitably resolves itself into the better one of preservation and government, and, having wasted much blood and treasure, we are compelled to do at last, what it were always more discreet, as well as more humane and just, to do at the beginning.

An illustration occurs to me not without its lesson. Two little expeditions made in the South since the spring of 1850—one against the Yumas, the other against Antonio Garra—cost the people of California at least $150,000. Will any one believe that their results have been commensurate with what the same sum would have effected, if differently applied among the same southern Indians? I have no hesitation in saying that such a sum would have put in operation and maintained three years, on the plan above proposed, the whole six Indian towns, and left them now flourishing and far on the road of progress!

Humanity, not war is the true policy for them. This is the voice of all experience.[71]

The reference to Antonio Garra and his movement is only one of several scattered throughout the sixty-nine page report, indicating that the opinions of the author were partially shaped by the recent outbreak.[72]

In January 1853 just before his departure for Washington, D.C., Beale was to be given the report in Los Angeles.[73] Just when he received the document is not known, but it is likely that he had either read it or was familar with its recommendations by the time he departed for the capital. Indeed, it seems to have been the foundation of the reservation system that he proposed to his superiors.[74] As Beale saw it, no treaties would be negotiated with the Indians; instead, they would be encouraged to settle on government lands where they would be given agricultural and domestic instruction. The reservation was to be a small, self-supporting, agricultural community. Beale was successful in his mission, and Congress authorized the president to establish five military reservations either in California or in the territories of Utah or New Mexico, and the sum of $250,000 was appropriated to cover expenses.[75]

Beale arrived in Los Angeles from Washington on

August 27, and together with nine assistants, including B. D. Wilson, soon departed for the Tejon Pass.[76] To Beale the pass was an ideal location for a reservation. First of all, its use by hostile Indians, traveling south to raid white settlements, would be prevented by the reservation's military garrison. Second, the area was fertile and capable of irrigation, thus perfect for the development of an Indian agricultural community.[77] On September 12, 1853, Beale explained his plan to more than one thousand assembled Indians.[78] Tejon's beginning was auspicious,[79] and Beale's successor, Thomas J. Henley, established three more reservations in California—Nome Lacke, Klamath, and Mendocino—all located in the northern regions of the state.[80] To deal with the Indians residing south of the Tejon Pass, several subagents, most of them rancheros, were appointed. They were to protect the Indians residing in their immediate vicinities, but their authority was ill defined, and they worked without pay.[81]

Again neglected by the white authorities, the Indians in the southernmost area of the state remained extremely discontented. To many local white residents, another Indian outbreak was imminent.

Chiefs and Americans

On January 21, 1852, Juan Antonio, with about one hundred followers, journeyed to Los Angeles to let the Americans know that he expected to be compensated for his actions in the late war. According to the *Los Angeles Star*, "Juan appears to be a prompt business man as well as a cunning chief, and a debt due by his white brethren is not soon forgotten." [1] Whether his mission was a success or not is unknown, but it was not long before the Cahuillas and, indeed, all the Indians of southern California came to realize that the goods and services promised in the treaty with O. M. Wozencraft were not forthcoming.

As a result, Indian raiding continued and intensified, especially by Cahuillas. In early February 1852, for example, Cahuillas raided Duff Weaver's ranch. [2] Late in the month or early in March, Rancho La Laguna was also attacked. The Indians were found eating one of the cows they had stolen. They fled toward San Gorgonio and were identified as Cahuillas. [3] While such raids were usually designed to secure food rather than to cause damage, many whites feared that the Indians were again planning to rise. "One great cause of dissatisfaction on the part of the Cahuillas," writes Major McKinstry in July 1852, "is the non-fulfillment by Dr. Wozencraft. . . . They complain of want of faith on my part and openly avow a want of confidence in all Americans. . . . My acquaintance with Cahuillas . . . indicates that they are seriously contemplating an outbreak." [4] This fear was shared by Lieutenant Thomas Sweeny who in November 1852 was back on the Colorado River. Sweeny mentions in his journal that "Juan Antonia [*sic*], chief of the Cahuillas, is said to have taken a trip out here, to stir up the tribes in this vicinity again to resistance. Time will tell,—I think there will be war soon." [5] In the same month, Paulino Weaver reported that Juan Antonio had gone to visit the Indians on the Colorado but for what purpose he did not know. Weaver interpreted a recent attack on his rancho as a violent manifestation of Indian discontent at not receiving the aid promised in the treaty with the United States. His house was robbed, all his animals were killed, and even his peach trees were cut down. In a letter to Indian agent B. D. Wilson, Weaver pleads with him to visit the area, for "if some steps are not taken soon to pacify these Indians, there will be bloodshed . . . between them and the whites." [6]

In July 1854 Isaac Williams of Rancho del Chino, writing to the *Los Angeles Star,* complains "that there are a great many wild Indians in the valley, and who have no other resource for a living than killing the stock from off the ranchos. Numbers of animals have been found, some killed and some wounded, and others partly consumed." [7] In November 1855 an Indian capitán admitted that the hostility was a result of governmental neglect. He felt that all the Indians to the north were being taken care of by the government. Consequently, those in the south were going to provide for themselves.[8]

During November it was also reported that all the Indians in the San Bernardino region were leaving for the mountains, where the women and children would remain while the men instigated a war against the whites. At Temecula a small party of armed Californios told an American that Juan Antonio had collected together all the Indians in the vicinity. They were in the mountains five miles away, supposedly to execute a criminal, but the Californios feared they had gathered for other reasons.[9] Writing to his brother in San Diego, a Temecula settler expresses his fears.

The moment that I arrived here I went to see Mr. Susiano and got information about the Indian troubles; this gentleman told me that there is not the slightest doubt that the Indian Juan Antonio wants to raise the Indians, because, for sometime previous he has been very angry with the Government, complaining that the lands for his people have not been designated. The same man told me, that he learned from an Indian, that Juan Antonio is holding a great Council, in the mountains, at the place where Captain Cabezon and his tribe reside. I learn from another person, by indirectly asking how the Indians are: "don't you know the news? all know that the Indians want to rise," and added that an Indian had said, that not only Juan Antonio, but all the Indians are angry, because they have not had justice done them.[10]

Realizing that something must be done, twenty Mormons, including Charles Rich and Jefferson Hunt, called upon Juan Antonio later in the month. The Cahuilla chief received them kindly and assured them he was still friendly to the Americans and ever wished to be. While complaining that whites on Weaver's rancho had taken some of his stock, he reemphasized his desire to remain at peace with the Americans. If they would only leave Indian stock alone, the whites would have nothing to fear from his people.[11] Superintendent Henley was also alarmed and sent a special agent to the region "to quiet any hostile feeling, that may have been produced by the little attention, that has been heretofore bestowed upon them." [12] Henley's agent reported that the Indians harbored no hostile feelings toward the whites. The rumors of an impending uprising, he suggests, were spread by those "who are anxious to have a Reservation established in this portion of the State." [13] Juan Antonio, however, continued to be suspect. In late December 1855 the assistant adjutant general, E. D. Townsend, reports that Juan Antonio had visited "in a suspicious manner, not only the Yumas [Quechans] and Mohaves, but the Tejon, Kern and Kings River Tribes." [14]

Captain H. S. Burton, commander of the military post at San Diego, fearing that hostilities were soon to begin, marched to Temecula in January 1856. Arriving on the nineteenth, he immediately sent for Manuelito Cota and Juan Antonio. On January 22, Antonio arrived, haughty and insolent, according to the captain. Burton asked why he had visited the Quechans in August. Antonio, apparently, was startled by the question, for it indicated to him that his movements for the past five months had been observed by the white authorities. Antonio's manner, claimed Burton, was completely subdued by the end of the conference. During the meeting, however, Antonio made several requests. He asked to see the superintendent so as to have a long talk with him about the twelve or thirteen American families that had settled on his land. He also wanted the plows, hoes, spades, and cattle promised in the treaty that he had signed with Commissioner Wozencraft in 1852.[15]

Burton advised Antonio "to go home to his people and keep them quiet, and probably something would be done for them; that their wishes would be made known to the general commanding the troops; and that they would be punished if they caused difficulties." The captain warned him that "six hundred well-armed men, with plenty cannon, could be brought against him immediately." Burton was convinced that between August and November 1855 Antonio had endeavored to form a combination with the Quechans and the Mohaves. His attempts had failed because the Quechans were not interested and because the Mohaves were too hesitant. Burton recommended to his superiors that Juan Antonio be kept under close surveillance, that once every four to six weeks a detachment of troops, twenty-five to thirty enlisted men under a commissioned officer, be sent to visit him.[16]

Adhering to his plan, Burton sent a detachment of troops, under Lieutenant William Winder, to Sahatapa in April. Juan Antonio complained to Winder that the promised farm implements had yet to arrive and that while some of his people had successfully grown food, most were nearly destitute owing to crop failures. The Cahuilla

chief requested that he be informed when the next detachment of troops was to arrive in order that he may assemble his capitanes in time.[17]

In his report, Winder stated that Juan Antonio would do
all in his power to preserve the peace but predicted that
serious hostilities would break out unless something was
done to alleviate the condition of the Indians. Because
whites in the region were taking their lands, Indians were
responding by raiding isolated forms and ranchos. Winder
mentioned that the whites had threatened to drive the Indians off their remaining lands unless the government put
a stop to their depredations. Winder was sufficiently
alarmed to suggest to his superiors in San Diego that it
would be cheaper to issue the Indians beef than to fight
them.[18]

One of the few white men in the region who gave assistance to the Indians was Isaac Williams of Rancho del
Chino. Writing on May 15, 1856, to George W. Manypenny, commissioner of Indian Affairs, Williams warned
that unless the white settlers were forced to cease their
encroachment upon Indian lands a serious Indian-white
conflict would ensue. He reported that local Indians were
complaining that groups to the north were receiving aid
and assistance while they were being neglected. With a
little aid from the government, these Indians would soon
become prosperous and contented. Williams also reported
that on May 25 all the Cahuilla were going to hold a council in the San Gorgonio Pass.[19]

At the time he wrote the letter, several Cahuilla leaders
had assembled at his rancho and had signed a petition
that was sent to the commissioner. Although obviously
drafted by Williams or another white man, it succinctly
presents the problems then facing the Indians.

The undersigned captains or chiefs of the various tribes comprising the Nation of Corveello [sic] Indians of California desire
to present the following history of their grievances and statement of their wants in order that the United States Government

being informed of their condition and necessities may adopt some measure for their assistance and relief.

The population of our nation is about 5000 of which about 1200 are men, the rest women and children. From time immemorial we have lived upon and occupied the lands of and adjacent to the Pass of San Gorgonia [sic] bounded on the North by the Cajon de los Negros and on the South and West by the Coast Range of Mountains. Since the occupation of California by the Americans and particularly within the last two or three years we have been encroached upon by the white settlers who have taken possession of a large portion of our best farming and grazing lands and by diverting the water from our lands depriving us to a great extent of the means of irrigation. In some instances the water privileges have been wholly monopolized by white settlers thereby depriving us of the most essential means for the successful cultivation of our crops consisting of corn, wheat, beans etc., etc. We have thus been frequently obliged to abandon portions of our improved lands greatly to the detriment and distress of our people.

While most if not all the tribes of Indians of California have received material aid and protection from the Government we have been wholly neglected. In the year 1850 [sic] a treaty was entered into with us by Oill [sic] Wozencraft an Agent of the Government but the said agent failed to comply with any of its conditions.

What we particularly desire and ask of the Government is that certain public lands may be set apart, for our use exclusively, (which lands we have long occupied and improved) and from which we may not be forced by white settlers. We would, also, ask that a reasonable amount of farming implements and oxen may be furnished us in accordance with a uniform custom of the Government, together with such amount of means as may be necessary to improve our means of irrigation.

We further desire to represent that we have received from time to time during a series of years past a limited supply of Beef Cattle and other important aids from Isaac Williams of Rancho del Chino all of which has been furnished us gratuitously. But for this timely assistance many of our people must have been driven to starvation and others have suffered great distress until our crops were properly matured and gathered.

In conclusion while hoping that this our petition may receive just and reasonable attention from the Government of the United States, we particularly desire that any action had for our relief and assistance may be communicated to us through Isaac Williams of Rancho del Chino, California.

The petition was signed by Juan Antonio as principal chief and contained the names of twenty-three other leaders, including Juan Bautista and Cabezon.[20]

In the meantime, to the south in San Diego County, Luiseño leaders Manuelito Cota and Pablo Apis and Diegueño officials Lázaro and Tomás made determined efforts to keep in good stead with the American authorities, assisting them whenever they could. In mid-May 1852, for instance, Apis captured two army deserters who were making their way north through the mountains near Temecula. Pretending to be unaware of their identity, Apis purchased their rifles from them and then got permission to examine their revolvers. Once disarmed, Apis put them under guard and later turned them over to the military in San Diego.[21]

In July the alcalde of the village of San José reported that Cupeños were returning to their villages and that Quechans were occupying the adjacent hills. Supposedly, a Quechan chief had crossed the desert to induce the local Indians into continuing the war against the Americans. He was to attack the next military supply train when it departed for the Colorado River.[22] This chief may have been Gerónimo, Garra's Kamia ally, who was spotted early in September near San Felipe.[23] Lázaro of Santa Isabel volunteered to capture Gerónimo if he received written permission to do so. Captain Magruder of San Diego gave Lázaro the authority he sought and promised him a reward if successful.[24] It was Tomás, however, who finally captured Gerónimo, but not before the Kamia chief had wounded two Diegueños. Tomás, who may have witnessed one of the military tribunals that had convicted

Garra and his allies, immediately convened a trial of his own. At the proceedings, he told Gerónimo that

when the Americans under General Kearny took possession of this country, routing our cowardly oppressors, you as a big Captain of your tribe swore to be their friend. I and my people did the same, and we aided the Americans in the war; we are and ever have been their friends. You are a liar—have not kept your word, and sided Antonio Garra last winter in the war against the Americans. You helped to kill the sheepmen on the desert; you are continually stealing from the Americans. . . . Geronimo you are to be shot, and I shall scalp you and cut off one of your ears to send to San Diego.[25]

Gerónimo admitted that he had come to continue the war against the Americans but claimed that he had only nine men with him. The Kamia chief was then led out and shot. Tomás, attended by a bodyguard armed with lances, took the scalp and one ear of Gerónimo to San Diego where he paid his respects to the principal officials. When he departed for Santa Isabel, Tomás was convinced that he had performed a great service to the American cause. A white resident of San Diego, however, feared that Gerónimo's followers, seeking revenge, would cross the desert and attack the Diegueños, perhaps igniting an inter-Indian war.[26]

Probably in recognition for his service in eliminating Gerónimo, Tomás was presented an American flag by General Hitchcock when he visited San Diego in March 1853. It was reported in the *San Diego Herald* that Tomás "was waited on by deputations from various other tribes, to whom he expressed his determination to preserve peace amongst them."[27] In February of the following year, Superintendent Beale designated Tomás "as Chief and General" of all the Indians in his district. Tomás was to consult the commanding officer in San Diego if he had any problems.[28]

In September 1853 Cave Couts (see pl. 15), Indian subagent for the Luiseños, appointed Manuelito Cota (see pl.

16) as captain general or chief over several villages. Couts
told Cota that he was only to follow the instructions of the
lawful Indian agents, that he had sole jurisdiction over
crimes committed between any of his people, that he
must report to Couts criminal cases between Indians and
whites, that he should visit the Indian agency when in the
vicinity, and that he should consult with Couts before issuing new orders to his people. Cota was given command
over the Luiseño villages of Puerta Cruz, La Puerta, La
Joya, Potrero Primero, Potrero Segundo, Pauma, Pala, Temecula, Aguanga, San Luis Rey, Santa Margarita, Las
Flores, and two others. Furthermore, he was also put in
charge of the Cupeño villages of Kupa and Wilakal and
the Cahuilla villages in Los Coyotes Canyon (see map
4).[29] The extent of Cota's influence before this appointment is not known. But it may have been limited, since
his name does not appear on the 1852 treaty with Wozencraft. Cota's chieftainship, therefore, was not his own creation but that of a white man—subagent Couts.

As white-appointed Indian leaders, Cota and Tomás
were continually being watched by the American authorities. In March 1854 the *Herald* reported that Tomás was
having problems governing his people and suggested that
it had been a mistake to appoint him captain general of
the Diegueños. The county sheriff had publicly whipped
him for stealing, and as a consequence he had lost the respect of his people. White residents in the area called
upon Cave Couts to extend his jurisdiction over the
Diegueños and to remove Tomás and appoint Panto in his
place.[30] When Superintendent Beale arrived in San Diego
in April or May, Major McKinstry prevailed upon him to
keep Tomás while Couts and others sought his removal.[31]
Tomás was replaced by Panto,[32] but he continued to act as
if he were still captain general. On one occasion he told
Panto that he was still the chief because he had received
his commission from the "General of the United States."
Apparently, Tomás continued to get instructions and encouragement from the military in San Diego. Panto, ex-

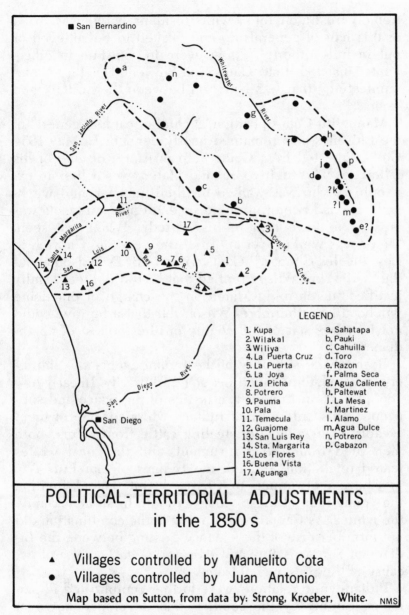

■ San Bernardino

LEGEND

1. Kupa	a. Sahatapa
2. Wilakal	b. Pauki
3. Wiliya	c. Cahuilla
4. La Puerta Cruz	d. Toro
5. La Puerta	e. Razon
6. La Joya	f. Palma Seca
7. La Picha	g. Agua Caliente
8. Potrero	h. Paltewat
9. Pauma	j. La Mesa
10. Pala	k. Martinez
11. Temecula	l. Alamo
12. Guajome	m. Agua Dulce
13. San Luis Rey	n. Potrero
14. Sta. Margarita	p. Cabazon
15. Los Flores	
16. Buena Vista	
17. Aguanga	

POLITICAL-TERRITORIAL ADJUSTMENTS
in the 1850 s

▲ Villages controlled by Manuelito Cota
● Villages controlled by Juan Antonio

Map based on Sutton, from data by: Strong, Kroeber, White.   NMS

Map 4

tremely frustrated, told a white resident that he was "tired of this half of generalship and wished to be relieved or put in full authority." If he were to continue in office, Panto insisted that Couts put an end to the "communicating" that was going on between the military and Tomás.[33]

Manuelito Cota's position as chief or captain general of the Luiseños also remained poorly defined. In May 1854 Cota requested from Couts help in capturing one of his followers. The fugitive, named Mateo, was a literate ex-neophyte who was wanted for theft, murder, and witchcraft. He had been in trouble several times, and Cota was anxious to have him in his custody. When last seen, Mateo was working for an American near San Gabriel, in Los Angeles County.[34] Couts wrote to B. D. Wilson about the matter, but Wilson replied that he did not feel legally justified in returning Mateo on the charge of practicing witchcraft. Furthermore, Wilson felt that a fugitive could not be taken out of the county on the request of an Indian.[35]

Because the authority of the Indian agents was imprecisely stated, they sometimes acted arbitrarily. In early July 1855, near San Luis Rey, a justice of the peace and subagent Couts ordered two Indians whipped, one of them a capitán, for allegedly stealing cattle from Couts. Both men died from the punishment, and the local whites feared retaliation. Indeed, the Indians of San Luis Rey may have sent runners to Kupa and Santa Isabel, inviting the young men of these villages to join in an attack upon the whites. As Captain Burton saw it, the combination did not form because of the jealousy existing between the Indians of San Luis Rey and those of Santa Isabel and because of the presence of troops.[36]

Indian-white relations were further complicated in San Diego County by the conflicts that developed between the subagents and the local military leaders concerning Indian jurisdiction. By April 1854 Captain Burton was issuing his own orders to various Indian leaders in the county. Writing to Cave Couts the following month, Burton insisted that he had not usurped the authority of the subagents but admitted that he had acted in the position of ex officio agent and that the Indians may have misinterpreted the nature of his authority on this account.[37]

In October 1855 Captain Burton sent a letter to the assistant adjutant general, E. D. Townsend, in which he identified four subagents who had dealt with the county's Indians in the past year: Cave Couts, W. W. Harvey, J. J. Warner, and John Rains. He suggested that if the superintendent would appoint one subagent whom the Indians could trust and then inform the local military leaders of such an appointment, future difficulties could be avoided. Burton admitted, however, that the Indians were easily governed by the advice and direction of the army officer who commands a detachment in their vicinity and that in many instances this officer may find it essential to give advice that would clash with that given by the subagent. "The Indians are sullen and discontented," claims Burton, "and only need a leader of determination and sagacity to commence an outbreak in a short time. Fortunately for the county, an unfriendly Indian, capable of forming a general combination against the whites, has not appeared as yet." [38]

To the *Los Angeles Star,* the situation in San Diego County was similar to that of November 1851.

Those of our readers who were resident in this county at the time of Antonio Garru's [sic] insurrection, will recollect that it was preceded by complaints from the Indians that the county of San Diego was collecting taxes from them. Several months ago, we understand that the same complaint was made by the Indians, whether well founded or not we do not know; and following upon that we hear that the Indians in San Diego county are exhibiting signs of restlessness.[39]

Superintendent Henley, however, felt that the Indians south of Los Angeles had no intention of opening hostilities with the whites.[40]

Writing to the superintendent in August 1855, Cave

Couts mentions that the Luiseños (see pls. 17 and 18) "are in fine condition—probably more prosperous than any west of the Rocky Mountains," and the Manuelito Cota "for honesty, industry and perseverance . . . is surpassed by but few of our countrymen *de razon*. His Indians have raised ample produce this year." Couts, however, is concerned over the condition of the Diegueños whom he claims raise nothing. "This results from the great number of Indian agents they have had over them the past year or two. They have not known who to obey." Couts recommended that a reservation be established in San Diego County which would encompass all the Diegueños and Luiseños and that one subagent be appointed over all the Indians. Furthermore, Manuelito Cota should be designated captain general of all the county's Indians and should be paid a salary of $50 per month.[41]

In late December 1855, Couts and J. J. Kendrick of the state assembly wrote to Superintendent Henley, requesting that one agent be appointed over the Indians of San Diego County and that Manuelito Cota be designated their captain general. "Our principal trouble," they complain, "has been the interference of the officers of the army . . . claiming to be *ex-officio* Indian agents." [42] Henley, however, was not in favor of giving to any Indian the kind of authority that this commission would have conferred. Instead, by occasionally issuing the Indians a few oxen and agricultural tools along with some blankets and clothing, Henley asserts that "their minds may be prepared for ultimate removal to the reservations, and peace in the meantime be preserved." [43]

In early July 1856 Couts again wrote to Henley and again requested that one agent be appointed over the Luiseños and Diegueños of the county. According to Couts, the agent should be paid and given the power to appoint an Indian leader over the two groups. Couts recommended that the chief should be Manuelito Cota and that he should be paid a salary of $30 to $40 per month. Moreover, the commander of the army detachment should be ordered not to interfere in Indian matters unless called upon by the civil authorities. Couts claimed that the military commander (obviously Captain Burton although his name is not mentioned) had canceled appointments made by the agents with the Indians and that several Indians in the vicinity of San Diego had lost their crops by obeying his numerous calls. One Indian declined to obey a summons from a justice of the peace because the commander had directed him " 'not to notice *any white man!* ' " Furthermore, stated Couts, in the previous month, this same commander had assembled some sixty or seventy capitanes and alcaldes to issue them various orders and instructions.[44] Replying to Couts, the superintendent said that he had passed on the complaint to the proper military authorities.[45]

In a letter to the assistant adjutant general, Captain Burton refuted the charges made by Couts. He admitted once calling about thirty-seven capitanes and alcaldes to the post, but that was in response to a request by Manuelito Cota. On two other occasions he sent for Cota individually. While Burton claims he "always charged the Indians particularly not to interfere with white men," he admits that he also told them that they "were not obliged to obey any white man except those properly placed over them by the General Government." [46]

Subagent J. J. Warner, in a July letter to Superintendent Henley, claims that

The management of the Indians (owing in a great measure to the former conflicting jurisdiction of these Agencies, and the consequent indifference of the Agents) has been assumed by the military department.

Strange as it may appear, the Captains and Alcaldes of the Indian villages upon and about the farms of the inhabitants, as well as of those more remotely situated, are appointed directly or indirectly by the Commander of the Military Post at San Diego Mission.

Such is the fact, but I am utterly ignorant of the source from whence he derives his authority to intermeddle with the affairs of your Superintendency,—There are within the boundaries of my Rancho no less than five Indian villages, the various Captains and Alcaldes of which, hold their appointment from a look to this officer as their superior or head. Such a state of things absolutely renders nugatory every act or measure which an *unepauleted* special agent may endeavor to introduce or enforce, either for the restraint or protection of the Indians. Why these things are so is to me a mystery. The only solution of which, that presents itself, is the desire of the Army officer at that Post to remain in those quarters. There can be no possible necessity for the continuance of the Post at San Diego Mission, and as some of the Army Officers have become proprietors of lands and herds in this county, they may have usurped the business of your department to afford a pretext for the continued occupation of the Post.[47]

Warner was the subject of a letter written the following month by Lieutenant Winder, who said that Tomás had told him that subagent Warner had threatened to confiscate all Indian animals having no brands. Winder felt that such action would be unjust, since many Indians owned mares with colts that had yet to be branded. Winder said that he had instructed Tomás to bring the animals to San Diego if an attempt was made to confiscate them. To the lieutenant, "this is one of many cases of injustices practiced upon these Indians, and by the very men whose duty it is to protect them, and I presume my action will be reported as 'an interference on the part of the military' with the *duties* of an agent." [48]

In early August 1856 the editor of the *San Diego Herald*, outraged at the state of Indian affairs in the county, published the following editorial:

Our present Superintendent of Indian Affairs, Col. Thomas J. Henley, is a useless "institution," for anything but political wire-pulling, and should be removed from his present position. . . . In this county there are some four or five Indian agents, with, in many cases, conflicting jurisdiction, so that the poor Indians who are disposed to do right, do not know whose orders to obey.

In the meantime the commander of a military Post, with a body guard of soldiers, in full uniform, makes his appearance

amongst them and declares that he is the person having jurisdiction over them. . . . Now we think it is full time to settle the
question who is to control the Indians in San Diego . . . and as
Col. Henley has never paid our county a visit since his appointment, we simply ask that he may be ousted and a man better fit-
ted for the office put in his place.[49]

It was to be two more years before Henley was finally dismissed—for gross irregularities involving the diversion to
his own use of funds appropriated for the Indians.[50]

As subagents and military authorities vied for Indian jurisdiction, Manuelito Cota attempted to make the best of a
most difficult situation and continued to offer his services
to the white authorities. In November 1854 he set out
after two murderers, an Indian and a Sonoran. The sheriff
of Los Angeles County offered a reward of $750, and the
Herald felt confident that Cota would capture the two
men.[51]

For such assistance, Cota received little governmental
support in return and found it impossible to keep whites
out of his territory. By July 1855 several families had
moved into the Temecula region where they were pastur-
ing several thousand head of cattle. Furthermore, entering the area were white merchants who traded liquor for
Indian-grown grain. As a result, some of Cota's followers
had become destitute and had turned to cattle raiding to
stay alive.[52]

When Captain Burton visited Temecula in January 1856,
Cota, whom he describes as "very intelligent and well informed, for his class," complained that he did not know
which of the Indian agents to obey. " 'Let us have one
agent,' " he pleads, " 'and we shall know what to do, but
as it is we are in trouble. . . . We wish the superintendent of the Indians to visit us, that he may see how we
are living; we wish to talk with him, and tell him our
wants.' " Cota seeks to know " 'why does he not come to
see us as well as the Indians of the Tulare and the Indians
in the north?' " [53]

While at Temecula, Burton discovered the deep hatred

that Cota held for Juan Antonio when the Luiseño chief offered him five hundred warriors if he went to war against Antonio's Cahuillas. Burton declined the offer, but suggested in his report that using friendly Indians against hostile ones might prove to be advantageous. Although impressed with Cota, Burton feared that making him captain general of all the Luiseños and Diegueños would not be wise. "This will be bad precedent. . . . It will give one Indian too much influence over the others." Burton warns that while "Manuel Cota deserves the most cordial appreciation for his management of the San Luis Rey Indians thus far . . . if he became discontented he can do great harm." [54]

A few months later, Cota resigned as head chief of the Luiseños. Visiting Captain Burton on May 19, 1856, he explained his actions. There were so many Indian agents, each issuing contradictory orders, that he did not know right from wrong. Because the government would not attend to the needs of his people, he was forced, at great expense, to sustain them himself. He told Burton that he would resume his duties as chief when he received his commission directly from the superintendent of Indian affairs and when one, and only one, subagent was appointed over his people.[55] The severe drought under which his people were then suffering may have contributed to his decision to resign.[56] In July it was reported that the crops of the Indians had failed for lack of water, and that many Luiseños, on the verge of starvation, were stealing to maintain themselves.[57] To Burton, it was unfortunate that Cota had resigned, since he regarded the chief to be the most influential man among the Luiseños and the only person who could curtail the Indians who were then stealing the stock of the local white settlers.[58] With the death of Pablo Apis the previous year, the Luiseños were now deprived of their two most effective leaders.[59]

Perhaps under pressure from Burton, Cota reconsidered, and with a party of thirty-seven journeyed to San

Diego on June 20 to inform the authorities that he was again assuming his position as chief.[60] At this time Cota controlled nearly twenty villages, each governed by a capitán and an alcalde, totaling between 2,500 and 2,800 persons.[61] According to subagent Couts, most of the Luiseños were Christians and many were literate in Spanish. They were good horsemen and cultivators and were very fond of liquor. They lived comfortably in their houses of tule or adobe, cultivated wheat and barley, gathered acorns, and stole cattle.[62] Cota possessed considerable means and lived on a rancho three miles east of the old asistencia of Pala and nine miles south of Temecula, in the center of his people.[63]

Cota continued to offer his services to the American authorities. In January 1857 when the sheriff of Los Angeles County and some of his men were murdered near San Juan Capistrano, Captain Burton wrote to Cota requesting that he assist the sheriff of San Diego County in pursuing the murderers. Burton also sent instructions to the capitanes of San Pasqual and Santa Isabel to place lookouts in the passes leading toward the desert and Baja California.[64] A few hours after the request, Cota had forty-eight armed and mounted men guarding the mountain passes in the vicinity of Temecula. They were out nine days, and Cota lost a horse worth $100. The chief felt that he and his men should be compensated for the expenses they had incurred. They received $20 from Andrés Pico.[65]

Throughout 1857 the Luiseños continued to suffer from the drought. In a letter written in April, John Ames, the editor of the *San Diego Herald*, reports that "the season has been so dry that there will be no crops and before the Indians starve they will prey on our ranchos." Apparently the citizens of San Diego were expecting trouble for Ames states that "there has been greater excitement in this place than I have witnessed since the great Indian outbreak here in 1852. . . . Just as sure as the troops are removed from here we should have trouble." [66] Reporting in October, subagent J. J. Kendrick notes that "in ordinary

years they raised not only a sufficiency to support themselves but have a surplus to dispose of." Cota told Kendrick that the drought had caused a poor harvest and that
three of his villages lacked sufficient food.[67]

Adding to Cota's problems was the interference by the
white authorities with his administration of justice. Cota
held court once a month to try offenders and to settle
disputes. Trial by a twelve man jury was the procedure.
But Cota's right to issue summary justice was challenged
at least twice by county officials. Some time in 1856 Cota
sentenced to death a follower who had been convicted of
beating his wife to death. But before the execution could
be carried out, the prisoner was released by the white
authorities. In 1858 a similar episode occurred. Cota tried
three individuals accused of poisoning two capitanes.[68]
The three men had long been suspected of being *hechi-
ceros,* or witches, and Cota believed that he had temporarily fallen under their influence. They were arrested,
tried, found guilty, and sentenced to be hanged.[69] Subagent Kendrick agreed with the verdict and informed
Cota that he would not interfere with the execution.[70]
Upon receiving word that three Indians were about to be
hanged at Pala, however, Judge Kurtz issued a writ of
habeas corpus, and Sheriff Lyons departed for Pala to rescue the condemned. Cota, having received word of the
impending visit and being very indignant over the interference, left Pala before the white authorities arrived. He
issued orders to a subordinate either to deliver the prisoners to the sheriff or to hang them. At Pala Lyons found
gathered a large number of Indians who had come to
witness the execution. He released the prisoners and
placed them in his custody.[71]

Later, Cota asked Kendrick what good was it to have Indian officials if they were not allowed to carry out their
own laws. Cota felt he was losing control over his people;
and rather than see his authority dwindle to nothing, he
again resigned as chief of the Luiseños. Kendrick, who
claimed there was not a better governed community in

the state than Cota's, was greatly disturbed over the resignation.[72] Superintendent Henley instructed Kendrick to
encourage Cota to reconsider. Henley promised to sustain
Cota's authority and to see that the officials in San Diego
County stop interfering in his internal affairs. He told
Kendrick to "buy for Manuel a comfortable suit of winter
clothes and present them to him for me." [73]

Nothing could make Cota change his mind, and the
problems of the Luiseños continued to mount. In late
February or early March 1859 an Indian deputation journeyed to San Diego to consult with the civil authorities
about the infiltration of white settlers.[74] The members of
the delegation spoke with the county judge, the district
attorney, the justice of the peace, and the Indian subagent. It was agreed that Kendrick and Judge Kurtz
would go to Temecula to look into the matter, and apparently they were able to remove the squatters.[75] Writing
to the *Semi-Weekly Vineyard* in April, however, a white
resident of San Luis Rey claimed that the county judge
was interfering with the authority of the Indian agent and
was thereby jeopardizing the peace. He warns:

We are now again on the eve of 1851, which you must have
fresh in mind. . . . Manuelito, the celebrated chief, who by his
own force of character and intelligence has kept these Indians
in subjection since the "Warner disaster" in 1851, retired from
his post as Captain-General, telling me himself that he feared a
difficulty. . . . Taking in view the out-break of 1851, last fall's
operations, Manuelito's retiring, the Temecula troubles and
threats, rather encouraged by ignorant parties in the town of
San Diego . . . no little apprehension has been caused among
the rancheros of the county.[76]

While the expected outbreak did not develop, Indian-
white relations in San Diego County remained tense and
unsettled.

In the meantime, to the north in San Bernardino
County, Juan Antonio's problems intensified when he became embroiled in local white politics. By 1856 San Bernardino was a thriving town of about two thousand per-

sons, the majority being Mormons. A visitor reports that politically the community was "divided into two separate parties known as the Mormons and Anti-Mormons. . . . The Anti-Mormons organized themselves on account of being unable to get any justice in the courts, the officers all being Mormons who are influenced by the priesthood." [77]

In mid-1856 members of the anti-Mormon party became alarmed when they discovered that a bishop in the Mormon church, Nathan C. Kinney, had been preaching among the Cahuillas. On the days of May 7, 8, and 9, Kinney visited the villages of Sahatapa, Yucaipa, and San Jacinto.[78] At Antonio's village, the bishop told the assembled Indians that he had been sent as a missionary to preach among them and to baptize those who so desired. He claimed that the Mormon religion was the only true religion, and he offered the Indians land on the San Bernardino Rancho which he felt was better than where they were then residing. When Kinney finished, Juan Antonio consulted with his followers and then informed the bishop that they did not want to be baptized again. Under the padres they had become Christians, and although they had been given plenty to eat, they were often beaten very severely for the slightest offense. They did not want to go through that again. Furthermore, Antonio told the bishop that the Americans had made the Indians free and that they were trying to get along with them as best they could. Only if the American government ordered them to accept the religion would they become Mormons. Concluding the discussion, Manuel Largo, who had been acting as translator, tells Kinney that "if you want us to be Christian, why don't you bring us some presents and lay them down before us . . . or why don't you give us money to put in our pockets?" The bishop then departed, Antonio having refused his request to baptize a young man.[79] At Yucaipa the bishop found capitán Marcus absent and left word that he would return some other day. At San Jacinto, the capitán, Vieto Ranno, told Kinney that if Juan

Antonio and his people were baptized, he and his followers would do the same.[80]

On May 20, 1856, various non-Mormon citizens met to discuss the activities of Bishop Kinney. Rumors had been spreading that Kinney was preaching sedition, that Mormons and Indians were conspiring against the Americans. It was resolved at the meeting that affidavits from certain Indians and whites be obtained to discover just what Kinney was up to, that the affidavits be forwarded to the governor as soon as possible, and that a committee of five be established to carry into effect the resolutions.[81]

On May 24 the anti-Mormon party held a second meeting, and the committee presented the affidavit of Juan Antonio who had appeared before John Brown, a justice of the peace, two days before. With Manuel Largo as interpreter, Antonio had sworn

that on or about the eighth day of May, A.D. 1856, one Nathan C. Kinney came to my village and called the Indians together, and stated that he (Kinney) had come on a mission to baptize the Indians into the Mormon church, and that the said Kinney proceeded to preach and admonish the Indians in the following language: That the Americans were a bad people, were not Christians, and were the enemies of the Mormons, and that the Americans were not to be relied on or believed in nowise, for the Americans were fools and devils, and should any one of them come among the Indians the Indians should in nowise believe them; and that the Mormons were the rulers of the country, and not the Americans; and the said Kinney furthermore proposed to gather the Indians into the settlement of San Bernardino, and there to partially provision or maintain them, and that the Mormons were not Americans, but a different people; that the Mormons and Indians were a good people, and the Americans were their enemies.[82]

Another affidavit was presented, this one by a white boy named Sidney van Luven. He stated that on May 10 an Indian with whom he was riding had asked him if he were a Mormon. "I told him I was not, and never should be. He then said I am going to kill you. I asked him what for? He said because Bishop Tinney [sic] had been among the Indians and told them that if we would kill you he (Tinney) would give the Indians the cattle and horses of the Americans." Van Luven attempted but failed to get more information from the Indian who, apparently, was afraid the boy would relay it to the white authorities.[83]

The day after the affidavits were taken, a party including Mormons Hunt, Rich, and Kinney, along with Judge Benjamin Hayes of Los Angeles, paid Juan Antonio a visit.[84] Hayes had journeyed to San Bernardino to witness an Indian celebration and to gather information as to their condition. Three or four times a year for the previous four years, Indians of the region had complained to him about white settlers depriving them of water. The interview lasted about two hours, the main subject being Bishop Kinney. Present were some one hundred Indians, old and young alike, who gave close attention to Antonio's remarks. The chief told Hayes and the Mormons how the bishop had sought permission to baptize his followers and why he had been refused.[85]

When Antonio finished, Hayes, who had listened intensely, addressed the chief in Spanish, Manuel Largo doing the translating. Hayes asked if Kinney had encouraged the Indians to rise against the Americans, to which Antonio replied that the bishop had not.[86] Antonio denied that Kinney had preached to his people in the way that his affidavit suggested.[87] Hayes then told Antonio that the American government would not force the Indians to choose a preacher, but he felt that their young children should be baptized. Largo translated this to the crowd which seemed to approve. With the interview over, a grand feast was held for the visitors. They returned to San Bernardino later that evening.[88]

Fear that Cahuilla-American conflict was imminent brought Captain Burton and a command of forty men to Antonio's village on May 29. With all his capitanes present, except Cabezon, Antonio tells Burton that

In former years I lived at the rancho of San Bernardino, when it belonged to the Luyo [sic] family. When the Mormons came there, I arranged with them to come and live here, (San Timeteo.) [sic] The Americans are now squatting here, and taking away my land, wood, and water. The man Weber [sic] living at San Gorgonio, has our animals killed whenever they go there. We have not land enough to plant; my people are poor and hungry; they want something from the government. Some Americans tell us we must go away to the mountains to live; other Americans tell us that we must all live together on some land. We do not understand it; we do not like it. A Mormon, Kinney, has been preaching to us that we must be baptized as Mormons—that the Mormons are our friends, the Americans are our enemies; they are fools, liars, bad people, and we must not believe them; that the Mormons always tell us the truth, the Americans never do; that soon the Mormons will whip the Americans, and then they and the Indians will live happy; that the Indians *must* be baptized as Mormons, and all of the Car-villa [sic] nation must come to live at San Bernardino; the Mormons, like good friends, will then help them to live, and not treat them as the Americans do. The Mormons and Americans are enemies, and will fight, I suppose. I do not tell lies; I tell the truth. You are an officer of the government—what shall we do? [89]

Burton replies:

I have heard you, and will relate what you have said to my general. If you have been wronged, he will endeavor to see you righted. You must remain quiet, keep your people so. You must mind your own affairs, and not permit bad people to put bad thoughts into your head. You must not permit any one to come to your village, or among your people, and preach as the Mormon Kinney has done. He has not told you the truth. The Mormons are living under and enjoying the protection of the American laws. You will not remove your people from their present location, unless you are directed to do so by the government. You will have nothing to do with the difficulties between the Americans and Mormons. You must not harm either; you will mind your own business, and keep your people quiet and peaceable. I will come to you again soon. The government is watching you, and if you do wrong you will be punished.[90]

Antonio promised to follow the advice, but Burton remained skeptical. In his report he recommends that "frequent visits to his people will be requisite, at least as long as the present excitement between the Americans and Mormons lasts." [91]

While Antonio was able to extricate himself from this

local white political squabble, he had a much more difficult time in dealing with the white settlers who had
encroached upon his lands. Essentially, the problem
arose because no land had been set aside for specific Cahuilla occupation. By mid-1857 Superintendent Henley
had in mind the establishment of a reservation in the San
Gorgonio Pass; but on receiving a report from a United
States surveyor, he changed his mind. The surveyor felt
that the pass area was unfit for a reservation in that its two
small streams would not afford more water than would ir-
rigate three or four hundred acres of land. Moreover,
settlers were already claiming and controlling the water.
According to the surveyor, somewhere on the Colorado
River would be the best location for a reservation.[92] Henley also considered Temecula, Rancho del Chino, and
Warner's rancho as possible sites but concluded that they
would be suitable for only a portion of the Indian population. Following the advice of the surveyor, Henley recommended to his superiors that a reservation be established
on the Colorado River, east of Fort Yuma.[93] Nothing, however, came of these plans.

For the Cahuilla, the year 1857 was especially bad. In
June, Major George Blake of San Diego spoke with most
of the principal leaders except one who was sick and
nearly starving to death. So poverty-stricken were the Indians that Blake felt obliged to purchase beef for them.
He reports that because they had no crops this season,
they were stealing cattle, "perhaps not to the extent complained of, but sufficient for a temporary satisfaction of
their appetites." [94]

Visiting several villages in October 1857, subagent J. J.
Kendrick reported that Juan Antonio was subsisting on a
few wild oats and some pumpkins, while most of his people were in the mountains gathering acorns that were
growing in abundance. Antonio told Kendrick that a
drought had cut short their crops, which in ordinary years
would have been sufficient for their support. Antonio
complained of the squatters, and Kendrick located two

white men, one of whom had already built a house, residing on Cahuilla land. By diverting most of the water to
their own fields, the settlers had caused the Indians to
lose nearly their entire crop, forcing them to rely on
acorns for their main staple. Kendrick and a local justice
of the peace contacted the squatters and read them the
laws of the state concerning Indian rights. The justice
promised Kendrick that in the future the laws would be
strictly enforced.[95]

Antonio told Kendrick that he would be willing to take
his people to a valley, located about forty-five miles from
San Bernardino, provided the government would pay him
for the improvements made on his present land. The only
qualms he had over removal was the fear that Americans
would come and drive him off as soon as he had become
settled. Rather than submit to such an injury, he would
prefer dying in defense of the territory he now occupied.
Estimating that the cost of compensating Antonio's Cahuillas for their land and removing them to the valley
would be about $1,500, Kendrick recommended resettle-
ment to Superintendent Henley.[96] No such plan was ever
implemented. Early the following year, Kendrick again
visited the region and reported that Juan Antonio's Cahuillas were cultivating about three hundred acres in
small gardens but that their water supply was severely
limited. Squatters had occupied nearly every remaining
tract that was agriculturally productive.[97]

Among the white community, rumors continued to
surface that Juan Antonio was up to no good. In November 1857, for instance, the San Diego Herald reported
that the Cahuillas were soon to leave their settlements
and join the Mormons.[98] José María Estudillo discussed
the matter with Juan Antonio who denied any intention of
forming an alliance with the Mormons. More than likely,
the rumor developed when Antonio and his people left
their villages to attend a ceremony with a neighboring
group.[99]

In early July of the following year, Los Angeles newspapers reported that Antonio had called his warriors into the mountains to secure alliance with other societies. Because the troops once stationed in San Bernardino had been removed, the whites in the region were very apprehensive.[100] Adding to the alarm was the report issued in mid-July that two white men had been killed by Indians on the Mohave River. One concerned citizen writes:

Much fear is felt here that this Indian attack upon quiet citizens is the precursor of what we may expect if the Indians meditate a general attack upon the frontier. There is not a more exposed place in the whole south than this, its location almost between two passes, either of which lead to the Indian country, and the fact that our population is so sparse that hostile forces of Indians could at any time enter at either of the passes, and carry away almost all stock in the county before a sufficient force could be rallied to hinder them; indeed I fear this attack bodes no good.[101]

The *Los Angeles Star,* however, assured its readers that it did not think an Indian war was imminent. Juan Antonio "is particularly friendly to the whites—always co-operates with them, and when his services are required turns out his men in support of the authorities. . . . From Juan Antonio and his men, we do not think there is anything to fear." [102]

Much of the problem resulted from governmental neglect. The Indians in the San Bernardino region were almost totally ignored by the federal authorities, and thus settlers were occupying Indian land without fear of prosecution. "Believe me," cries a resident of San Bernardino in October 1861,

that a good and efficient agent is . . . much needed here. . . . The Indians of Southern California are an interesting race of people. We regret to say that, now, they are more neglected than they ever have been before. They are left absolutely without any attention at all from the officers of the Federal Government, and they are consequently exposed to great annoyance and oppression from worthless whites, who worm themselves, on one pretense or another, into the neighborhood of their villages. This begets an irritated feeling among the Indians themselves, that is apt to endanger the peace of the community. The Insurrection of 1851 . . . was caused by the improper interference of whites with the rights of the Indians.[103]

Disputes over judicial matters also contributed greatly to Cahuilla-American tensions. Juan Antonio and the local white authorities had an understanding that the chief had full judicial authority when crimes were committed among Indians. Late in November 1861, however, the sheriff of San Bernardino jailed a follower of Antonio who had killed an Indian of another group. In early December, Antonio, accompanied by forty or fifty men, mounted on horses, mules, and donkeys, rode into San Bernardino and proceeded to the residence of the county judge, A. D. Boren. When Antonio demanded the prisoner be released in his custody, the judge refused, referring the chief to Justice Herring. When located, the justice agreed to listen to Antonio's demands.[104]

Speaking in Cahuilla but through his interpreter, the chief let the white citizens of San Bernardino know exactly how he felt.

Judges, Captains, and Gentlemen of San Bernardino: I come not here as a child to play, but as an old gray-headed chief to transact business, and talk with the white man. I come because my people asked me; they sent for me. I was far away from my village when they came and told me that murders were being charged upon my people. I took some of my old men who do not steal and murder, and come a long way to meet you. On our way we caught an Indian who murdered a Sonoranian named Antonio. But being few in number, last night he made his escape. But my Indians are on his trail, and he cannot escape if he remains in Indian country. He is a bad Indian and should be hung. I am an American—my people are all Americans, although we are Indians. If we should hear of armed men in these mountains, we should come and tell you, and help you to fight them. If bad men should come here to fight you, we should fight with you. This is our country, and it is yours. We are your friends, we want you to be ours.

Some of my people are bad men and commit crimes. But all are not bad. *He alone* should be punished who murders and steals; *he* should pay *all* the debt. If the Governor of the United

States should say my people were all bad, and must be all killed, then you should kill us. But the Governor does not say so, and he never will. He sends warriors to fight for all of us. That is the reason they are here now. My people come here to the white people, and walk about, and the white men give them whiskey, and then they try to get their squaws, and then they fight. My people are buried all around, killed by white men. I shall take my people all away from this place, and then there will be no more of this. When white men want Indians to work, they can come and get a recommend from our village, and then they will get good men. Now I want when one of my people commits a crime, to have him punished. I will deliver up any white man who commits a crime to be dealt with by *his* people, and I wish to punish my people my own way. If they deserve hanging I will hang them. If a white man deserves hanging, let the white man hang him. I am done.

The speech concluded, Justice Herring ordered the prisoner released and delivered to Antonio.[105]

Whenever an Indian killed a white man, however, the American authorities insisted that he be tried in their courts. In mid-May 1862 a former deputy sheriff of San Bernardino County, Rich Dickey, journeyed to Fort Yuma but failed to return. A few weeks later four men went in search. On the desert they encountered a group of Cahuillas and sought from its capitán information on Dickey. At first the capitán claimed to know nothing, but when threatened he admitted that some of his men had recently killed a white man. One of those responsible was located and turned over to the whites who took him back to San Bernardino to await trial. A posse of fifteen, accompanied by Juan Antonio, set out in early June to bring in the rest of the guilty Indians, but it found the Cahuilla camp deserted. Juan Antonio went in search and brought in six Indians, one of them an alcalde. Apparently, they were not expecting to be arrested, for when about to be handcuffed they dashed for cover. Juan Antonio called upon the whites to shoot, and a fight erupted. Armed only with bows and arrows, the Indians put up a stiff resistance and eventually forced the posse to withdraw. Three or four Indians may have been killed, however.[106]

The Cahuilla who had been captured earlier was brought to trial in San Bernardino after being indicted on his own confession. He admitted that he and a brother had killed Dickey.[107] He was executed, and Cabezon captured and killed his accomplice, perhaps preventing a serious Indian-white conflict.[108] The whites, however, remained fearful of an Indian outbreak, especially after Juan Antonio informed them that some Cahuillas were threatening to kill every white man they could find.[109] "Fortunately," editorializes the Los Angeles Star of July 5, 1862, "the chiefs, Juan Antonio and Cabezon are well disposed at present, but it must be easily conceived, that this atrocious murder, with that of Don Antonio Savedia (of a previous date) are calculated to leave no little irritation on the minds of the whites." [110]

Perhaps in response to this affair an Indian agent visited the area in August 1862. He found the Indians in the vicinity of San Bernardino peaceful and industrious but destitute. Beans, rice, and agricultural implements were ordered for them. At the time of the visit, Juan Antonio's people were in the mountains searching for food.[111]

Early the following year a smallpox epidemic struck the San Bernardino region. The Cahuillas fled from the San Timoteo Canyon, leaving behind a dying Juan Antonio. A white neighbor, Duff Weaver, on hearing of Antonio's condition, sent over provisions with a Mexican who gave the chief what help he could. Antonio, apparently, was attempting to rid himself of the disease by sweating and then plunging into cold water.[112] On February 28, 1863, the Los Angeles Star reported that Juan Antonio had died of smallpox. It also carried the rumor that the bodies of Antonio and three other Indians were being mutilated by dogs and hogs.[113] The territory vacated by Juan Antonio's Cahuillas was immediately occupied by white settlers.[114]

8

Conclusion

With the resignation of Manuelito Cota in 1858 and the death of Juan Antonio in 1863, the historical narrative of this study is concluded. This is not to say that the subsequent activity of the Cahuillas, Luiseños, and Cupeños, as they continued to interact with one another and with the whites, is not of historical interest or importance. From the 1860s on, these peoples came under increasing white pressure, finally to be placed on reservations.[1] How they responded to this pressure, how their societies were further altered, and how all this affected the whites are themes worthy of serious investigation. For now, however, the preceding historical developments will be analyzed and, hopefully, put into perspective.

By the middle of the eighteenth century, the Indians of southern California had developed a highly specialized hunting and food-gathering economy based on a vast ecological knowledge. They were divided into politically autonomous, localized patrilineages. But while all lineages were structurally similar, there were basic differences in demography and modes of lineage interaction. Cupeño lineages were limited to a small area and were distributed between only two main villages, producing a good deal of social and political integration. Cahuilla lineages were quite dispersed and were grouped into several clans. The Luiseño apparently lacked clans, and their lineages remained isolated from and often hostile to one another. Not without its shortcomings, the lineage was perhaps the best form of social organization a people could devise for exploiting the abundant natural resources in what was for them a heavily populated region. The lineage was small enough to allow for the mobility a hunting and gathering people need, yet large enough for defensive purposes and collective enterprises. The lineage, however, was a delicate mechanism that could be easily upset by natural or human catastrophies.

The Spanish, who ushered in a period of intense social, political, and religious change, represent perhaps the greatest human catastrophe these people had yet witnessed. Lineages located where the missions were constructed came under immediate Spanish influence, although the degree of missionary success was often determined by the specific policies of the resident priests and on the state of interlineage relations. Lineages that put up the least opposition to Spanish pressure were of the Luiseño language division. Father Peyri of Mission San Luis Rey introduced a policy of gradual incorporation and acculturation and therefore did not too rapidly disrupt traditional lineage society. Furthermore, the often hostile relationships existing among Luiseño lineages accounts for, at least in part, their rapid incorporation, since it was virtually impossible for them to unite in opposition to the Spanish.[2]

Although Indians of other language divisions were perhaps not as receptive or as vulnerable to the Spanish as were the Luiseño, large numbers were eventually brought into the mission system. Indian response to mission life, of course, varied from individual to individual. Those born at a mission or incorporated at an early age knew no other life and probably were reasonably contented. Others, especially those forced into the system, often found mission life intolerable. Part of the problem stemmed from the difference in size between mission and lineage society. The lineage in southern California seldom contained more than one hundred members, and it was in this small kin group that the Indian found his social contentment and physical well-being. The Spaniards, however, forced the Indians into large nonkin aggregations, each of which eventually included over one thousand members. According to Sherburne Cook, an authority on the California Indians, "this centrifugal mission trend naturally conflicted violently with the innate Indian centripetal preference." [3]

Structurally, the lineage and the mission were also very different. Although the lineage was ranked, having hereditary officers and a secret association, it recognized and rewarded individual qualities. The mission, in contrast, was a highly stratified community, into which all Indians were incorporated on the same differential basis. They all entered the lowest stratum of the structure where the only change for advancement lay in becoming an alcalde, page, or some other kind of privileged person. But even those neophytes who acquired special status were prevented from entering the highest stratum of the mission community, that being the exclusive domain of the gente de razón.[4] In short, the neophytes found themselves in a completely alien social environment, and it is not difficult to understand why so many escaped. The Spanish, of course, were troubled at losing converts, but they were sometimes more concerned, and rightfully so, that the runaways would foster anti-Spanish sentiments among interior societies.

In the final analysis, the Spanish were only partially successful in colonizing the Indians of southern California. With few exceptions, the interior groups were able to hold the foreigners to their coastal missions, presidios, and immediate inland ranchos and asistencias. While many Luiseños were incorporated into the mission system, the Cahuilla and Cupeño remained outside Spanish political control, although they obviously came under a certain amount of Spanish cultural influence.

During the two-and-a-half decades that Mexico laid claim to California, several significant historical developments occurred which greatly affected Indian-white relations. One of the most important was the secularization of the missions. Released from both religious and secular control and often cheated out of their promised lands, homeless and destitute ex-neophytes saturated parts of southern California. Many wandered into the towns, especially Los Angeles, where they intermittently worked, drank, and gambled. These "urban" Indians were what we would call today displaced persons, and they contributed greatly to the social unrest that was so prevalent at the time.

Another important development was the rise of powerful territorial chiefs. The process of political centralization had begun with the appointment of prominent lineage headmen and neophytes as capitanes of mission districts. But it intensified after secularization when Indians were forced into making the necessary political and social adjustment that would reestablish some order and meaning to their lives. "The chiefs," according to the anthropologist Alfred L. Kroeber, "were therefore thrust forward by pressure of opinion both on the native side and from the Caucasians." [5]

Also correlated to the breakup of the mission system was the establishment of land-grant ranchos and the intensification of Indian-white conflicts on or about these ranchos. And clearly the initiative lies with the Indian horse and cattle raiders. They could penetrate the old Spanish "frontier" almost at will, and the expeditions sent against them were generally ineffective.[6] During the 1830s and 1840s, as the historian Hubert Howe Bancroft has pointed out, Indian raiding was so intense that southern California resembled other more famous "frontier" regions.

Notwithstanding the fragmentary nature of the records, it is evident that in all these years the frontier ranchos were continually ravaged by Indians, and that there was no security for either life or property. The condition of this more than any other part of California resembled that of the Apache frontier in Sonora and Chihuahua, though the loss of life was much less. The marauders were the gentile tribes of the mountains, reenforced by renegade neophytes, allied with more distant Colorado tribes, and having a secret understanding with Indian servants on the ranchos. Fortunately, of the five or six chieftains who commanded the tribes of that region, one or two were generally allied with the gente de razon and rendered valuable aid.[7]

Indeed, the assistance given by Juan Antonio's Cahuillas to the Lugo family was instrumental in the survival of Rancho San Bernardino. So interdependent was the relationship that it should be viewed as an alliance of equals rather than as a simple employer-employee arrangement. Given the size of the rancho and the wide dispersal of the Cahuilla, there seems to have been little if any competition between Indians and Californios over land. Many of Antonio's followers lived beyond the rancho; thus only occasionally did they come into direct contact with the gente de razón. At Warner's rancho, however, the situation was significantly different. Warner employed Cupeños on an individual basis and was not above using coercive measures, such as flogging, to wrench the necessary work out of them. Moreover, the Cupeños competed directly with Warner for the same land.

It seems, then, that the different demographic, social, and economic conditions that prevailed on or about these two ranchos helped shape the structure of Indian-white relations in the interior of southern California. Furthermore, the kinds of relationships established between rancheros and Indians also affected inter-Indian affairs. For example, when Manuelito Cota and young Pablo Apis murdered eleven Californios shortly after the Battle of San Pasqual, Juan Antonio and his Cahuillas, under orders from the Lugos, retaliated and killed thirty-eight Luiseños and Cupeños. Whether the subsequent hostility between Antonio Garra and Juan Antonio stemmed from this incident or had its origin further back in time is not known. But it definitely influenced the course of both inter-Indian and Indian-white relations. These relations, of course, took a turn for the worse in late 1851.

Although it is virtually impossible to isolate and analyze all the contributing factors that led to the Garra Uprising, guarded speculation on the matter seems to be in order. Many local whites and even Garra himself claimed that the Indians rose in rebellion because they were forced to pay taxes. This explanation, however, does not explain why Luiseños and Diegueños, who were also taxed, refused to take part in the hostilities. Neither does it explain why Los Coyotes Cahuillas joined the resistance. Considered "wild" Indians by the white authorities, they were outside county jurisdiction and therefore were not liable to pay taxes. Certainly, the Cupeños resented being taxed. It not only hurt them economically but the very act of contributing money to the Americans was an admission of their political subordination. Nevertheless, Cupeño discontent was probably the result of more fundamental causes.

Sociological theory has it that during a period of economic and social improvement a people generate expectations about continued improvement. But if the fulfillment of these expectations is checked, extreme frustration often sets in.[8] While unrealized aspirations produce disappointment, unrealized expectations produce feelings of deprivation. Disappointment is generally tolerable, but deprivation often is not[9] and may drive a people to violence.[10]

In the decade following the breakup of the missions, the Cupeño had undertaken significant economic and political developments. Having become mainly agriculturalists and pastoralists, they were economically self-sufficient and had unified under the strong leadership of Antonio Garra. One might suppose that they expected continued improvement. But the Cupeños, much more so than the Luiseños and most of the Cahuillas, took the initial brunt of the American (and Mexican) arrival in southern California. Cupeño territory rested directly in the path of white immigration into the region, and what Garra and his people witnessed was not so much an invasion as an inundation of foreigners. By the middle of 1851, therefore, the Cupeños were probably reaching the conclusion that the Americans posed a definite threat to their economic well-being and political sovereignty. That feelings of intense deprivation were being felt seems evident.

When Garra decided upon insurrection is impossible to discern. But perhaps he reached his decision after United States Indian Commissioner George W. Barbour canceled his treaty-making visit to the south. It seems likely that Garra would have been greatly disappointed at the postponement, since he probably had heard that the commissioners were setting aside land for the northern Indians. It is not known when he began sending out emissaries in an attempt to unify the Indians of southern California, but it may have been after the nonfulfillment of the promised treaties.

The uprising he instigated was the last in a series of resistance movements that began as soon as the Spanish arrived in southern California. In this sense, Garra was only one in a long line of militant Indian leaders who sought to rid their lands of the white foreigners. But while the neophytes and others who attacked the missions and initiated uprisings were clearly expressing their discontent with the Spanish presence, their resistance was fragmented and localized; that is, piecemeal they sought to drive the foreigner from the immediate areas. Furthermore, while it is known that conspiracies formed during the 1830s to drive the Californios from the region, most of those who attacked the ranchos were seeking food or wealth rather than expressing a political ideology.

Garra, in contrast, as a literate ex-neophyte and powerful territorial chief, possessed a broader vision. Not accepting Indian political fragmentation to be a permanent condition, he sought to create a powerful alliance that would, through careful and long-range planning, eliminate the Americans from the entire region of southern California. That there was to be a place in the area for Sonorans and Californios indicates that Garra was not attempting to destroy all traces of the colonial present so as to recreate the "utopia" of the aboriginal past. Instead, he probably looked forward to a time when Indians would be secure on their lands and at peace with their Spanish-speaking neighbors. The uprising he instigated, therefore, was clearly a manifestation of hope and a commitment to the future.

Because Garra was more concerned with the condition of the Indian in general than with that of the Cupeño in particular, he was expressing a nascent form of pan-Indianism or ethnic nationalism. And in doing so he forced a decisional crisis upon the Indian leaders of southern California, a crisis in which they had to weigh the benefits of victory against the consequences of defeat. Those of Los Coyotes Cahuilla, a society that had a long and very close relationship with the Cupeño, were the most receptive to Garra's plans, perhaps because first hand they too saw the inundation of the whites. Most leaders, however, either concluded that the risks were too great or expressed no desire to go to war against the Americans.

Why Garra failed in his unification efforts can never be fully known, but part of the answer may rest in the nature of his movement. Created in response to an external threat rather than generated from an internal need for reorganization or revitalization, the movement's single objective was political—the elimination of the Americans from southern California. As such, it would have appealed only to those leaders who realized that the Americans posed a threat to Indian political sovereignty. Most failed to see the danger, probably because the Americans had yet to occupy, to any significant degree, interior Indian territory.

Transcending his single political objective was perhaps the only way Garra could have enlisted the support of southern California's Indian leaders. The anthropologist Peter Worsley makes a relevant statement.

In a society split into numerous component units, jealous of each other but seeking to unite on a new basis, a political leader must avoid identification with any particular section of that society. He must avoid being seen as the representative of the interests of any one group, particularly, of course, his own. He must therefore show that he seeks to establish his movement on the basis of a higher loyalty. By projecting his message on to the supernatural plane, he clearly demonstrates that his authority comes from a higher sphere, and that it transcends the narrow province of local gods and spirits associated with particular clans, tribes or villages. He is thus able to build upon existing social foundations, to use the small units of village and clan as elements in his organizational scheme whilst at the same time transcending the cramping limitations of these units by incorporating them in a wider framework.

By this projection on to the supernatural plane he thus avoids sectional discord. This is always backed up by specific injunctions to love one another, by calls to forget the narrow loyalties of the past, to abandon those things that divide them and to practice a new moral code of brotherly love.[11]

The enticing, but extremely limited, bit of evidence suggesting that Garra believed he could turn the white man's bullets into water is the only indication that his movement may have had a supernatural aspect to it.[12] It seems, however, that Garra could not or did not project his message onto a supernatural plain, and this probably hurt his chances for unifying the region's Indians.

Perhaps it is for this reason that he failed to bring the powerful Quechans to his banner. It will be remembered that their resistance to the white foreigner began back in 1781 when they destroyed the Spanish missions and settlements in their territory. Seventy years later, they were well aware of the seriousness of the American invasion. They knew the extent of white immigration and had witnessed American arrogance and hostility on the Colorado River. That they eliminated A. L. Lincoln and his ferrymen in one surprise attack may have convinced Garra that he had a ready-made ally. But Garra's encouragement that they attack the tiny military post at the crossing, while perhaps the only way he could get them committed to all-out war, was poor strategy. The garrison posed no threat to the Quechans, let alone to those Indians far to the west where the uprising was to have its real importance.

Garra's thoughts must have been quite grim as he rode back to Los Coyotes Canyon in mid-November 1851. Not only had he failed to overrun Camp Independence but the quarrel with the Quechans over the distribution of the stolen sheep had severed whatever unity he had been able to forge with the river Indians. By the time he arrived at the canyon, he may have developed second thoughts about the wisdom of instigating an uprising against the Americans, for in one of his testimonies he stated that he had been against the attack on Warner's rancho. Furthermore, Garra's disclosure that he had remained silent after the attack and had gone to meet Juan Antonio only under pressure suggests that he had become despondent and had lost his supreme position among the rising Indians. One suspects that when he left to meet Juan Antonio, Garra knew he was riding into a trap.

By 1851 Juan Antonio certainly had his own grievances. He was very disturbed when, having waited five days at the rancho of Isaac Williams, Commissioner Barbour canceled his treaty-making trip to the south. Antonio had heard that Indians to the north were receiving lands and supplies from the Indian commissioners, and he believed that he was as deserving as they. Just how upset he was over the cancelation is not known; but when individuals compare their own situation with that of a reference group that they think has what they want, a sense of deprivation often develops.[13] It was probably after Barbour failed to appear that Antonio sent couriers north to the Tulareños, seeking their support in a war against the Americans. The Tulareños refused to join because they had recently signed a treaty with the United States government and as yet had no reason to believe that the Americans would not honor it. Perhaps their refusal to join convinced Antonio that the Indians of southern California would never coalesce and that resistance would be foolhardy without complete unification.

Still, there is a considerable difference between planning to rise against the Americans and performing valu-

able service for them. When Antonio decided to capture
Garra is impossible to discern, but it may have been after
receiving a letter from a Los Angeles county judge warning him not to get involved with the rising Indians. Indeed, a short time later Antonio wrote to Garra suggesting
they meet on the desert. The actual decision to capture
Garra may have been the result of Paulino Weaver's influence, since the rancher provided Antonio with mules and
provisions for his journey and probably went along as
well. But given the mistrust that existed between the two
chiefs, Antonio probably undertook the task with great
eagerness. He was resentful of Garra's increasing influence among the southern Indians, especially among Los
Coyotes Cahuillas whom he probably wanted to place
under his own jurisdiction. Capturing Garra, therefore,
was less a demonstration of loyalty to the Americans than
a tactic in an inter-Indian political struggle.

Historical hindsight tells us that even with Juan Antonio's assistance, Garra had little chance of driving the
Americans from southern California, that the time had
passed for an Indian uprising to be successful. True, it
seems unlikely that he could have held up American colonization for any length of time, but it would be a mistake
to suggest that his movement was doomed to immediate
failure. The Americans in the region were limited in
numbers and weapons, were without sufficient military
protection, and were totally ignorant of Indian strengths
and weaknesses. A vulnerable white enclave in a vast Indian territory, their initial response to the outbreak bor-
dered on hysteria and justifiably so. Had Garra been only
partially successful in his organizational goals, the Americans might have suffered numerous casualties.

Once effectively organized, however, they terminated
the uprising rather easily, and the four military tribunals
that convicted and executed seven Indians, one American, and a Sonoran were designed to find guilt at whatever cost and to eliminate what were thought to be the
principal leaders of the outbreak. The fact that Bill Mar-

shall ran the store at Kupa and was the husband of José Noca's daughter indicates that he might have had a say in village affairs, but there is no real proof that he encouraged Garra to rise or was directly involved in the planning and execution of the uprising. Apparently, the tribunal could not accept the validity of Indian grievances and came to the conclusion that the Indians had been stirred up by renegades, "outside agitators" of the mid-nineteenth century.

When it came to investigating what part, if any, was played in the uprising by two prominent Californios, the American authorities, however, were not quite so eager to find guilt. Garra's tribunal absolved José Joaquin Ortega and José Antonio Estudillo of any envolvement, probably to prevent the already wide breach between Americans and Californios from expanding even farther. But it makes little sense that Garra would first write to them and then later accuse them of involvement if, indeed, they had not been somehow implicated.

It is quite likely that an Indian outbreak, if directed only against the Americans, would not have been unwelcomed by many Californios. After all, when the uprising began, California had been American territory for only four years, and certainly many Californios resented American rule and the oppressive tax system that accompanied it. If Ortega did encourage Garra to rise, it was probably after he returned from a state political convention in Santa Barbara where he failed in his efforts to have California divided so as to reduce the heavy tax burden suffered by all the people in the south. Be that as it may, Garra was executed without receiving the opportunity to prove his accusations.

Garra's death brought the uprising to an end; and compared to other Indian resistance movements, its historical significance might seem quite limited. There is, however, more to it than would appear: even though the uprising involved relatively few people, both Indian and white, it set in motion actions and ideas that had far-reaching repercussions. Remember that four months after the federal commissioner was to visit the Indians of southern California no meeting had taken place. Yet shortly after the start of hostilities, O. M. Wozencraft journeyed to the south, and in early January 1852 he negotiated one treaty with the Serranos, Cahuillas, and Luiseños and another with the Diegueños. This is not to say that without hostilities no treaties would have been made, but the outbreak certainly convinced the commissioners that the southern Indians could no longer be ignored. In this sense the uprising acted as a catalyst, forcing white authorities to undertake immediate diplomatic action.

Considering that the treaties were negotiated by a colonizing power, they were quite fair and even generous to the Indians. For accepting the authority, protection, and jurisdiction of the United States government, the Indians were to receive assistance in the form of agricultural instructors and implements, foodstuffs, farm animals, schools and teachers. The territory set aside for Indian occupation corresponded in general to the region where they were then residing. In theory, therefore, the treaties represented a kind of mid-nineteenth-century "foreign aid scheme"; and had they been ratified and, once ratified, had the United States government kept its word, it seems that the Indians would have benefited greatly from the arrangement.

Of course, the treaties were not ratified, so the Indians gained nothing from them. But the uprising did convince the federal authorities that more attention must be paid to the southern Indians. A major result of this attention was the B. D. Wilson Report. It called for the introduction of a system of benevolent control over the Indians so as to eliminate the conditions that were causing them, and therefore the local whites, so much discontent. Written within a year of a serious Indian-white conflict, the report makes several references to Antonio Garra and his movement. This clearly indicates that the author's views were

partly shaped by the uprising. Certainly, without so recent an outbreak, the call for controlling the Indians
would not have been so urgent.

The military reservation system introduced by Edward
Fitzgerald Beale was so similar to the plan submitted by
B. D. Wilson that there seems to be little doubt that the
superintendent was greatly influenced by the report. The
Garra Uprising, therefore, by drawing attention to the condition of the southern Indians, stimulated thought among
the white authorities. This, in turn, contributed to the formation of a new federal Indian policy for California. Repercussions of the outbreak, then, extended far beyond
the local setting where the violence took place.

The type of military reservation proposed by Wilson
and implemented by Beale, however, was never established south of the Tejon Pass, and Indian discontent
in the extreme southern portion of the state persisted. It
stemmed largely from the disappointment at not receiving
the goods and services promised in the treaty with Wozencraft and from the belief that Indians to the north were
receiving preferential treatment. By comparing their situation to what they thought existed among northern
groups, their sense of deprivation increased; and as a consequence, their horse and cattle raiding continued. Most
raids were sporadic and isolated, but they kept alive in
the minds of the whites the realization that another Indian outbreak was still possible. When the whites were
honest enough to admit that the condition of the Indians
had failed to improve since November 1851, the Garra
Uprising was fearfully recalled. Indeed, the number of
references made to Antonio Garra throughout the 1850s
and into the 1860s suggests that the chief and what he
stood for were never far from their thoughts.

Although the whites in southern California were not to
witness another uprising, it was certainly not because
they had solved their Indian problem. Instead, it was
owing to the way in which the two most powerful Indian

leaders dealt with their white problem. During these years, Manuelito Cota and Juan Antonio sought to adjust to what was obviously a permanent American presence. But since their backgrounds and aspirations varied so greatly and since federal Indian policy in southern California lacked consistency and continuity, their politics of survival differed dramatically.

As a white-appointed chief, Manuelito Cota had definite obligations to the American officials and so implemented policies of loyalty and cooperation. But federal Indian policy was much too ill defined and the power of the local subagents much too weak for Cota to be without options in dealing with the authorities. In fact, the competition for Indian jurisdiction that developed between the subagents and the local military officers actually contributed to Cota's independence. It is true that he complained of too much governmental interference, but the vying for Indian jurisdiction prevented any one agency from exercising full control over his people.

It would be a mistake, therefore, simply to view Cota as a puppet of the government, even though his appointment was certainly designed to achieve this end. As in many colonial situations, where "puppet" leaders do not always conform to the dictates of their "masters," Cota used his position as chief to further his own ambitions. He was able to expand the jurisdiction initially appropriated to him and to improve his own financial situation. That he could twice publicly resign as captain general is more an indication of his independence from, rather than dependence on, the United States government. One suspects that these acts were carefully staged to let the authorities know that he would not be taken for granted, for it seems that he kept his chieftainship active while he was officially in retirement. Under his guidance the Luiseño became the most prosperous Indian group in southern California, and for the first time in their history were unified under one political banner. Furthermore, since his administration encompassed the Cupeño and Los Coyotes

Cahuilla, Cota represents perhaps one of the first truly pan-Indian leaders in southern California.

While Manuelito Cota complained of too much governmental interference, Juan Antonio suffered from governmental neglect. A permanent subagent was not appointed to the Cahuillas, and this allowed whites to settle upon Indian lands with little fear of official reproach. As a result, Antonio may have considered rising against the Americans in late 1855. If he had toyed with the idea of joining Garra in 1851, there is no reason why, when conditions became much worse, resistance was not again given consideration. Perhaps he changed his mind when informed by the military that his movements had been carefully observed. But even after 1855, when he sought to remain in good stead with the Americans, he carefully maintained his independence, cooperating with the whites on some occasions but demanding concessions from them on others. Until his death, Juan Antonio remained one of the most powerful individuals, Indian or white, in all of southern California.

With the conclusion of this study, certain paradoxes become apparent. For example, one tends to see in Antonio Garra an individual who courageously resisted the American colonization of southern California and who bravely gave his life in the process. Yet, in the final analysis, Garra not only failed to unify the region's Indians but allowed himself to be captured by a chief whose reliability he surely must have questioned. In contrast, one initially looks upon Manuelito Cota as a leader who blindly attempted to accommodate his people to a new social order that obviously had no place in it for the Indian and whose loyalty to the American authorities was completely out of proportion to what benefits he received in return. But in terms of political longevity and economic prosperity, he far outlasted Antonio Garra in the former and greatly surpassed Juan Antonio in the latter. Finally, one is tempted to condemn Juan Antonio for capturing Garra and to view his death by the white man's disease as ironic justice. Still, by maintaining his society during such trying times and by keeping the whites pondering his next move, Antonio exhibited all the characteristics of an extremely skillful leader and astute diplomat.

Notes

INTRODUCTION

1. While many Indian societies were obliterated as the whites pushed westward, ethnically the Indian has survived. According to one authority, of the estimated three hundred Indian languages spoken north of Mexico at the time of initial white contact, at least half are currently in use. Few Indian cultures have completely disappeared, and the current rate of growth of the Indian population in the United States exceeds that of the general population. See D'Arcy McNickle, *The Indian Tribes of the United States: Ethnic and Cultural Survival* (London: Oxford University Press, 1962), pp. 1–4.

2. For a theoretical discussion of the importance of inter-Indian relations in the historical study of the Indian, see Robert F. Berkhofer, Jr., "The Political Context of a New Indian History," *Pacific Historical Review*, vol. 40, no. 3 (August, 1971).

3. To date, only one scholar has seriously investigated postcontact Indian activity in California. See Sherburne Cook, *The Conflict between the California Indian and White Civilization: I, The Indian Versus the Spanish Mission*, Ibero-Americana 21 (Berkeley: University of California Press, 1943); *The Conflict between the California Indian and White Civilization: II, The Physical and Demographic Reaction of the Nonmission Indians in Colonial and Provincial California*, Ibero-Americana 22 (Berkeley: University of California Press, 1943); *The Conflict between the California Indian and White Civilization: III, The American Invasion, 1848–1870*, Ibero-Americana 23 (Berkeley: University of California Press, 1943).

4. See, for example, Elman R. Service, *Primitive Social Organization: An Evolutionary Perspective* (New York: Random House, 1968), p. 62.

5. Interestingly, the nineteenth-century California historian, Hubert Howe Bancroft, included more Indian material in his works than have later historians in theirs. While Bancroft lacked the methodological sophistication to incorporate much Indian activity into his general narrative, at least he had the good sense to include it in footnotes.

6. For an account of the vast ecological knowledge accumulated by a southern California Indian people see Lowell John Bean and Katherine Siva Saubel, *Temalpakh: Cahuilla Indian Knowledge and Usage of Plants* (Banning: Malki Museum Press, 1972). Concerning the intricate nature of California Indian political and economic systems, see Lowell John Bean and Thomas F. King, eds., *Antap: California Indian Political and Economic Organization*, Anthropological Paper No. 2 (Ramona: Ballena Press, 1974).

7. See John G. Ames, "Report of Special Agent John G. Ames in Regard to the Conditions of the Mission Indians of California, with Recommendations" (Washington: Government Printing Office, 1873); Helen Hunt Jackson, "The

Present Condition of the Mission Indians in Southern California," *Century Magazine* (August, 1883); Helen Hunt Jackson and Abbot Kinney, "Report on the Condition and Needs of the Mission Indians of California Made by Special Agents Helen Jackson and Abbot Kinney, to the Commissioner of Indian Affairs" (Washington: Government Printing Office, 1883); also published in *A Century of Dishonor: A Sketch of the United States Government's Dealing with Some of the Indian Tribes.* First published in 1881. New edition, enlarged by the addition of the Report of the Needs of the Mission Indians (Boston: Roberts Brothers, 1886); C. C. Painter, "A visit to the Mission Indians of California" (Philadelphia: Indian Rights Association, 1887); Charles Wetmore, "Report of Charles A. Wetmore, Special U.S. Commissioner of Mission Indians of Southern California" (Washington: Government Printing Office, 1875).

8. For an account of how Helen Hunt Jackson distorted the California past, see Carey McWilliams, *Southern California Country: An Island on the Land* (New York: Duell, Sloan and Pearce, 1946), pp. 70–83.

9. While ignored by California's better-known historians, these chiefs have been given some attention by local scholars. For Antonio Garra see William Edward Evans, "The Garra Uprising: Conflict between San Diego Indians and Settlers in 1851," *California Historical Society Quarterly* 45 (1966). Millard F. Hudson, "The Last Indian Campaign in the Southwest," *The Pacific Monthly* 17 (1907). Noel Loomis, "The Garra Uprising of 1851," *Brand Book No. Two* (The San Diego Corral of the Westerners, 1971). June Reading, "New Light on the Garra Uprising," Paper read before the First Annual San Diego Historical Conference, San Diego, California, March 20, 1965. Arthur Woodward, "The Garra Revolt of 1851," *The Westerners Brand Book* (Los Angeles Corral, 1947). William Smythe, *History of San Diego, 1542–1908, Vol. I., Old Town* (San Diego: The History Company, 1908), pp. 186–193. Richard Pourade, *The History of San Diego, Vol. III, The Silver Dons* (San Diego: The Union-Tribune Publishing Company, 1963), pp. 177–185. For Juan Antonio, see Marjorie Wolcott, "The Lugos and Their Indian Ally—How Juan Antonio Aided in the Defense and Development of Rancho San Bernardino," *Touring Topics*, vol. 21, no. 12 (December, 1929). George William Beattie and Helen Pruitt Beattie, *Heritage of the Valley, San Bernardino's First Century* (Pasadena: San Pasqual Press, 1939), pp. 61–66, 84, 87–88, 184–185, 189–190, 213, 233, 236, 247, 249. Gerald Smith, Raymond Sexton, and Elsie Koch, "Juan Antonio, Cahuilla Indian Chief, a Friend of the Whites," *Quarterly of San Berardino County Museum Association*, vol. 3, no. 1 (Fall, 1969). For Manuelito Cota, see Horace Parker, "The Temecula Massacre," *The Westerners Brand Book* (Los Angeles Corral No. 10, 1963). Millard Hudson, "The Pauma Massacre," *Annual Publication of the Historical Society of Southern California and the Tenth Annual Publication of the Pioneers of Los Angeles County* (1906). Arthur Woodward, "Bad Indians at Pauma," *Westways*, vol. 28, pt. 1, no. 8 (1936).

CHAPTER 1

THE CAHUILLA, LUISEÑO, AND CUPEÑO

1. Robert F. Spencer, Jesse D. Jennings, et al., *The Native Americans* (New York: Harper and Row, 1965), p. 229.

2. For an ethnographic survey of these Indians, see Alfred L. Kroeber, *Handbook of the Indians of California*, Smithsonian Institution, Bureau of American Ethnology Bulletin 78 (Washington: Government Printing Office, 1925). The

terms Luiseño, Gabrielino, Fernandino, Juaneño and Diegueño derive from the Indians' association with missions San Luis Rey, San Gabriel, San Fernando, San Juan Capistrano, and San Diego respectively.

3. Ruth Underhill, *Indians of Southern California,* Bureau of Indian Affairs (Washington: Department of the Interior, 1941), pp. 15–19. The Americans labeled these Indians "Diggers" because of their mode of subsistance. As Underhill has pointed out (p. 17), however, the Indians of southern California did more "picking" than "digging," mainly because the soil was too dry for the moist edible roots of the lily family.

4. David Barrows, *The Ethno-Botany of the Coahuilla Indians of Southern California* (Chicago: University of Chicago Press, 1900), p. 69.

5. Underhill, *Indians of Southern California,* pp. 7–12.

6. *Ibid.,* pp. 21–25.

7. Barrows, *Ethno-Botany,* p. 46.

8. Underhill, *Indians of Southern California,* pp. 27–29.

9. *Ibid.,* pp. 33–35.

10. *Ibid.,* pp. 36–37.

11. *Ibid.,* pp. 39–43.

12. *Ibid.,* pp. 45–46.

13. Edwin F. Walker, "Indians of Southern California," *Southwest Museum Leaflets* 10 (Los Angeles: Southwest Museum, n.d.), pp. 14–15. About the middle of the eighteenth century a universal religion may have been spreading inland from the nearby islands of San Clemente, Santa Catalina, and San Nícolas, occupied by Shoshonean-speaking Gabrielino Indians. Known as Chinigchnich, meaning high god, punisher, or avenger, the religion superimposed itself over the older, more localized, religious beliefs of some mainland peoples. Chinigchnich resided in the heavens and gave all humans certain rules to follow, including industry, kindness, respect for the old, and hospitality to guests. He had numerous watchers on earth to see that the people followed his dictates. Those who failed were punished. Most information about the religion comes from Fr. Gerónimo Boscana, *Chinigchinich: A Historical Account of the Origin, Customs, and Traditions of the Indians at the Missionary Establishment of St. Juan Capistrano, Alta California; Called the Acagchemem Nation,* trans. Alfred Robinson, in Alfred Robinson, *Life in California* (New York: Wiley & Putnam, 1846).

14. Underhill, *Indians of Southern California,* pp. 46–50.

15. *Ibid.,* pp. 53–54.

16. The lineage has been defined as "a consanguineal kin group practicing unilinear descent. . . . It includes only persons who can actually trace their relationship to a common ancestor; that is, a lineage is all the unilateral descendants of a known common ancestor or ancestress." See Ernest L. Schusky, *Manual for Kinship Analysis* (New York: Holt, Rinehart and Winston, 1965), pp. 23–26.

17. See Edward Gifford, "Miwok Lineages and the Political Unit in Aboriginal California," *American Anthropologist* 28 (1926), 389–401. The basic sociopolitical unit of the California Indians has been identified as the band by Underhill, the lineage by Gifford, the clan by Goldschmidt, and the tribelet by Kroeber. See respectively, Underhill, *Indians of Southern California,* pp. 31–32; Gifford, "Miwok Lineages," p. 392; Walter Goldschmidt, "Social Organization in Native California and the Origin of Clans," *American Anthropologist* 50 (July–September, 1948), 444–456; and Alfred Kroeber, "The Nature of Land-Holding Groups in Aboriginal California," in Robert F. Heizer, ed., *Aboriginal California: Three Studies in Culture History* (Berkeley: University of California Archaeological Research Facility, 1963), p. 94.

18. For a theoretical discussion of the political nature of the lineage, see M.

G. Smith, "On Segmentary Lineage Systems," *Journal of the Royal Anthropological Institute,* 86, 2 (1956), 39–80.

19. See Edward W. Gifford, *Clans and Moieties in Southern California,* University of California Publications in American Archaeology and Ethnology, vol. 14, no. 2 (March 29, 1918). The basic difference between the lineage and the clan is that clan members tend to forget their exact relationships with one another, even though they all supposedly derive from a common ancestor. See Lucy Mair, *An Introduction to Social Anthropology* (London: Oxford University Press, 1965), p. 71.

20. Gifford, "Miwok Lineages," pp. 399–400. According to another authority, the lineage (he uses the term "clan") system developed in California largely as a result of population density. "When . . . the population of a society grows more dense, its members will be increasingly surrounded by persons less intimately known. . . . Under such circumstances they will increasingly react toward persons in terms of some symbolic system. The clan system furnishes such a set of symbols and it therefore fulfills a need that has grown either from technological developments or from environmental circumstances." See Goldschmidt, "Social Organization in Native California," p. 453.

21. For description of the territorial locations of these language divisions see Alfred Kroeber, *Ethnography of the Cahuilla Indians,* University of California Publications in American Archaeology and Ethnology 8 (June 20, 1908), 32–37. Kroeber, *Handbook,* pp. 615–616, 620–621, 636, 648–649, 689–690, 693–694. Lowell Bean, "The Wanakik Cahuilla," *The Masterkey* 34 (July–September, 1960), 114–116. Philip Sparkman, *The Culture of the Luiseño Indians,* University of California Publications in American Archaeology and Ethnology 8 (August 7, 1908), 189.

22. Bean, "The Wanakik Cahuilla," pp. 112–114. Bean uses the term "sib" which has been replaced by "clan" in this study.

23. Lowell Bean, *Mukat's People: The Cahuilla Indians of Southern California* (Berkeley, Los Angeles, London: University of California Press, 1972), p. 87.

24. *Ibid.,* p. 76.

25. *Ibid.,* p. 87.

26. *Ibid.,* p. 85.

27. *Ibid.,* p. 76.

28. *Ibid.*

29. *Ibid.,* pp. 104–105. Many of the anthropologists consulted for this chapter identify the lineage leader as a chief. The term "headman" is substituted because it suggests a leader who governed with the consensus of kinsmen. A chief, in contrast, is seen as a leader who possessed a political following that was not just made up of kinsmen and who ruled through the use of power.

30. *Ibid.,* pp. 105–106.

31. The association has been defined "as an organized and corporate group, membership in which does not follow automatically from birth or adoption into a kin or territorial unit. Assocations with important authoritative functions are, in the main, permanent and have continuous organization." See Paula Brown, "Patterns of Authority in West Africa," *Africa* 21 (October, 1951), 267–271.

32. Bean, *Mukat's People,* pp. 105–106.

33. Gifford, *Clans and Moieties,* p. 177.

34. Kroeber, *Handbook,* p. 649.

35. Raymond White, *Luiseño Social Organization,* University of California Publications in American Archaeology and Ethnology 48 (1963), 127. Similar territorial units were formed by the Diegueño. See Katherine Luomala, "Flexibility in Sib Affiliation Among the Diegueño," *Ethnology* 2 (July, 1963), 282–301.

36. Kroeber, *Handbook,* p. 636.

37. White, *Luiseño Social Organization,* p. 159. White calls this unit a ranchería, a term the Spanish applied to any village or settlement. Because of its ambiguity, the term is not used in this study except in a quotation.

38. William Duncan Strong, *Aboriginal Society in Southern California,* University of California Publications in American Archaeology and Ethnology 26 (1929), 297.

39. Raymond White, "The Luiseño Theory of 'Knowledge,' " *American Anthropologist* 59 (February, 1957), 1–3.

40. *Ibid.,* pp. 10–14.

41. In the historical documentation, these Indians are called the Agua Caliente people after the Spanish name of one of their villages. The term "Cupeño," which derives from "Kupa," the name of their principal village, was not introduced into the ethnographic literature until 1918. See Gifford, *Clans and Moieties,* p. 177. As early as 1908, the term had been introduced into the historical literature. See William E. Smythe, *History of San Diego, 1542–1908, Vol. I, Old Town* (San Diego: The History Company, 1908), p. 186. In 1902, however, the term was used by an early supporter of Indian rights in Southern California. See Charles F. Lummis, "The Exiles of Cupa," *Out West,* vol. 16, no. 5 (May, 1902). In much of the documentation consulted for this study, the Cupeños are classified as Luiseños, mainly because numerous Indians from Mission San Luis Rey settled in Cupaño territory after the mission was disbanded.

42. William Bright and Jane Hill, "The Linguistic History of the Cupeño," in Dell H. Hymes, ed., *Studies in Southwestern Ethnolinguistics* (The Hague: Mouton and Company, 1967), p. 363.

43. Kroeber, *Handbook,* pp. 689–690.

44. In August 1795, when the Spanish first entered the valley, they recorded that the language spoken was Mau, i.e., Yuman. Perhaps Diegueños were then in occupation of the area, only to be forced out later by Cupeños. See "Diary of Fray Juan Mariner, August, 1795," in Joseph Hill, *The History of Warner's Ranch and Its Environs* (Los Angeles: [privately printed], 1927), p. 188.

45. Kroeber, *Handbook,* pp. 689–690.

46. Gifford, "Miwok Lineages," pp. 395–396.

47. *Ibid.*

48. Strong, *Aboriginal Society,* p. 221. It is known that in 1851 the political leader of Wilakal was Francisco Mocate, who was appointed to his position by Antonio Garra of Kupa. See Record Group 393, Pacific Division, Proceedings of a Council of War Convened in the Valley Los Coyotes, December 23, 1851, H-4 (1852). U.S. National Archives.

49. Strong, *Aboriginal Society,* pp. 249–253.

50. Gifford, "Miwok Lineages," pp. 394–395.

51. Strong, *Aboriginal Society,* p. 158.

52. *Ibid.,* pp. 270–273.

53. Lucille Hooper, *The Cahuilla Indians,* University of California Publications in American Archaeology and Ethnology 16 (April 10, 1920), 355.

54. Alfred Kroeber, *Elements of Culture in Native California,* University of California Publiations in American Archaeology and Ethnology 13 (1922), 296–297.

55. Strong, *Aboriginal Society,* pp. 262–263.

56. *Ibid.,* p. 98.

57. James T. Davis, "Trade Routes and Economic Exchange Among the Indians of California" in Heizer, ed., *Aboriginal California,* pp. 12–13.

58. Malcolm F. Farmer, "The Mojave Trade Route," *The Masterkey* 9 (September, 1935), 156–157.

59. Bernice Eastman Johnston, *California's Gabrielino Indians* (Los Angeles: Southwest Museum, 1962), p. 76.

60. Davis, "Trade Routes," p. 24.

61. *Ibid.*, p. 21.
62. *Ibid.*, p. 26.
63. *Ibid.*, p. 24.
64. *Ibid.*, pp. 33–34.
65. *Ibid.*, p. 28.
66. Strong, *Aboriginal Society*, p. 183.

CHAPTER 2

FOREIGN INFLUENCE

1. John W. Caughey, *California* (Englewood Cliffs: Prentice-Hall, 1953), pp. 107–108.

2. Fr. Francisco Palóu, O.F.M., *Historical Memoirs of New California*, ed. Herbert Eugene Bolton (Berkeley: University of California Press, 1926), II, 268–272.

3. *Ibid.*, III, 214–215.

4. Fr. Zephyrin Engelhardt, *The Missions and Missionaries of California, Vol. II, Upper California, Part I, General History* (San Francisco: The James H. Barry Company, 1912), p. 169.

5. Fr. Pedro Font, "Diary of an Expedition to Monterey by Way of the Colorado River, 1775–1776," in Herbert Eugene Bolton, ed. and trans., *Anza's California Expeditions, Vol. IV, Font's Complete Diary of the Second Anza Expedition* (Berkeley: University of California Press, 1930; reprint, New York: Russell & Russell, 1966), p. 182.

6. Palóu, *Historical Memoirs*, II, 325–326.

7. Quoted in Thomas Workman Temple II, "The Founding of Misión San Gabriel Arcángel, Part II," *The Masterkey* 33 (October–December, 1959), 159–160.

8. *Ibid.*

9. Palóu, *Historical Memoirs*, III, 219–220.

10. Font, "Diary," pp. 178–181.

11. Palóu, *Historical Memoirs*, III, 219–220.

12. Font, "Diary," pp. 180–181.

13. Mission San Gabriel, "Preguntas y Respuestas, 1813–1814," trans. Fr. Maynard Geiger, Old Mission Archives, Santa Barbara.

14. John W. Caughey, ed., *The Indians of Southern California in 1852: The B. D. Wilson Report and A Selection of Contemporary Comment* (San Marino: Huntington Library, 1952), pp. 7–8.

15. Pedro Fages, *A Historical, Political, and Natural Description of California by Pedro Fages, Soldier of Spain*, trans. Herbert Ingram Priestly (Berkeley: University of California Press, 1937), p. 20.

16. Palóu, *Historical Memoirs*, IV, 62–64.

17. *Ibid.*, pp. 63–64.

18. Font, "Diary," pp. 197–201.

19. *Ibid.*, pp. 204–213.

20. Fr. Zephyrin Engelhardt, O.F.M., *San Juan Capistrano Mission* (Los Angeles: The Standard Printing Co., 1922), pp. 6–10.

21. Raymond White, "A Reconstruction of Luiseño Social Organization" (Ph.D. diss., University of California, Los Angeles, 1959), p. 15.

22. Engelhardt, *San Juan Capistrano Mission*, p. 16.

23. Engelhardt, *The Missions*, pt. 1, pp. 350–352.

24. Fr. Zephyrin Engelhardt, O.F.M., *San Gabriel Mission and the Beginnings of Los Angeles* (San Gabriel: Mission San Gabriel, 1927), pp. 342–344.

25. Engelhardt, *The Missions*, pt. 1, p. 357.

26. Thomas Workman Temple II, "Toypurina the Witch and the Indian Uprising at San Gabriel," *The Masterkey* 32 (September–October, 1958), 136–152.

27. Fr. Zephyrin Engelhardt, O.F.M., *San Luis Rey Mission* (San Francisco: The James H. Barry Co., 1921), p. 220.

28. White, "Reconstruction," pp. 18–19.

29. Raymond White, "The Luiseño Theory of 'Knowledge,'" *American Anthropologist* 59 (February, 1957), 14.

30. George W. Beattie, "Mission Ranchos and Mexican Grants," *San Bernardino County Historical Society* 2 (1942), 3–4.

31. Marguerite Eyer Wilbur, ed., *Duflot de Mofras' Travels on the Pacific Coast* (Santa Ana: Fine Arts Press, 1937), I, 183.

32. Robert F. Heizer, ed., *The Indians of Los Angeles County: Hugo Reid's Letters of 1852* (Los Angeles: Southwest Museum, 1968), p. 84.

33. Fr. Juan Caballeria, *History of San Bernardino Valley, from the Padres to the Pioneers* (San Bernardino: Times-Index Press, 1902), pp. 37–39.

34. *Ibid.*, pp. 37–40.

35. *Ibid.*, pp. 67–68.

36. Joseph John Hill, *The History of Warner's Ranch and Its Environs* (Los Angeles: [privately printed], 1927), pp. 37–38.

37. Engelhardt, *San Luis Rey Mission*, p. 35.

38. Quoted in Hill, *History of Warner's Ranch*, pp. 42–43.

39. Pablo Tac, *Conversion of the San Luiseños of Alta California*, ed. and trans. Minna and Gordon Hewes (San Luis Rey: Old Mission, 1958), p. 17.

40. Quoted in Hill, *History of Warner's Ranch*, pp. 42–43.

41. Hubert Howe Bancroft, *History of California, Vol. II, 1801–1824* (San Francisco: A. L. Bancroft and Company, 1885), p. 553.

42. Hill, *History of Warner's Ranch*, pp. 37–38.

43. Engelhardt, *The Missions*, pt. 1, pp. 261–262.

44. *Ibid.*, pp. 253–255.

45. Florian F. Guest, "The Indian Policy Under Fermín Francisco de Lasuén, California's Second Father President," *California Historical Society Quarterly* 45 (September, 1966), 206.

46. Engelhardt, *San Gabriel Mission*, p. 44.

47. Tac, *Conversion of the San Luiseños*, pp. 19–20.

48. Timothy Flint, ed., *The Personal Narrative of James O. Pattie of Kentucky* (Chicago: The Lakeside Press, 1930), pp. 347–348.

49. Heizer, ed., *The Indians of Los Angeles County*, p. 85.

50. Alfred Robinson, *Life in California During a Residence of Several Years in that Territory Comprising a Description of the Country and the Missionary Establishments, with Incidents, Observations, Etc., Illustrated with Numerous Engravings* (New York: Wiley & Putnam, 1846), pp. 25–26.

51. Tac, *Conversion of the San Luiseños*, pp. 20–21.

52. Robinson, *Life in California*, p. 24.

53. William Duncan Strong, *Aboriginal Society in Southern California*, University of California Publications in American Archaeology and Ethnology 26 (1929), 148–149.

54. Mission San Diego, "Preguntas y Respuestas."

55. Mission San Luis Rey, "Preguntas y Respuestas."

56. Mission San Gabriel, "Preguntas y Respuestas."

57. Mission San Juan Capistrano, "Preguntas y Respuestas."

58. Mission San Diego, "Preguntas y Respuestas."

59. Friar Gerónimo Boscana, *Chinigchinich: A Historical Account of the Ori-*

gin, *Customs, and Traditions of the Indians at the Missionary Establishment of St. Juan Capistrano, Alta-California; Called The Acagchemen Nation,* in Robinson, *Life in California,* pp. 326–328.

60. *Ibid.,* p. 338.

61. Sherburne Cook, *The Conflict Between the California Indian and White Civilization: I, The Indian Versus the Spanish Mission,* Ibero-Americana 21 (Berkeley: University of California Press, 1943), 73–90.

62. Sherburne Cook, *Population Trends Among the California Mission Indians,* Ibero-Americana 17 (Berkeley: University of California Press, 1940), 27.

63. Quoted in Fr. Zephyrin Engelhardt, O.F.M. *Santa Barbara Mission* (San Francisco: The James H. Barry Company, 1923), pp. 80–81.

64. Quoted in Fr. Zephyrin Engelhardt, O.F.M., *The Missions, Vol. II, Upper California, Part II, General History* (1913), pp. 33–34.

65. George William Beattie, *California's Unbuilt Missions* ([privately printed], 1930), p. 35.

66. Quoted in *ibid.,* p. 39.

67. Fr. Zephyrin Engelhardt, O.F.M., *San Diego Mission* (San Francisco: The James H. Barry Company, 1920), p. 150.

68. Engelhardt, *San Juan Capistrano Mission,* pp. 39–40.

69. *Ibid.,* p. 197.

70. Engelhardt, *San Gabriel Mission,* p. 90.

71. Mission San Gabriel, "Preguntas y Respuestas."

72. Engelhardt, *San Gabriel Mission,* p. 268.

73. Engelhardt, *San Juan Capistrano Mission,* p. 175.

74. Engelhardt, *San Diego Mission,* p. 300.

75. Engelhardt, *San Luis Rey Mission,* p. 220.

76. Dr. Thomas Coulter, "Notes on Upper California," paper read on March 9, 1835, to the Royal Geographical Society, reprinted from the *Journal of the Royal Geographical Society,* 1835 (Aldine Book Co., August, 1925), p. 67.

77. C. Alan Hutchinson, "The Mexican Government and the Mission Indians of Upper California, 1821–1835," *The Americas* 21, (1965), 336.

78. *Ibid.,* p. 335.

79. Quoted in *ibid.,* pp. 338–339.

80. *Ibid.*

81. *Ibid.,* p. 335.

82. *Ibid.,* p. 340.

83. Engelhardt, *San Juan Capistrano Mission,* pp. 81–82.

84. F. W. Beechey, *Narrative of a Voyage to the Pacific and Beering's Strait in the Years 1825–1828,* Part II (London: Henry Colburn and Richard Bentley, 1831), pp. 582–583.

85. Hutchinson, "The Mexican Government," pp. 351–352.

86. C. Alan Hutchinson, *Frontier Settlement in Mexican California: The Híjar-Padrés Colony, and Its Origins, 1769–1835* (New Haven and London: Yale University Press, 1969), pp. 255–260.

87. Quoted in Engelhardt, *San Luis Rey Mission,* pp. 96–97.

88. *Ibid.,* pp. 102–103.

89. Quoted in *ibid.,* pp. 104–105.

90. *Ibid.,* pp. 121–122. In 1852 it was reported that there were some fifty Indian proprietors of land in southern California. See Caughey, ed., *The Indians of Southern California in 1852,* p. 24.

91. Quoted in Arthur Woodward, *Lances at San Pasqual* (Oakland: Westgate Press, 1948), p. 21.

92. *Ibid.*

93. Engelhardt, *San Diego Mission,* p. 267.

94. Richard Henry Dana, Jr., *Two Years Before the Mast: A Personal Narrative of Life at Sea* (New York: Harper and Brothers, 1840), p. 210.

95. Wilbur, ed., *De Mofras' Travels*, p. 179.

96. Bancroft, *History of California, Vol. III, 1825–1840*, p. 359.

97. Quoted in A. P. Nasatir, "Pueblo Postscript: San Diego During the Mexican period 1825–1840," *Journal of San Diego History* 13 (January, 1967), 38–40.

98. William Ellison and Francis Price, eds., *The Life and Adventures in California of Don Agustín Janssens 1834–1856* (San Marino: Huntington Library, 1953), p. 103.

99. *Ibid.*, p. 99.

100. Caballeria, *History of San Bernardino Valley*, pp. 102–104.

101. *Ibid.*, pp. 74–76.

102. Hutchinson, *Frontier Settlement in Mexican California*, pp. 278–281.

103. Caballeria, *History of San Bernardino Valley*, p. 82.

104. Horace Bell, *Reminiscences of a Ranger or Early Times in Southern California* (Los Angeles: Yarnell, Caystile & Mathes, Printers, 1881), pp. 281–283.

105. Caballeria, *History of San Bernardino Valley*, pp. 102–104.

106. Arthur Woodward, ed., "Benjamin David Wilson's Observations on Early Days in California and New Mexico," as told to Thomas Savage of Bancroft Library, Lake Vineyard, December 6, 1877, *Annual Publication of the Historical Society of Southern California* (1934), pp. 89–91.

107. *Ibid.*, p. 92.

108. *Ibid.*, pp. 93–94.

109. Strong, *Aboriginal Society*, pp. 53–54. The *Los Angeles Star* of October 22, 1859, reports that "Cabezon has, from time to time, received certificates of white men, for favors rendered them; these are sometimes of a questionable character, and convey intimations anything but complimentary to the chief; but they have all been strictly preserved."

110. What to call this political organization remains a problem. American anthropologists would probably identify it as a composite band because it developed as a result of white contact. See Elman R. Service, *Primitive Social Organization: An Evolutionary Perspective* (New York: Random House, 1968), pp. 83–107. British anthropologists, however, might label it a kind of "primitive" state because of its centralized authority. See Lucy Mair, *An Introduction to Social Anthropology* (London: Oxford University Press, 1965), pp. 112–125.

CHAPTER 3

CHIEFS AND CALIFORNIOS

1. John Brown, Jr., and James Boyd, *History of San Bernardino and Riverside Counties* (Chicago: The Lewis Publishing Company, 1922), I, 31.

2. *Ibid.*, p. 27.

3. Quoted in *ibid.*, II, 680.

4. *Ibid.*

5. Benjamin Hayes, "Notes," nos. 120–133, C-E 81:10, Bancroft Library, Berkeley.

6. *Los Angeles Star*, June 7, 1851.

7. Marjorie Tisdale Wolcott, ed., *Pioneer Notes from the Diaries of Judge Benjamin Hayes, 1849–1875* (Los Angeles: [privately printed], 1929), p. 277.

8. William Duncan Strong, *Aboriginal Society in Southern California*, Uni-

versity of California Publications in American Archaeology and Ethnology 26 (1929), 152.

9. *Ibid.*, p. 149.

10. *Ibid.*, p. 150.

11. Lieut. A. W. Whipple, *Reports of Explorations and Surveys to Ascertain the Most Practicable and Economical Route for a Railroad from the Mississippi River to the Pacific Ocean 1853–1854*, U.S. Congress. Senate, 33d Cong., 2d Sess., *Exec. Doc.* 78 (Washington: Beverly Tucker, 1856), III, 134.

12. John W. Caughey, ed., *The Indians of Southern California in 1852: The B. D. Wilson Report and a Selection of Contemporary Comment* (San Marino: Huntington Library, 1952), pp. 7–8.

13. Wolcott, ed., *Pioneer Notes*, pp. 275–276.

14. George William Beattie and Helen Pruitt Beattie, *Heritage of the Valley: San Bernardino's First Century* (Pasadena: San Pasqual Press, 1939), pp. 61–62. Juan Antonio's Cahuillas probably settled on the rancho in 1846. According to a historian, Indian depredations were so serious from March to August, 1846, that the rancheros decided to station guards near the Cajon Pass. Six Yuta families were invited to settle at Jurupa. See Hubert Howe Bancroft, *History of California, Vol. V, 1846–1848* (San Francisco: The History Company, 1886), p. 624. An anthropologist also accepts 1846 as the year Antonio settled at Jurupa, claiming that the term "Yuta" probably refers to the five lineages that Antonio commanded. See Strong, *Aboriginal Society*, pp. 150–151. Another anthropologist accepts the year 1846 as correct but asserts that Juan Antonio was allowed to settle in what was Wanakik (Pass) Cahuilla territory because he had a Wanakik wife. See Lowell John Bean, "The Wanakik Cahuilla," *The Masterkey* 34 (1960), 116.

15. Arthur Woodward, *Lances at San Pasqual* (Oakland: Westgate Press, 1948), pp. 37–39.

16. Millard F. Hudson, "The Pauma Massacre," *Annual Publication of the Historical Society of Southern California and the Tenth Annual Publication of the Pioneers of Los Angeles County* (1906), p. 16.

17. Benjamin Hayes, *San Diego Union*, July 12, 1874.

18. José Antonio Serrano and Petitioners, Testimony Sworn to Cave J. Couts, Justice of the Peace, San Louis Rey Township, San Diego County, State of California, December 28, 1859, Cave Johnson Couts Collection, Indian Affairs, CT 199 (1–11) Huntington Library, San Marino.

19. Benjamin Hayes, "Scrapbooks," vol. 38, Bancroft Library, Berkeley, p. 210.

20. Hudson, "The Pauma Massacre," p. 15.

21. Hayes, "Scrapbooks," pp. 230–231.

22. *Ibid.*, p. 210.

23. *Ibid.*, p. 232.

24. José María Estudillo, "Datos Históricos sobre la Alta California por José María Estudillo vecino de San Diego," dictated to Thomas Savage, North San Diego, January 17, 1878, Bancroft Library, Berkeley, pp. 46–47.

25. Relatives of the slain remembered the tragedy taking place between *Dia de la Virgen* (December 8) and *Guadalupe* (December 12). See Wolcott, ed., *Pioneer Notes*, p. 285.

26. *Ibid.*, p. 286.

27. John S. Griffin, "Diary," in Benjamin Hayes, "Emigrant Notes," pt. 4, Bancroft Library, p. 763. For a detailed version of the killings based on oral testimony, see Hudson, "The Pauma Massacre." According to a local historian, when General Kearny talked with the Indians at Kupa, he may have suggested to them that if they attacked Californios the Americans would not be disappointed. See Horace Parker, "The Temecula Massacre," *The Westerners Brand*

Book, Los Angeles Corral No. 10 (1963), pp. 176–188. An anthropologist claims that the Cahuillas, as allies of the Californios, saw the Americans as invaders while the Luiseño, who had lost their lands to the Californios, looked upon the Americans as liberators. The battle at Aguanga was the natural result of this situation. See Strong, *Aboriginal Society*, p. 149.

28. Estudillo, "Datos Históricos," p. 49.

29. Wolcott, ed., *Pioneer Notes*, pp. 285–286.

30. Ralph P. Bieber, ed., "Cooke's Journal of the March of the Mormon Battalion, 1846–1847," in *Exploring Southwestern Trails 1846–1854 by Philip St. George Cooke, William Henry Chase Whiting, Francois Xavier Aubry* (Glendale: The Arthur H. Clark Company, 1938), pp. 228–229.

31. Antonio Serrano and Petitioners to Cave J. Couts, Huntington Library.

32. Don José del Carmen Lugo, "Life of a Rancher," as told to Thomas Savage of the Bancroft Library, 1877, *Historical Society of Southern California Quarterly* 32 (September, 1950), 208–209.

33. Bieber, ed., "Cooke's Journal," pp. 228–229. See also *Daily Alta California*, December 19, 1851.

34. Quoted in Beattie, *Heritage of the Valley*, pp. 76–78.

35. *Ibid.*, p. 84.

36. *Los Angeles Star*, August 16, 1851.

37. In December 1851 Juan Antonio signed a treaty of peace with Major General J. H. Bean of the state militia in which he designated himself "Chief of the Cahuilla Nation." See *Los Angeles Star*, January 3, 1852. A petition sent to the Commissioner of Indian Affairs in the mid-1850s was signed by twenty-four Cahuilla leaders with Juan Antonio identified as principal chief. See Isaac Williams to G. W. Manypenny, Rancho del Chino, May 15, 1856, Letters Received by the Office of Indian Affairs 1824–1881, California Superintendency, Microcopy 234, Roll 35, U.S. National Archives.

38. *Los Angeles Star*, January 24, 1852.

39. Caughey, ed., *Indians of Southern California*, p. 29.

40. Quoted in Marjorie Tisdale Wolcott, "The Lugos and Their Indian Ally— How Juan Antonio Aided in the Defense and Development of Rancho San Bernardino," *Touring Topics* 21 (November 12, 1929), 23.

41. Capt. C. S. Lovell, "Report in Relation to the Cohuilla Indians," n.d., Record Group 393, Pacific Division, Register of Letters Received and Sent, Reports 1848–1851, vol. 1/2, Reports Received Pertaining to Indian Customs 1853–1854, U.S. National Archives. Lovell estimated that the population of the Cahuilla was between 3,000 and 3,500. According to an anthropologist, they numbered between 2,500 and 3,000. See Herbert Raymond Harvey, "Population of the Cahuilla Indians: Decline and Its Causes," *Eugenics Quarterly* 14 (September, 1967), 191.

42. Hayes, "Emigrant Notes," pt. 4, p. 751.

43. *Ibid.*, p. 751.

44. Quoted in Wolcott, "The Lugos and Their Indian Ally," p. 24.

45. Tom Hughes, *History of Banning and San Gorgonio Pass* (Banning: Banning Record Print, 1938), pp. 107–108.

46. Joseph Lancaster Brent, *The Lugo Case: A Personal Reminiscence* (New Orleans: Searcy and Pfaff, 1926), pp. 57–59.

47. *Ibid.*, pp. 10–18.

48. *Ibid.*, pp. 47–50.

49. Lugo, "Life of a Rancher," pp. 213–214.

50. "The Coroner's Inquest," *Los Angeles Star*, June 7, 1851.

51. *Ibid.*

52. *Ibid.*, May 31, 1851.

53. Lugo, "Life of a Rancher," p. 214.

54. Brent, *The Lugo Case*, pp. 64–65.
55. *Los Angeles Star*, June 7, 1851.
56. Caughey, ed., *Indians of Southern California*, pp. 10–11.
57. *Ibid.*, p. 11.
58. *Los Angeles Star*, June 7, 1851.
59. *Ibid.*, June 14, 1851.
60. Caughey, ed., *Indians of Southern California*, pp. 10–11.
61. *Los Angeles Star*, August 2, 1851.
62. *Ibid.*, August 9, 1851.
63. Stephen Clark Foster, "Reminiscences: My First Procession in Los Angeles, March 16, 1847," *Historical Society of Southern California* (1887), p. 50.
64. John Russell Bartlett, *Personal Narrative of Explorations and Incidents in Texas, New Mexico, California, Sonora, and Chichuahua* (New York: D. Appleton and Company, 1854), II, 82.
65. Caughey, ed., *Indians of Southern California*, pp. 21–22.
66. *Ibid.*
67. Horace Bell, *Reminiscences of a Ranger or Early Times in Southern California* (Los Angeles: Yarnell, Caystile & Mathes, Printers, 1881), pp. 47–49. On the complaint of any resident white citizen, a vagrant Indian could be brought before a justice of the peace, mayor, or recorder. If found guilty, the Indian could be hired out for a term up to four months. See *The Statutes of California Passed at the First Session of the Legislature* (San Jose: J. Winchester, State Printer, 1850), p. 410.
68. Quoted in W. W. Robinson, *The Indians of Los Angeles: Story of the Liquidation of a People* (Los Angeles: Glen Dawson, 1952), pp. 1–3.
69. Bell, *Reminiscences*, pp. 47–49.
70. Brent, *The Lugo Case*, pp. 7–8.
71. *Daily Alta California*, November 13, 1851.
72. *Los Angeles Star*, November 1, 1851.
73. Caughey, ed., *Indians of Southern California*, pp. 8–9.
74. Strong, *Aboriginal Society*, pp. 150–151.
75. Caughey, ed., *Indians of Southern California*, pp. 8–9.
76. Joseph John Hill, *The History of Warner's Ranch and Its Environs* (Los Angeles: [privately printed], 1927), pp. 201–202.
77. George Walcott Ames, Jr., ed., "A Doctor Comes to California: The Diary of John S. Griffin, Assistant Surgeon with Kearny's Dragoons 1846–47," *California Historical Society Quarterly*, 21, 4 (December, 1942), 333.
78. *Ibid.*, no. 3 (September, 1942), p. 220.
79. *Ibid.*, no. 4 (December, 1942), p. 333.
80. *Ibid.*, no. 3 (September, 1942), p. 220.
81. *Ibid.*, no. 4 (December, 1942), p. 334.
82. Jane H. Hill and Rosinda Nolasquez, eds., *Mulu'wetam: The First People, Cupeño Oral History and Language* (Banning: Malki Museum Press, 1973), pp. 26a–27a.
83. Ames, ed., "A Doctor Comes to California," no. 3 (September, 1942), p. 220.
84. "Confession of William Marshall, San Diego, December 10 and 11, 1851," *Los Angeles Star*, December 27, 1851.
85. *San Diego Herald*, December 18, 1851.
86. "Confession of William Marshall," *Los Angeles Star*, December 27, 1851.
87. Wolcott, ed., *Pioneer Notes*, pp. 52–53.
88. Ames, ed., "A Doctor Comes to California," no. 4 (December, 1942), p. 334.
89. *Daily Alta California*, December 18, 1851. How well educated was Garra is not clear. A letter written by Garra to a Californio was reported to be in half

Spanish and half Indian dialect. See Edward H. Fitzgerald to J. Hooker, San Diego, November 27, 1851, Letters Received by the Office of the Adjutant General (Main Series) 1881–1889, Microcopy 689, Roll 470, U.S. National Archives.

90. "Confession of Antonio Garra, Rancho del Chino, December 13, 1851," *Daily Alta California*, January 2, 1852. Because Garra called himself a "St. Louis" Indian does not mean that he was a Luiseño. He probably identified himself as such because he had been a neophyte at Mission San Luis Rey.

91. Caughey, ed., *Indians of Southern California*, pp. 7–8.

92. *Ibid.*, p. 59. The report also states (p. 59) that General Kearny breveted Juan Antonio a general. A report on the condition of the Indians of southern California issued in 1883 states that the aged captain of the Cupeños possessed "a memorandum of a promise from General Kearny, who assured them that in consideration of their friendliness and assistance to him they should retain their homes without molestation, 'although the whole State should fill with white men.'" See Helen Jackson and Abbot Kinney, "Report on the Condition and Needs of the Mission Indians of California," in Helen Hunt Jackson, *A Century of Dishonor: A Sketch of the United States Government's Dealings with Some of the Indian Tribes, Enlarged by the Addition of the Report of the Needs of the Mission Indians* first published in 1881 (Boston: Roberts Brothers, 1886), p. 486.

93. Strong, *Aboriginal Society*, pp. 249–250.

94. Record Group 393, Pacific Division, Proceedings of a Council of War Convened in the Valley Los Coyotes, December 23, 1851, H-4 (1852), U.S. National Archives.

95. *San Diego Herald*, November 27, 1851.

96. Bieber, ed., "Cooke's Journal," pp. 228–229. A historian claims that it was "Garra's band of Cahuillas and fugitive ex-neophytes of San Luis Rey" who killed the eleven Californios and who were, in turn, ambushed at Aguanga by Juan Antonio's Cahuillas. Furthermore, he asserts that Bill Marshall instigated the murders because the Americans would have approved of such action. See Hubert Howe Bancroft, *History of California*, V, 267–268.

97. Bieber, ed., "Cooke's Journal," pp. 228–229.

98. Two Indians with the name "Juan Bautista" (Baupista or Baptista) appear in this study. The one who also went by the name "Coton" was an active participant in the 1851 uprising and was executed by the military authorities. The one who spoke with Cooke came to the aid of the Americans and later signed, along with other Cahuilla leaders, a treaty with the United States government. The treaty identifies Bautista as a subordinate of Juan Antonio's. See Charles Kappler, ed., *Indian Affairs: Laws and Treaties* (Washington: Government Printing Office, 1929), IV, 1124–1126.

99. Bieber, ed., "Cooke's Journal," p. 231. The chastisement was probably unnecessary, for an Indian leader who had recently killed Cupeños would not have been at Kupa. The ambush was undertaken by Juan Antonio and his closest followers.

100. *Ibid.*, pp. 233–234.

101. Sgt. Daniel Tyler, *A Concise History of the Mormon Battalion in the Mexican War, 1846–1847* (Glorieta, N.M.: The Rio Grande Press, 1964), p. 251.

102. Bieber, ed., "Cooke's Journal," p. 234.

103. Colonel Couts Diary, Bancroft Library, Berkeley, p. 119. The statement "whipping the Mexicans during the war" may refer to the killing of the eleven Californios. If so, it clearly implicates Garra in the murders.

104. Wolcott, ed., *Pioneer Notes*, pp. 52–53.

105. *Ibid.*, pp. 57–58.

106. Hayes, "Emigrant Notes," pt. 2, p. 308.

107. Wolcott, ed., *Pioneer Notes*, p. 52.

108. William H. Emory, *Notes of a Military Reconnaissance from Fort Leavenworth, in Missouri, to San Diego, in California, Arkansas, Del Norte, and Gila Rivers* (Washington: Wendell and van Benthuysen, 1848), pp. 105–106.

109. Wolcott, ed., *Pioneer Notes*, pp. 57–58.

110. Emory, *Notes*, pp. 105–106.

111. Wolcott, ed., *Pioneer Notes*, p. 57.

112. *Ibid.*, pp. 52–53.

113. *Ibid.*, p. 57.

114. *Ibid.*, p. 59.

115. *Ibid.*, p. 58.

116. "Journal of Captain A. R. Johnston, First Dragoons," U.S., Congress, House, 30th Cong., 1st. Sess., *House Exec. Doc.* 41, pp. 613–614. See also "Johnston's Journal," *Out West* 18 (January to June, 1903), 746.

117. Ames, ed., "A Doctor Comes to California," no. 4 (December, 1942), p. 334.

118. Emory, *Notes*, pp. 105–106.

119. Bieber, ed., "Cooke's Journal," pp. 228–229.

120. Wolcott, ed., *Pioneer Notes*, p. 84.

121. Hayes, "Emigrant Notes," pt. 2, p. 308.

122. Lt. J. D. Stevenson to Col. R. B. Mason, Los Angeles, June 28, 1847, Pacific Division, Records of the 10th Military Department, 1846–1851. Microcopy 210, Roll 2, U.S. National Archives.

123. Citizens' Letter and Petition, San Diego, June 27, 1847, Pacific Division, Records of the 10th Military Department, 1846–1851, Microcopy 210, Roll 5, U.S. National Archives.

124. Lt. J. D. Stevenson to Col. R. B. Mason, Los Angeles, June 28, 1847, Pacific Division, Records of the 10th Military Department, 1846–1851, Microcopy 210, Roll 2, U.S. National Archives.

125. Lt. J. D. Stevenson to Col. R. B. Mason, Los Angeles, July 12, 1847, Pacific Division, Records of the 10th Military Department, 1846–1851, Microcopy 210, Roll 2, U.S. National Archives.

126. Lt. W. T. Sherman to J. D. Hunter, Santa Barbara, August 1, 1847, Pacific Division, Records of the 10th Military Department, 1846–1851, Microcopy 210, Roll 1, U.S. National Archives.

127. Agostin Haraszthy to Editors, San Diego, December 22, 1851, *Los Angeles Star*, December 27, 1851.

128. *Ibid.* According to the *Los Angeles Star* of December 20, 1851, "from three rancherias commanded by Antonio Garra, the tax collector of San Diego County collected $250 in money, and drove off eighteen gentile milch cows, and five gentile horses and mules. Persons have called upon us and offered to produce proof of these facts, stating themselves to have been eye-witnesses of the proceedings. From the rancheria where Garra lives $150 in money was collected."

129. José Joaquin Ortega to Editors, San Diego, December 20, 1851, *Daily Alta California*, January 11, 1852.

130. Colonel Couts Diary, p. 130.

131. Ortega to Editors, *Daily Alta California*, January 11, 1852.

132. *Daily Alta California*, December 4, 1851.

133. William H. Ellison, "The Federal Indian Policy in California, 1846–1860," *Mississippi Valley Historical Review* 9 (1922), 48–49.

134. George W. Barbour to Luke Lea, Near Los Angeles, U.S., Congress, Senate, June 16, 1851, 33d Cong., Sp. Sess., *Exec. Doc.* 4, March 4, 1853, no. 668, pp. 257–260.

135. *Los Angeles Star*, July 19, 1851.

136. "Indians of San Bernardino and San Diego Counties," *Los Angeles Star,* March 8, 1856.

137. *Ibid.,* July 19, 1851.

CHAPTER 4

THE UPRISING

1. Cave J. Couts to W. H. Emory, Santa Isabel, September 17, 1849, Cave J. Couts Documentary File, San Diego Historical Society, Serra Museum and Library, San Diego.

2. J. M. Guinn, "Yuma Depredations and the Glanton War," *Annual Publication of the Historical Society of Southern California and the Pioneers of Los Angeles County,* vol. 6, pt. 1 (1903), pp. 50–51.

3. Quoted in Douglas D. Martin, *Yuma Crossing* (Albuquerque: University of New Mexico Press, 1954), pp. 140–141.

4. "Origin of the Troubles Between the Yumas and Glanton, Deposition of Jeremiah Hill" in Guinn, "Yuma Depredations," pp. 57–59. See also "Petition of Thomas W. Sutherland and Others and Affidavit of William Carr," Record Group 393, Pacific Division, Letters Received 1849–1853, 1850, A1-W14, U.S. Army Continental Commands, 1821–1920, Box 2, U.S. National Archives.

5. Guinn, "Troubles Between the Yumas and Glanton," pp. 57–59.

6. Arthur Woodward, ed., *Journal of Lt. Thomas W. Sweeny 1849–1853* (Los Angeles: Westernlore Press, 1956), pp. 135–137.

7. *Daily Alta California,* January 8, 1851.

8. Woodward, ed., *Journal,* pp. 135–137.

9. Guinn, "Troubles Between the Yumas and Glanton," pp. 60–61.

10. See "Yuman Indian Depredation on the Colorado in 1850, a Deposition," *Annual Publication of the Historical Society of Southern California* vol. 7, pts. 2–3, (1907–1908), pp. 202–203.

11. George A. Johnson, "Life of Captain George A. Johnson," Typed manuscript, n.d. The California State Library, Sacramento, pp. 4–5.

12. J. M. Guinn, *History of the State of California and Biographical Record of Coast Counties, California* (Chicago: The Chapman Publishing Company, 1904), pp. 226–227.

13. Johnson, "Life," pp. 5–6.

14. Guinn, *History,* pp. 226–227.

15. Robert W. Frazer, "Camp Yuma—1852," *Historical Society of Southern California Quarterly* 52 (June, 1970), 170–171.

16. Capt. S. P. Heintzelman to Gen. R. Jones, June 5, 1851, Letters Received by the Office of the Adjutant General (Main Series) 1881–1889, Microcopy 689, Roll 470, U.S. National Archives.

17. Frazer, "Camp Yuma," p. 171.

18. "Memorandum of Claim of J. E. Iaeger for Property Taken, Used, and Destroyed by Order of Capt. D. Davidson, 2d U.S. Infantry Commanding at Camp Yuma, Calif. in 1851 with Statement of Loss by Indians, etc., December 6, 1851," Letters Received by the Office of the Adjutant General (Main Series) 1881–1889, Roll 470, U.S. National Archives.

19. Woodward, ed., *Journal,* pp. 55–56.

20. *Ibid.,* pp. 120–121.

21. W. J. Ankrim to Editors, November 27, 1851, *San Diego Herald,* November 27, 1851.

22. "Confession of Antonio Garra," Rancho del Chino, December 13, 1851, *San Diego Herald*, December 18, 1851.

23. "Court Martial of Antonio Garra, January 10–17, 1852, San Diego," Cave Johnson Couts Collection, Indian Affairs, CT 1974, Huntington Library, San Marino.

24. Ankrim to Editors, *San Diego Herald*, November 27, 1851.

25. *Ibid.*

26. Lt. E. Murray to Capt. S. P. Heintzelman, November 18, 1851, *San Diego Herald*, December 5, 1851.

27. Ankrim to Editors, *San Diego Herald*, November 27, 1851.

28. Isaac Williams to Editors, Rancho del Chino, November 27, 1851, *Los Angeles Star*, November 29, 1851.

29. Capt. S. P. Heintzelman to Lt. Col. J. Hooker, San Diego, November 28, 1851, Letters Received by the Office of the Adjutant General (Main Series) 1881–1889, Roll 470, U.S. National Archives.

30. *San Diego Herald*, November 27, 1851.

31. Richard R. Hopkins, "Journal of Richard R. Hopkins," November 28, 1851, Office of the Church Historian, Salt Lake City, pp. 61–62.

32. *San Diego Herald*, January 10, 1852. According to a report on the southern Indians, written in 1852, "the Tulareños live in the mountain wilderness of the Four Creeks, Porsiuncula (or Kern's or Current) river and the Tejon, and wander thence towards the headwaters of the Mojave and the neighborhood of the Cahuillas. Their present common name belongs to the Spanish and Mexican times, and is derived from the word *tulare* (a swamp with flags). They were formerly attached to the Missions of Santa Ynes, Santa Barbara, La Purissima, and San Buenaventura, in Santa Barbara county, and San Fernando, in Los Angeles county. They are all of one family: there is very little difference in the languages spoken by the several rancherias (villages). . . . They speak the Santa Ynes tongue." See John W. Caughey, ed., *The Indians of Southern California in 1852: The B. D. Wilson Report and a Selection of Contemporary Comment* (San Marino: Huntington Library, 1952), pp. 4–5. From their association with the missions in the Santa Barbara region, many of the Tulareños were probably Chumash Indians. See Leif C. W. Landberg, *The Chumash Indians of Southern California*, Southwest Museum Report, no. 19 (Los Angeles: Southwest Museum, 1965), p. 21.

33. O. M. Wozencraft to Luke Lea, n.d., Letters Received by the Office of Indian Affairs, 1824–1881, California Superintendency, 1849–1880, 1849–1852, Microcopy 234, Roll 32, U.S. National Archives. See also *Los Angeles Star*, December 20, 1851; and Charles Kappler, ed., *Indian Affairs: Laws and Treaties* (Washington: Government Printing Office, 1929), IV, 1101–1103.

34. Capt. S. P. Heintzelman to Maj. E. D. Townsend, Fort Yuma, July 15, 1853, U.S. Congress, House, 34th Cong. 3d Sess., *Exec. Doc.* 74, p. 40.

35. Woodward, ed., *Journal*, pp. 176–177.

36. *Ibid.*, pp. 146–147.

37. *Los Angeles Star*, November 22, 1851.

38. Heintzelman to Townsend, July 15, 1853, 34 Cong., pp. 50–51.

39. "Confession of Antonio Garra," *San Diego Herald*, December 18, 1851.

40. Lt. E. Murray to Capt. D. Davidson, Camp Independence, December 4, 1851, Letters Received by the Office of the Adjutant General (Main Series) 1881–1889, Roll 470, U.S. National Archives.

41. "Declaration of Antonio Garra," Rancho del Chino, December 16, 1851, *Los Angeles Star*, December 20, 1851.

42. "Trial of Antonio Garra," *San Diego Herald*, January 17, 1852.

43. *Daily Alta California*, December 3, 1851.

44. Trial of Bill Marshall, Benjamin Hayes, "Scrapbooks," vol. 39, Bancroft Library, Berkeley.

45. Record Group 393, Pacific Division, Proceedings of a Council of War Convened in the Valley Los Coyotes, December 23, 1851, H-4 (1852), U.S. National Archives.

46. Trial of Bill Marshall, Hayes, "Scrapbooks."

47. Proceedings of a Council of War, U.S. National Archives.

48. *Ibid.*

49. *Los Angeles Star,* November 29, 1851.

50. "Trial of Antonio Garra," *San Diego Herald,* January 17, 1852.

51. *Ibid.*

52. *Los Angeles Star,* November 29, 1851.

53. Statement of Juan José Warner, U.S. Congress, Senate, 33d Cong., Sp. Sess., *Exec. Doc.* 4.

54. Trial of Bill Marshall, Hayes, "Scrapbooks."

55. *Ibid.*

56. *San Diego Herald,* December 5, 1851.

57. Francis Engle Patterson to Edward H. Fitzgerald, San Luis Rey, November 30, 1851, Cave Johnson Couts Collection, Indian Affairs, CT 1755, Huntington Library, San Marino.

58. Domingo Tule to Manuel Cota, San Luis Rey, November 30, 1851, Cave Johnson Couts Collection, Indian Affairs, CT 2321, Huntington Library, San Marino.

59. "Declaration of Antonio Garra," *Los Angeles Star,* December 20, 1851.

60. Trial of Bill Marshall, Hayes, "Scrapbooks."

61. *San Diego Herald,* December 5, 1851.

62. Antonio Garra to Juan Antonio, literal translation, Los Coyotes, December 2, 1851, *Los Angeles Star,* December 20, 1851.

63. Hopkins, "Journal," November 26, 1851, p. 60.

64. Augustín Olvera to Juan Antonio, Los Angeles, November 25, 1851, "La Estrella," *Los Angeles Star,* December 13, 1851.

65. Juan Antonio to Augustín Olvera, San Gorgonio, December 8, 1851, "La Estrella," *Los Angeles Star,* December 13, 1851.

66. Trial of Bill Marshall, Hayes, "Scrapbooks."

67. W. H. R. to Editors, *Los Angeles Star,* December 13, 1851.

68. Trial of Bill Marshall, Hayes, "Scrapbooks."

69. *Los Angeles Star,* December 20, 1851.

70. Trial of Bill Marshall, Hayes, "Scrapbooks." See also "Declaration of Antonio Garra," *Los Angeles Star,* December 20, 1851.

71. Trial of Bill Marshall, Hayes, "Scrapbooks."

72. "Declaration of Antonio Garra," *Los Angeles Star,* December 20, 1851.

73. "Confession of Bill Marshall," *Los Angeles Star,* December 27, 1851.

74. *Daily Alta California,* December 12, 1851.

75. Horace Bell, *Reminiscences of a Ranger or Early Times in Southern California* (Los Angeles: Yarnell, Caystile & Mathes, Printers, 1881), p. 165.

76. Gen. J. H. Bean to Gov. J. McDougal, November 30, 1851, California State Archives. See also *Daily Alta California,* December 12, 1851.

77. *Daily Alta California,* December 13, 1851.

78. Thomas Whaley to Anna Eloise, San Diego, December 17, 1851. Whaley House, San Diego.

79. Hopkins, "Journal," November 25, 1851, p. 60.

80. Luther Ingersoll, *Ingersoll's Century Annals of San Bernardino County 1769–1904* (Los Angeles: [privately printed], 1904), pp. 133–135.

81. *Los Angeles Star,* November 29, 1851.

82. *Ibid.*
83. *Ibid.*, December 6, 1851.
84. *Ibid.*, December 8, 1851.
85. Capt. S. P. Heintzelman to Lt. Col. J. Hooker, San Diego, November 28, 1851, Letters Received by the Office of the Adjutant General (Main Series) 1881–1889, Roll 470, U.S. National Archives.
86. Capt. D. Davidson to Maj. S. P. Heintzelman, Santa Isabel, December 18, 1851, Letters Received by the Office of the Adjutant General (Main Series) 1881–1889, Roll 470, U.S. National Archives.
87. *Ibid.*
88. Memorandum of J. E. Iaeger, U.S. National Archives.
89. Woodward, ed., *Journal*, p. 137.
90. *Ibid.*, pp. 140–142.
91. *San Diego Herald*, November 27, 1851.
92. *Daily Alta California*, December 3, 1851.
93. Thomas Whaley to Mother and Sister, San Diego, December 2, 1851, Whaley House, San Diego.
94. *San Diego Herald*, November 27, 1851.
95. *Los Angeles Star*, November 29, 1851.
96. *Ibid.*
97. *San Diego Herald*, December 5, 1851.
98. Whaley to Mother, December 2, 1851. Whaley House, San Diego.
99. *San Diego Herald*, December 5, 1851.
100. Maj. E. H. Fitzgerald to Col. J. Hooker, San Diego, December 9, 1851, Record Group 393, Pacific Division, Letters Received, 1849–1853, 1850, A1-W14, U.S. Army Continental Commands, 1821–1920, Box 3, U.S. National Archives.
101. *Ibid.*
102. José María Estudillo, "Datos Históricos sobre la Alta California por José María Estudillo vecino de San Diego," dictated to Thomas Savage, North San Diego, January 17, 1878, Bancroft Library, Berkeley, p. 52.
103. *Los Angeles Star*, December 13, 1851.
104. Estudillo, "Datos Históricos," p. 53.
105. Fitzgerald to Hooker, December 9, 1851, U.S. National Archives.
106. *Daily Alta California*, December 11, 1851.
107. Col. E. A. Hitchcock to Bvt. Maj. Gen. R. Jones, Benicia, December 12, 1851, Record Group 393, Pacific Division, Letters Sent 1851–1852, U.S. National Archives.
108. Whaley to Eloise, December 17, 1851. Whaley House, San Diego.
109. *San Diego Herald*, December 25, 1851.
110. *Ibid.*, January 5, 1852.
111. *Ibid.*
112. *Ibid.*, January 24, 1852.
113. Woodward, ed., *Journal*, pp. 142–144.
114. *Los Angeles Star*, December 6, 1852.
115. *Daily Alta California*, January 6, 1852.
116. *Ibid.*
117. Fitzgerald to Hooker, December 9, 1851, U.S. National Archives.
118. *Daily Alta California*, January 6, 1852.
119. "Treaty of Peace, Amity and Friendship made and concluded between Major General J. H. Bean, commanding the 4th Division, California State Militia, on the part and behalf of the people of the said State; and Juan Antonio, Chief of the Cahuilla Nation, December 20, 1851," *Los Angeles Star*, January 3, 1852.
120. *Daily Alta California*, January 6, 1852.

121. Gen. J. H. Bean to Gov. J. McDougal, Rancho del Chino, January 1, 1852, Adjutant General Record Group, Misc. Files, 1851, California State Archives, Sacramento.

122. *Los Angeles Star*, January 24, 1852.

123. Davidson to Heintzelman, December 18, 1851, U.S. National Archives.

124. Capt. S. P. Heintzelman, "Expeditions Against the Indians of Los Coyotes and Destruction of their Village, December 21, 1851," Record Group 393, Pacific Division, H-24 (1851), U.S. National Archives. See also *Los Angeles Star*, January 24, 1852. A local historian claims that the battle was fought where the present-day mouth of Collins Valley encounters Coyote Creek in the vicinity of Santa Catarina Spring. See Horace Parker, "The Treaty of Temecula," *The Historic Valley of Temecula*, Librito 2 (Balboa Island: Paisano Press, 1967), p. 7.

125. *San Diego Herald*, December 25, 1851. See also *Daily Alta California*, January 2, 1852.

126. Heintzelman, "Expeditions," U.S. National Archives.

127. Thomas W. Sweeny, "Journal of Thomas W. Sweeny," Sweeny Collection, 1 13 B 5, Huntington Library, San Marino.

128. Heintzelman, "Expeditions," U.S. National Archives.

129. *Ibid.*

130. Capt. S. P. Heintzelman to Capt. F. Steel, near Temecula, December 30, 1851, Letters Received by the Office of the Adjutant General (Main Series) 1881–1889, Roll 470, U.S. National Archives.

131. *Ibid.*

132. *Los Angeles Star*, January 24, 1852.

133. Heintzelman to Steel, December 30, 1851, U.S. National Archives.

134. *San Diego Herald*, January 10, 1852.

135. Heintzelman to Steel, December 30, 1851, U.S. National Archives.

136. Capt. E. D. Townsend to Maj. S. P. Heintzelman, Benicia, January 16, 1852, Letters Received by the Office of the Adjutant General (Main Series) 1881–1889, Roll 470, U.S. National Archives.

137. Maj. S. P. Heintzelman to Capt. E. D. Townsend, Junction of the Gila and Colorado Rivers, February 29, 1852, Letters Received by the Office of the Adjutant General (Main Series) 1881–1889, Roll 470, U.S. National Archives.

138. See Jack Forbes, *Warriors of the Colorado: The Yumas of the Quechan Nation and Their Neighbors* (Norman: University of Oklahoma Press, 1965), pp. 332–340.

CHAPTER 5

MILITARY JUSTICE

1. Trial of Bill Marshall, Benjamin Hayes, "Scrapbooks," vol. 39, Bancroft Library, Berkeley.

2. "Confession of William Marshall, San Diego, December 10–11, 1851," *Los Angeles Star*, December 27, 1851. See also Hayes, "Scrapbooks."

3. "Confession of William Marshall," *Los Angeles Star*.

4. Trial of Bill Marshall, Hayes, "Scrapbooks."

5. *San Diego Herald*, December 5, 1851. According to California law, "in no case shall a white man be convicted of any offense upon the testimony of an Indian, or Indians." See *The Statutes of California Passed at the First Session of the Legislature* (San Jose: J. Winchester, State Printer, 1850), p. 409.

6. Trial of Bill Marshal, Hayes, "Scrapbooks."

7. *Ibid.*
8. *Ibid.*
9. *Ibid.*
10. *Ibid.*
11. *Ibid.*
12. *Ibid.*
13. "Court Martial of William Marshall, José Verdugo, and Santos Suna, December 9–12, 1851, San Diego," Cave Johnson Couts Collection, Indian Affairs, CT 1973, Huntington Library, San Marino.
14. *San Diego Herald*, December 18, 1851.
15. "Court Martial of William Marshall," Huntington Library.
16. *San Diego Herald*, December 18, 1851.
17. Record Group 393, Pacific Division, Proceedings of a Council of War Convened in the Valley Los Coyotes, December 23, 1851, H-4 (1852), U.S. National Archives.
18. O. M. Wozencraft to Luke Lea, n.d., Letters Received by the Office of Indian Affairs, 1824–1881, California Superintendency, 1849–1880, 1849–1852, Microcopy 234, Roll 32, U.S. National Archives.
19. *San Deigo Herald*, January 10, 1852.
20. Proceedings of a Council of War, U.S. National Archives.
21. *Ibid.* See also *San Diego Herald*, January 17, 1852.
22. Proceedings of a Council of War, U.S. National Archives.
23. *Ibid.*
24. *Ibid.*
25. Wozencraft to Lea, U.S. National Archives.
26. *San Diego Herald*, January 10, 1852.
27. Wozencraft to Lea, U.S. National Archives.
28. *San Diego Herald*, January 10, 1852.
29. *Los Angeles Star*, January 3, 1852.
30. General Court Martial, Rancho del Chino, Benjamin Hayes, "Scrapbooks," vol. 39, Bancroft Library, Berkeley.
31. *Ibid.*
32. *Ibid.*
33. *Ibid.*
34. *Ibid.*
35. *Los Angeles Star*, January 3, 1852.
36. Capt. C. S. Lovell to Gen. J. H. Bean, Rancho del Chino, December 27, Benjamin Hayes, "Scrapbooks," vol. 38, Bancroft Library, Berkeley.
37. Gen. J. H. Bean to Gov. J. McDougal, Rancho del Chino, January 1, 1852, Adjutant General Record Group, Misc. Files, 1851, California State Archives, Sacramento.
38. "Confession of Antonio Garra, Rancho del Chino, December 13, 1851," *San Diego Herald*, December 18, 1851. Also published in the *Daily Alta* California, January 2, 1852. Garra's statement about "the ferrymen" refers to the killing of A. L. Lincoln, Jack Glanton, and others in 1850 by Quechans at the Colorado River crossing.
39. "Declaration of Antonio Garra, Rancho del Chino, December 16, 1851," *Los Angeles Star*, December 20, 1851.
40. *San Diego Herald*, January 10, 1852.
41. Arthur Woodward, ed., *Journal of Lt. Thomas W. Sweeny 1849–1853* (Los Angeles: Westernlore Press, 1956), pp. 146–147.
42. William E. Smythe, *History of San Diego, 1542–1908, Vol. I Old Town* (San Diego: The History Company, 1908), pp. 191–192.
43. Dr. O. M. Wozencraft, "Statement," 1877, Indian Affairs, 1849–1850, C-D 204, Bancroft Library, Berkeley, pp. 10–13.
44. *San Diego Herald*, January 10, 1852.

45. *Ibid.*, January 17, 1852.
46. Woodward, ed., *Journal*, pp. 146–147.
47. *San Diego Herald*, January 17, 1852.
48. *Ibid.*
49. "Court Martial of Antonio Garra, January 10–17, San Diego, 1852," Cave Johnson Couts Collection, Indian Affairs, CT 1974, Huntington Library, San Marino.
50. *San Diego Herald*, January 17, 1852.
51. "Court Martial of Antonio Garra," Huntington Library.
52. *San Diego Herald*, January 17, 1852.
53. *Ibid.*, January 10, 1852.
54. *Ibid.*, January 17, 1852.
55. *Ibid.*
56. Woodward, ed., *Journal*, pp. 146–147.
57. *San Diego Herald*, January 17, 1852.
58. Cave J. Couts to Abel Stearns, San Diego, January 11, 1852, Cave Johnson Couts Collection, S.G. Box 18, Huntington Library, San Marino.
59. "Gordito" to Editors, *Daily Alta California*, January 15, 1852.
60. *San Diego Herald*, January 17, 1852.
61. *Ibid.*, January 24, 1852.
62. One postscript to the uprising was the capture on February 14, 1852, of Cosme by Juan Bautista. Cosme, who had fled to Santa Ana, was turned over to the military authorities at Rancho del Chino. Interviewed by Captain Lovell, Isaac Williams, and others, Cosme gave his account of what took place at Kupa at the time of the murders. He claimed that fifteen had participated in the killing of the four Americans; and that while young Garra had been in overall command, Bill Marshall and Juan Verdugo had been the most active. For his part in the affair, Cosme told his captors that he deserved and expected to die. After his confession had been reduced to writing, Cosme was placed in the guardhouse, securely ironed hand and foot. During the night, however, he somehow got possession of a rope and hanged himself. By late February, then, only a few of the principal rebels, such as Panito, had not been captured, tried, and sentenced. See *Los Angeles Star*, February 21, 1852.

CHAPTER 6

REPERCUSSIONS

1. "Confession of Antonio Garra, Rancho del Chino, December 13, 1851," *San Diego Herald*, December 18, 1851.
2. *Los Angeles Star*, November 22, 1851.
3. Richard R. Hopkins, "Journal of Richard R. Hopkins," November 23, 1851, Office of the Church Historian, Salt Lake City, p. 58.
4. Gen. J. H. Bean to Gov. J. McDougal, Los Angeles, November 30, 1851, Indian War Files, 1850–1859, Box 1, California State Archives, Sacramento. See also *Daily Alta California*, December 12, 1851.
5. Agostin Haraszthy to Gov. J. McDougal, November 26, 1851, *Daily Alta California*, December 3, 1851.
6. *San Diego Herald*, November 27, 1851.
7. Thomas Whaley to Mother and Sister, San Diego, December 2, 1851, Whaley House, San Diego.
8. *Daily Alta California*, December 3, 1851.
9. Duff Weaver to Editors, San Bernardino, December 4, 1851, *Los Angeles Star*, December 6, 1851.
10. *San Diego Herald*, November 27, 1851.

11. *Los Angeles Star*, November 29, 1851.
12. *Daily Alta California*, December 12, 1851.
13. *San Diego Herald*, December 25, 1851. See also *Daily Alta California*, January 2, 1852.
14. *San Diego Herald*, January 1, 1852.
15. *Ibid.*
16. Joaquin Ortega to Editors, San Diego, December 30, 1852, *Daily Alta California*, January 11, 1852.
17. *Los Angeles Star*, n.d. (probably early January, 1852).
18. Quoted in William E. Smythe, *History of San Diego, 1542-1908, Vol. I Old Town* (San Diego: The History Company, 1908), pp. 191-192.
19. *Los Angeles Star*, n.d. (probably early January, 1852).
20. *San Diego Herald*, January 17, 1852.
21. "Justica" to Editors, Los Angeles, January 24, 1852, *Los Angeles Star*, January 24, 1852.
22. Gen. J. H. Bean to Editors, *Los Angeles Star*, January 31, 1852.
23. "Confession of William Marshall, San Diego, December 10-11, 1851," *Los Angeles Star*, December 27, 1851.
24. Benjamin Wilson to Editors, Los Angeles, January 5, 1852, *Los Angeles Star*, January 10, 1852.
25. Charles C. Rich to Editors, San Bernardino, January 1, 1852, *Los Angeles Star*, January 10, 1852.
26. O. M. Wozencraft to Luke Lea, n.d., Letters Received by the Office of Indian Affairs 1824-1881, California Superintendency, 1849-1880, 1849-1852, Micocopy 234, Roll 32, U.S. National Archives.
27. Adam Johnston to A. H. H. Stuart, San Francisco, December 3, 1851, Report of the Secretary of the Interior, U.S. Congress, House, 33d Cong. 1st Sess., *Exec. Doc.* 61, April 15, 1852.
28. *Daily Alta California*, December 4, 1851.
29. *Ibid.*, December 27, 1851.
30. *Los Angeles Star*, December 20, 1851.
31. *San Diego Herald*, February 3, 1852.
32. *Los Angeles Star*, December 20, 1851.
33. *Ibid.*, January 24, 1852.
34. Wozencraft to Lea, n.d., U.S. National Archives.
35. *San Diego Herald*, January 10, 1852.
36. *Ibid.*, January 1, 1852.
37. Dr. O. M. Wozencraft, "Statement," 1877, Indian Affairs, 1849-1850, C-D 204, Bancroft Library, Berkeley, pp. 10-13.
38. *San Diego Herald*, January 10, 1852.
39. Wozencraft, "Statement," Bancroft Library, pp. 10-13.
40. *Ibid.*
41. *San Diego Herald*, January 10, 1852.
42. Wozencraft to Lea, n.d., U.S. National Archives. See also *Los Angeles Star*, December 20, 1851.
43. Wozencraft, "Statement," Bancroft Library, pp. 10-13.
44. Wozencraft to Lea, n.d., U.S. National Archives.
45. Wozencraft, "Statement," Bancroft Library, pp. 10-13.
46. Charles Kappler, ed., *Indian Affairs: Laws and Treaties* (Washington: Government Printing Office, 1929), IV, 1124-1126.
47. *Ibid.*
48. *Ibid.*
49. *Ibid.*
50. *Ibid.* See also *San Diego Herald*, January 10, 1852.
51. Wozencraft to Lea, n.d., U.S. National Archives.

52. Kappler, ed., *Indian Affairs*, pp. 1124–1126.

53. *San Diego Herald*, January 10, 1852.

54. Kappler, ed., *Indian Affairs*, pp. 1127–1128. See also *San Diego Herald*, January 10, 1852. While Cupeño Chief José Noca signed as a Luiseño, Cupeño territory was included within the territory set aside for Diegueños.

55. Wozencraft to Lea, n.d. U.S. National Archives.

56. Quoted in Richard E. Crouter and Andrew F. Rolle, "Edward Fitzgerald Beale and the Indian Peace Commissioners in California 1851–1854," *Historical Society of Southern California Quarterly* 42 (June, 1960), 117.

57. Quoted in Kenneth M. Johnson, *K-344 or the Indians of California vs. the United States* (Los Angeles: Dawson's Book Shop, 1966), pp. 56–57.

58. *Journal of the Third Session of the Legislature of California* (G. K. Fitch and Co., and V. E. Geiger and Co., State Printers, 1852), pp. 105–106.

59. William H. Ellison, "The Federal Indian Policy in California, 1846–1860," *Mississippi Valley Historical Review* 9 (1922), 57–58.

60. *Ibid.*, p. 59.

61. Edward Fitzgerald Beale to B. D. Wilson, San Francisco, October 8, 1852, Wilson Collection, 1847–1853, Huntington Library, San Marino.

62. *Los Angeles Star*, October 16, 1852.

63. Marjorie Tisdale Wolcott, ed., *Pioneer Notes From the Diaries of Judge Benjamin Hayes 1849–1875* (Los Angeles: [privately printed], 1929), p. 94.

64. John W. Caughey, ed., *The Indians of Southern California in 1852: The B. D. Wilson Report and a Selection of Contemporary Comment* (San Marino: Huntington Library, 1952), p. 37.

65. *Ibid.*, pp. 36–38.

66. *Ibid.*, p. 52.

67. *Ibid.*, p. 48.

68. *Ibid.*, pp. 53–54.

69. *Ibid.*, pp. 55–57.

70. *Ibid.*, p. 59.

71. *Ibid.*, pp. 67–68.

72. *Ibid.*, see pp. 8, 11, 30, 32, 55, 59, 67, and 68.

73. *Los Angeles Star*, January 8, 1853.

74. According to the *Los Angeles Star* of August 1, 1868, "this report was transmitted at the time to the authorities at Washington, and was the foundation for the recommendations made by the agent for the establishment of the Tejon Reservation and the building of the military post at Fort Tejon."

75. Crouter and Rolle, "Edward Fitzgerald Beale," pp. 120–124.

76. *Los Angeles Star*, September 3, 1853.

77. Crouter and Rolle, "Edward Fitzgerald Beale," pp. 123–124.

78. *Daily Alta California*, September 22, 1853.

79. *Los Angeles Star*, June 24, 1854.

80. Ellison, "The Federal Indian Policy," pp. 63–65.

81. Thomas Henley to Maj. E. D. Townsend, San Francisco, December 31, 1855, Letters Received by the Office of Indian Affairs, 1824–1881, California Superintendency, Microcopy 234, Roll 35, U.S. National Archives.

CHAPTER 7

CHIEFS AND AMERICANS

1. *Los Angeles Star*, January 24, 1852.

2. Duff Weaver to J. H. Bean, San Gorgonio, February 12, 1852, Benjamin Hayes, "Scrapbooks," vol. 39, Bancroft Library, Berkeley.

3. *Los Angeles Star*, March 6, 1852.

4. Maj. J. McKinstry to Capt. E. D. Townsend, San Diego, July 20, 1852, Record Group 393, Pacific Division, Letters Received 1849–1853, 1852, II-W73, U.S. Army Continental Commands 1821–1920, Box 5, U.S. National Archives.

5. Thomas W. Sweeny, "Journal of Thomas W. Sweeny," Sweeny Collection 1 13 B 5, Huntington Library, San Marino.

6. Paulino Weaver to B. D. Wilson, San Bernardino, November 10, 1852, *Los Angeles Star*, November 20, 1852.

7. *Los Angeles Star*, July 25, 1854.

8. *San Diego Herald*, November 10, 1855.

9. *Ibid.*, November 17, 1855.

10. *Ibid.*

11. *Los Angeles Star*, December 1, 1855. See also *The Weekly Chronicle*, December 15, 1855; and Richard R. Hopkins, "Journal of Richard R. Hopkins," November 23–24, 1855, Office of the Church Historian, Salt Lake City, p. 29.

12. Thomas Henley to George W. Manypenny, San Francisco, December 18, 1855, Letters Received by the Office of Indian Affairs, 1824–1881, California Superintendency, Microcopy 234, Roll 35, U.S. National Archives.

13. W. H. Harvey to Thomas Henley, February 23, 1856, Letters Received by the Office of Indian Affairs, 1824–1881, California Superintendency, Microcopy 234, Roll 35, U.S. National Archives.

14. Maj. E. D. Townsend to Thomas Henley, Benecia, December 27, 1855, Letters Received by the Office of Indian Affairs, 1824–1881, California Superintendency, Microcopy 234, Roll 35, U.S. National Archives.

15. Capt. H. S. Burton to Maj. E. D. Townsend, January 27, 1856, U.S., Congress, House, 34th Cong., 3d Sess., *Exec. Doc.* 76, pp. 114–116.

16. *Ibid.*

17. Lieut. William Winder to Capt. H. S. Burton, Old Mission, San Diego, April 29, 1856, U.S., Congress, House, 34th Cong., 3d Sess., *Exec. Doc.* 74, pp. 123–124.

18. *Ibid.*

19. Isaac Williams to George W. Manypenny, Rancho del Chino, May 15, 1856, Letters Received by the Office of Indian Affairs 1824–1881, California Superintendency, Microcopy 234 Roll 35, U.S. National Archives.

20. *Ibid.*

21. Arthur Woodward, ed., *Journal of Lt. Thomas W. Sweeny 1849–1853* (Los Angeles: Westernlore Press, 1956), p. 161. See also *Los Angeles Star*, June 26, 1852.

22. McKinstry to Townsend, July 20, 1852, U.S. National Archives.

23. Woodward, ed., *Journal*, pp. 176–177.

24. Capt. J. B. Magruder to Maj. E. D. Townsend, Mission San Diego, October 2, 1852, Record Group 393, Pacific Division. Letters Received 1849–1853, 1852, II-W73, U.S. Army Continental Commands, 1821–1920, Box 5, U.S. National Archives.

25. Letter to a Newspaper (probably the *Daily Alta California*, n.d.), September 15, 1852, Benjamin Hayes, "Scrapbooks," vol. 38, Bancroft Library, Berkeley.

26. *Ibid.* See also Woodward, ed., *Journal*, pp. 258–259.

27. *San Diego Herald*, March 12, 1853. See also *Daily Alta California*, March 31, 1853.

28. Edward Fitzgerald Beale to General Thomas, Indian Chief, San Diego, February 16, 1854, Cave Johnson Couts Collection, Indian Affairs, CT 83, Huntington Library, San Marino.

29. Cave J. Couts to Manuel Cota, Rancho Quajome, September 1, 1853, Cave Johnson Couts Collection, Indian Affairs, CT 297, Huntington Library,

San Marino. Couts was a subagent from June 1853 until April 1856. See Moss
v. Warner, April 1856, 1st District Court, Testimony of Cave J. Couts, San
Diego County Law Library.

30. *San Diego Herald,* March 18, 1854.

31. Cave J. Couts to B. D. Wilson, Guajomito, May 7, 1854, Wilson Collection, WN 195, Huntington Library, San Marino.

32. *Ibid.*

33. M. Sexton to Cave J. Courts, La Mesa, September 14, 1854, Cave Johnson
Couts Collection, Indian Affairs, CT 2075, Huntington Library, San Marino.

34. Couts to Wilson, May 7, 1854, Huntington Library.

35. B. D. Wilson to Cave J. Couts, Los Angeles, May 15, 1854, Cave Johnson
Couts Collection, Indian Affairs, CT 2406, Huntington Library, San Marino.

36. Capt. H. S. Burton to Maj. E. D. Townsend, Mission San Diego, October
29, 1855, Letters Received by the Office of Indian Affairs, 1824–1881, California
Superintendency, Microcopy 234, Roll 35, U.S. National Archives.

37. Capt. H. S. Burton to Cave J. Couts, Mission San Diego, May 3, 1854,
Cave Johnson Couts Collection, Indian Affairs, CT 145, Huntington Library,
San Marino.

38. Burton to Townsend, October 29, 1855, U.S. National Archives.

39. Quoted in *The Weekly Chronicle,* November 17, 1855, from the *Los
Angeles Star,* n.d.

40. Thomas Henley to Maj. E. D. Townsend, San Francisco, December 31,
1855, Letters Received by the Office of Indian Affairs 1824–1881, California Superintendency, Microcopy 234, Roll 35, U.S. National Archives.

41. Cave J. Couts to Thomas Henley, Guajome, August 24, 1855, Letters
Received by the Office of Indian Affairs, 1824–1881, California Superintendency, Microcopy 234, Roll 34, U.S. National Archives.

42. Cave J. Couts and J. J. Kendrick to Thomas Kenley, December 29, 1855,
Letters Received by the Office of Indian Affairs 1824–1881, California Superintendency, Microcopy 234, Roll 35, U.S. National Archives.

43. Thomas Henley to G. W. Manypenny, April 1, 1856, Letters Received by
the Office of Indian Affairs 1824–1881, California Superintendency, Microcopy
234, Roll 35, U.S. National Archives.

44. Cave J. Couts to Thomas Henley, July 7, 1856, *San Diego Herald,* August
2, 1856.

45. Thomas Henley to Cave J. Couts, San Francisco, July 21, 1856, Cave
Johnson Couts collection, Indian Affairs, CT 1071, Huntington Library, San
Marino.

46. Capt. H. S. Burton to Maj. W. W. Mackall, Mission San Diego, September
2, 1856, Record Group 393, Pacific Division, Letters Received 1854–1858, 1856,
A1–Q1, U.S. Army Continental Commands 1821–1920, Box 10, U.S. National
Archives.

47. J. J. Warner to Thomas Henley, San Diego, July 9, 1856, *San Diego
Herald,* July 12, 1856.

48. Lt. William Winder to Maj. W. W. Mackall, Mission San Diego, August
23, 1856, Record Group 393, Pacific Division, Letters Received 1854–1858,
1856, RI–B74, Box 11, U.S. National Archives.

49. *San Diego Herald,* August 2, 1856.

50. Edward Everett Dale, *The Indians of the Southwest: A Century of Development under the United States* (Norman: University of Oklahoma Press, 1949),
p. 40.

51. *San Diego Herald,* November 11, 1854.

52. *The Weekly Chronicle,* July 14, 1855.

53. Burton to Townsend, January 27, 1856, U.S. Congress, House, 34th
Cong., 3d Sess., pp. 114–117.

54. *Ibid.*

55. Capt. H. S. Burton to Capt. D. R. Jones, Mission San Diego, May 19, 1856, Record Group 393, Pacific Division, Letters Received 1854–1858, 1856, A1-Q1, U.S. Army Continental Commands 1821–1920, Box 10, U.S. National Archives.

56. Maj. George Blake to Maj. W. W. Mackall, Mission San Diego, May 8, 1856, Record Group 393, Pacific Division, Letters Received 1854–1858, 1857, A1–B74, Box 11, U.S. National Archives.

57. Thomas Henley to George W. Manypenny, San Francisco, September 4, 1856, *Report of the Commissioner of Indian Affairs, 1856, Accompanying the Annual Report of the Secretary of the Interior* (Washington: A. O. P. Nicholson, 1857), p. 243.

58. Burton to Jones, May 19, 1856, U.S. National Archives.

59. J. Q. A. Stanley to Austin Wiley, San Francisco, May 19, 1865, *Report of the Commissioner of Indian Affairs for the Year 1865* (Washington: Government Printing Office, 1865), pp. 125–127.

60. Burton to Mackall, September 2, 1856, U.S. National Archives.

61. John Rains to Thomas Henley, July 24, 1856 in Thomas Henley to George W. Manypenny, September 4, 1856, *Report of the Commissioner of Indian Affairs 1856*, p. 243.

62. Cave J. Couts to Thomas Henley, July 7, 1856, in Thomas Henley to George W. Manypenny, September 4, 1856, *Report of the Commissioner of Indian Affairs 1856*, pp. 240.

63. J. J. Kendrick to Thomas Henley, San Diego, October 19, 1857, Letters Received by the Office of Indian Affairs 1824–1881, California Superintendency, Microcopy 234, Roll 35, U.S. National Archives.

64. Capt. H. S. Burton to Maj. W. W. Mackall, Mission San Diego, February 8, 1857, Record Group 393, Pacific Division, Letters Received 1854–1858, 1857, A1-B74, U.S. Army Continental Commands, 1821–1920, Box 11, U.S. National Archives.

65. Kendrick to Henley, October 19, 1857, U.S. National Archives.

66. John Ames to Col. Fauntleroy, San Diego, April 9, 1857, Record Group 393, Pacific Division, Letters Received 1854–1858, 1858, A4-H50, U.S. Army Continental Commands, 1821–1920, Box 13, U.S. National Archives.

67. Kendrick to Henley, October 19, 1857, U.S. National Archives.

68. J. J. Kendrick to Thomas Henley, San Diego, November 5, 1858, Letters Received by the Office of Indian Affairs 1824–1881, California Superintendency, Microcopy 234, Roll 37, U.S. National Archives. See also *California Farmer, Journal of Useful Sciences*, March 1, 1861.

69. Alex S. Taylor, "The Indianology of California," *California Farmer, Journal of Useful Sciences*, March 1, 1861.

70. Kendrick to Henley, November 5, 1858, U.S. National Archives.

71. Taylor, *California Farmer*, March 1, 1861. See also *Southern Vineyard*, October 2, 1858.

72. Kendrick to Henley, November 5, 1858, U.S. National Archives.

73. Thomas Henley to J. J. Kendrick, San Francisco, December 10, 1858, Letters Received by the Office of Indian Affairs, 1824–1881, California Superintendency, Microcopy 234, Roll 37, U.S. National Archives.

74. *San Diego Herald,* March 5, 1859.

75. *Ibid.,* March 26, 1859.

76. *Semi-Weekly Vineyard,* April 15, 1859.

77. Henry Miller, *Account of a Tour of the California Missions, 1856: The Journal and Drawings of Henry Miller* (The Book Club of California, 1952), p. 52.

78. *San Diego Herald,* July 5, 1856.

79. Benjamin Hayes to Charles C. Rich, Los Angeles, n.d., Benjamin Hayes, "Scrapbooks," vol. 38, Bancroft Library, Berkeley.

80. *San Diego Herald,* July 5, 1856.

81. "Meeting Called by the Citizens of the City and Country of San Bernardino, San Bernardino, May 20, 1856," U.S., Congress, House, 34th Cong., 3d Sess., *Exec. Doc.* 76, pp. 127–128.

82. "Citizens of San Bernardino Met in Large Numbers at the Democratic Headquarters, San Bernardino, May 24, 1856," U.S., Congress, House, 34th Cong., 3d Sess., *Exec. Doc.* 76, pp. 128–129.

83. *Ibid.*

84. *San Diego Herald,* July 12, 1856.

85. Hayes to Rich, Hayes, "Scrapbooks."

86. *Ibid.*

87. Bishop Kinney to Editors, San Bernardino, June 20, 1856, *San Diego Herald,* July 5, 1856.

88. Hayes to Rich, Hayes, "Scrapbooks."

89. Capt. H. S. Burton to Capt. D. R. Jones, June 15, 1856, U.S., Congress, House, 34th Cong., 3d Sess., *Exec. Doc.* 76, pp. 125–127.

90. *Ibid.*

91. *Ibid.*

92. Thomas Henley to J. W. Denver, San Francisco, October 27, 1857, Letters Received by the Office of Indian Affairs 1824–1881, California Superintendency, Microcopy 234, Roll 35, U.S. National Archives.

93. Thomas Henley to Charles E. Mix, San Francisco, February 18, 1858, Letters Received by the Office of Indian Affairs 1824–1881, California Superintendency, Microcopy 234, Roll 36, U.S. National Archives.

94. Maj. George Blake to Maj. W. W. Mackall, Mission San Diego, June 23, 1857, Record Group 393, Pacific Division, Letters Received 1854–1858, 1857, A1-B74, U.S. Army Continental Commands, 1821–1920, Box 11, U.S. National Archives.

95. Kendrick to Henley, November 5, 1858, U.S. National Archives.

96. *Ibid.*

97. J. J. Kendrick to Thomas Henley, San Diego, February 22, 1858, Letters Received by the Office of Indian Affairs, 1824–1881, California Superintendency, Microcopy 234, Roll 36, U.S. National Archives.

98. *San Diego Herald,* November 21, 1857.

99. *Ibid.,* December 5, 1857.

100. *Los Angeles Star,* July 3, 1858. See also *Southern Vineyard,* July 3, 1858.

101. *Southern Vineyard,* July 24, 1858.

102. *Los Angeles Star,* July 24, 1858.

103. *Ibid.,* October 26, 1861.

104. *San Bernardino Weekly Patriot,* December 7, 1861.

105. *Ibid.*

106. Porter to Editors, San Bernardino, June 10, 1862, *The Semi-Weekly Southern News,* June 13, 1862.

107. *Ibid.*

108. P. H. Wentworth to William P. Dole, San Francisco, August 30, 1862, *Report of the Secretary of the Interior* (Washington: Government Printing Office, 1862), pp. 470–471.

109. Porter to Editors, *The Semi-Weekly Southern News,* June 13, 1862.

110. *Los Angeles Star,* July 5, 1862.

111. Wentworth to Dole, August 30, 1862, *Report of the Secretary of the Interior,* pp. 470–471.

112. *Los Angeles Star,* February 21, 1863.

113. *Ibid.,* February 28, 1865. It has been claimed that one of the graves ac-

cidently uncovered on October 4, 1956, at El Casco in the San Timoteo Canyon contained the remains of Juan Antonio. This is inferred because Hazen G. Shinn in his *Shoshonean Days* (p. 93) mentioned that General Bean gave Antonio an old army coat with epaulettes and that in the grave of an adult male was found the remains of an army coat with part of an epaulette still in place. See Gerald A. Smith, Raymond Sexton, and Elsie J. Koch, "Juan Antonio, Cahuilla Indian Chief, A Friend of the Whites," *Quarterly of San Bernardino County Museum Association* 3 (Fall, 1960), 13, 28–30. According to Benjamin Hayes, however, Juan Antonio died of the pestilence in San Jacinto, the region of his birth, having left San Timoteo twelve months before. See Majorie Tisdale Wolcott, ed., *Pioneer Notes from the Diaries of Judge Benjamin Hayes, 1849–1875* (Los Angeles: [privately printed], 1929), p. 277.

114. W. K. Lovett to Austin Wiley, May or June, 1865, *Report of the Commissioner of Indian Affairs for the Year 1865* (Washington: Government Printing Office, 1865), pp. 121–123.

CHAPTER 8

CONCLUSION

1. Juan Antonio was succeeded by his longtime associate and translator, Manuel Largo, who successfully governed part of the Cahuillas until 1877 when he resigned as chief. Some Cahuillas moved to the Cahuilla Valley with Largo while others remained in the region of the San Gorgonio Pass where they intermarried with the Serrano. Cabezon continued to rule the desert Cahuilla long after the death of Juan Antonio. In 1883 it was reported that he still had great influence with his people, governing at least eight villages totaling about five hundred individuals. He died a year or so later. In 1865 Manuelito Cota was reappointed chief of the Luiseños by an Indian agent, only to be deposed and permanently retired by his own people in 1871.

2. Raymond C. White, "The Luiseño Theory of 'Knowledge,'" *American Anthropologist* 59 (February, 1957), 13–14.

3. Sherburn F. Cook, *The Conflict between the California Indian and White Civilization: I, The Indian Versus the Spanish Mission*, Ibero-Americana 21 (Berkeley: University of California Press, 1943), 71.

4. Consisting of three distinct strata (the Spanish padres and soldiers, the Indian officials, and the general Indian population), the mission clearly fits the model of the "total institution," as defined by sociologist Erving Goffman. A corporate structure in which the majority of the inmates are controlled by a small supervisory staff, the "total institution" is characterized by sharp divisions between its members. The responsibility of the staff is not the guidance or periodic inspection of the inmates, as in many employer-employee relations, but surveillance. Because of these divisions, staff and inmates may look upon one another as stereotypes. The staff may view the inmates as untrustworthy, bitter, secretive, while the inmates may see the staff as condescending, highhanded, and mean. The staff also considers itself superior and righteous, whereas the inmates are often made to feel inferior and guilty. See Erving Goffman, *Asylums: Essays in the Social Situation of Mental Patients and Other Inmates* (New York: Doubleday and Company, 1962), pp. 6–7.

5. Alfred L. Kroeber, "The Nature of Land-Holding Groups in Aboriginal California," in Robert F. Heizer, ed., *Aboriginal California: Three Studies in Culture History* (Berkeley: University of California Archaeological Research Facility, 1963) p. 108.

6. Sherburne F. Cook, *The Conflict between the California Indian and White Civilization: II, The Physical and Demographic Reaction of the Nonmission Indians in Colonial and Provincial California,* Ibero-Americana 22 (Berkeley: University of California Press, 1943), 35.

7. Hubert Howe Bancroft, *History of California Vol. IV, 1840–1845* (San Francisco: A. L. Bancroft and Company, 1886), p. 70.

8. Ted Robert Gurr, *Why Men Rebel* (Princeton: Princeton University Press, 1970), p. 113.

9. *Ibid.,* p. 39.

10. *Ibid.,* p. 9.

11. Peter Worsley, *The Trumpet Shall Sound: A Study of "Cargo Cults" in Melanesia,* second, augmented edition (New York: Schocken Books, 1968), p. 237.

12. The belief that the white man's bullets will turn into water crops up all over the world in millenarian resistance movements. It is found in the 1890–1891 Sioux outbreak against the Americans in South Dakota; in the 1905–1906 Maji-Maji uprising against the Germans in southern Tanzania; and in the 1939 Mansren movement against the Dutch in the South Pacific. See, respectively, James Mooney, *The Ghost Dance Religion and the Sioux Outbreak of 1890,* Bureau of American Ethnology Annual Report, 1892–1893, abridged, with an introduction by Anthony F. C. Wallace (Chicago: University of Chicago Press, 1965), pp. 115–118; John Iliffe, "The Organization of the Maji Maji Rebellion, *Journal of African History* 8 (1967), 502; and Worsley, *The Trumpet Shall Sound,* p. 141.

13. Gurr, *Why Men Rebel,* p. 105.

Bibliography

GOVERNMENT DOCUMENTS

Ames, John G. "Report of Special Agent John G. Ames in Regard to the Conditions of the Mission Indians of California, with Recommendations." Washington: Government Printing Office, 1873.

California State Archives. Adjutant General Records Group. Miscellaneous Files, 1851.

———. Jotham Bixby et al., plaintiffs and appellants, v. H. K. W. Bent et al., defendants and respondents, transcript on appeal, No. 5449, 65, 120, December 16, 1879, The Supreme Court of the State of California.

———. Indian War Files, 1850–1859.

Democratic State Journal, The, vol. 1, no. 6. Sacramento, Wednesday, February 11, 1852.

Emory, William. *Notes of a Military Reconnaissance from Fort Leavenworth, in Missouri, to San Diego, in California, Arkansas, Del Norte, and Gila Rivers.* Washington: Wendell and van Benthuysen, 1848.

Jackson, Helen Hunt, and Abbot Kinney. "Report on the Condition and Needs of the Mission Indians of California Made by Special Agents Helen Jackson and Abbot Kinney to the Commissioner of Indian Affairs." Washington: Government Printing Office, 1883.

Journal of the Third Session of the Legislature of California. G. K. Fitch and Company and V. E. Geiger and Company. State Printers, 1852.

Journals of the Legislature of the State of California at its Second Session: Journal of the Senate. Eugene Casserly, 1851.

Kappler, Charles, ed. *Indian Affairs: Laws and Treaties.* Vol. IV. Washington: Government Printing Office, 1929.

Letters of the Commissioners of Indian Affairs to Secretary of the Interior, Report Book, 1838–1885, no. 7, June 28, 1851–April, 1854. U.S. National Archives.

Letters Received by the Office of the Adjutant General (Main Series) 1881–1889, Microcopy 689, Roll 470. U.S. National Archives.

Letters Received by the Office of the Adjutant General, 1822–1860, Microcopy 567, Roll 464. U.S. National Archives.

Letters Received by the Office of Indian Affairs, 1824–1881, California

Superintendency, 1849–1880, Microcopy 234, Rolls 32, 34, 35, 36, 37. U.S. National Archives.

Moss v. Warner, April, 1856, 1st District Court. Testimony of Cave J. Couts, San Diego County Law Library.

Pacific Division, Records of the 10th Military Department, 1846–1851, Microcopy 210, Rolls 1, 2, 5. U.S. National Archives.

Record Group 393, Pacific Division, Letters Received 1849–1853, U.S. Army Continental Commands, 1821–1920, U.S. National Archives.

Record Group 393, Pacific Division, Letters Received 1854–1858, U.S. Army Continental Commands, 1821–1920. U.S. National Archives.

Record Group 393, Pacific Division, Letters Received, Miscellaneous, 1857–1862, U.S. Army Continental Commands, 1821–1920. U.S. National Archives.

Record Group 393, Pacific Division, Letters Sent 1851–1852, U.S. Army Continental Commands, 1821–1920. U.S. National Archives.

Record Group 393, Pacific Division, Register of Letters Received 1848–1861, U.S. Army Continental Commands, 1821–1920. U.S. National Archives.

Record Group 393, Pacific Division, Register of Letters Received and Sent, Reports 1848–1851, vol. 1/2, Reports Received Pertaining to Indian Customs 1853–1854, U.S. Army Continental Commands, 1821–1920. U.S. National Archives.

Record Group 393, Pacific Division. Expeditions Against the Indians of Los Coyotes and Destruction of their Village, December 21, 1851, H-24 (1851), U.S. Army Continental Commands, 1821–1920. U.S. National Archives.

Record Group 393, Pacific Division. Proceedings of a Council of War Convened in the Valley Los Coyotes, December 23, 1851, H-4 (1852), U.S. Army Continental Commands, 1821–1920. U.S. National Archives.

Report of the Commissioner of Indian Affairs, 1856, Accompanying the Annual Report of the Secretary of the Interior. Washington: A. O. P. Nicholson, 1857.

Report of the Commissioner of Indian Affairs Accompanying the Annual Report of the Secretary of the Interior for the Year 1857. Washington: William Harris, 1858.

Report of the Commissioner of Indian Affairs for the Year 1865. Washington: Government Printing Office, 1865.

Report of the Secretary of the Interior. Washington: Government Printing Office, 1862.

Report of the Secretary of the Interior. 33d Cong., 1st Sess., *House Exec. Doc.* 61, April 15, 1852.

Report of the Secretary of the Interior. 37th Cong., 3d Sess., *House Exec. Doc.,* 1862.

Royce, C. C. *Indian Land Cessions in the U.S.* Annual Report, 1897, Part II. Bureau of American Ethnology, Washington, 1899.

Statutes of California Passed at the First Session of the Legislature, The. San Jose: J. Winchester, State Printer, 1850.

U.S., Congress, House. 30th Cong., 1st Sess., *Exec. Doc.* 41.

U.S., Congress, House. 34th Cong., 3d Sess., *Exec. Docs.* 74, 76.

U.S., Congress, Senate. 33d Cong., Sp. Sess., *Exec. Doc.* 4.

Wetmore, Charles. "Report of Charles A. Wetmore, Special U.S. Commissioner of Mission Indians of Southern California." Washington: Government Printing Office, 1875.

Whipple, A. W. *Reports of Explorations and Surveys to Ascertain the Most Practicable and Economical Route for a Railroad from the Mississippi River to the Pacific Ocean, 1853–1854,* Vol. III, Part I. Washington: Beverly Tucker, 1856.

Williamson, R. S. *Report of Explorations in California for Railroad Routes to Connect with Routes Near the 35th and 32nd Parallels of North Latitude.* 33d Cong., 3rd Sess., *House Exec. Doc.* 91, 1853.

LETTERS, UNPUBLISHED MANUSCRIPTS, AND COLLECTIONS

Bancroft, Hubert Howe. Bancroft Reference Notes, California Indians 1851–1852. Bancroft Library, Berkeley, California.

Beale, Edward Fitzgerald. Beale File. Huntington Library, San Marino, California.

Couts, Cave Johnson. Couts Collection. Huntington Library, San Marino, California.

———. Cave J. Couts Documentary File. San Diego Historical Society. Serra Museum and Library, San Diego, California.

———. Colonel Couts Diary. Bancroft Library, Berkeley, California.

De Ridington, Dona Juana Machado Alipaz. "Times Gone by in Alta California," 1878. Translated and annotated by Raymond S. Brandes. San Diego Historical Society. Serra Museum and Library, San Diego, California.

Estudillo, José María. "Datos Históricos sobre la Alta California por José María Estudillo vecino de San Diego." Dictated to Thomas Savage, North San Diego, January 17, 1878. Bancroft Library, Berkeley, California.

Garra, Antonio. Three English Translations of Antonio Garra's Letter to José Antonio Estudillo. Whaley House, San Diego, California.

Hayes, Benjamin. "Documentos para de la Historia de California, 1874." Bancroft Library, Berkeley, California.

———. "Emigrant Notes," part 2. Bancroft Library, Berkeley, California.

———. "Notes." Bancroft Library, Berkeley, California.

———. "Scrapbooks," vol. 38. Bancroft Library, Berkeley, California.

———. "Scrapbooks," vol. 39. Bancroft Library, Berkeley, California.

Hopkins, Richard R. "Journal of Richard R. Hopkins." Office of the Church Historian, Salt Lake City, Utah.

Indian Affairs, 1849–1850, 1877. Bancroft Library, Berkeley, California.

Jenson, Andrew. "Manuscript History of San Bernardino." Office of the Church Historian, Salt Lake City, Utah.

Johnson, George A. "Life of Captain George A. Johnson," Typed

Manuscript, n.d. The California State Library, Sacramento, California.

"Preguntas y Respuestas, 1813–1814." Translated by Fr. Maynard Geiger. Old Mission Archives, Santa Barbara, California.

Stearn, Abel. Stearn Collection. Huntington Library, San Marino, California.

Sweeny, Thomas W. "Journal of Thomas W. Sweeny." Sweeny Collection. Huntington Library, San Marino, California.

Whaley, Thomas. Letters of Thomas Whaley to his Mother and Sister. Whaley House, San Diego, California.

Wilson, Benjamin. Letters to and from Benjamin Wilson. Wilson Collection, 1847–1853. Huntington Library, San Marino, California.

Wozencraft, O. M. "Statement." Indian Affairs, 1849–1850, C-D 204. Bancroft Library, Berkeley, California.

NEWSPAPERS

California Farmer, Journal of Useful Sciences, 1860–1861.
Daily Alta California, 1851–1853.
Los Angeles Star, 1851–1863.
San Bernardino Weekly Patriot, 1861.
San Diego Herald, 1851–1859.
San Diego Union, 1874.
Semi-Weekly Southern News, 1862.
Semi-Weekly Vineyard, 1859.
Southern Californian, 1854.
Southern Vineyard, 1858.
The Weekly Chronicle, 1855–1859.

PUBLISHED DIARIES, DEPOSITIONS, JOURNALS, PERSONAL REMINISCENCES, AND REPORTS

Ames, George Walcott, Jr., ed. "A Doctor Comes to California, The Diary of John S. Griffin, Assistant Surgeon with Kearny's Dragoons 1846–47," *California Historical Society Quarterly,* vol. 21, no. 3 (September, 1942).

Bartlett, John Russell. *Personal Narrative of Explorations and Incidents in Texas, New Mexico, California, Sonora, and Chihuahua.* Vol. II. New York: D. Appleton and Company, 1854.

Bean, Lowell, and William Mason, eds. *Diaries and Accounts of the Romero Expeditions in Arizona and California 1823–1826.* Los Angeles: Ward Ritchie Press, 1962.

Beechey, F. W. *Narrative of a Voyage to the Pacific and Beering's Strait in the Years 1825–1828.* Part II. London: Henry Colburn and Richard Bentley, 1831.

Bell, Horace. *Reminiscences of a Ranger or Early Times in Southern California.* Los Angeles: Yarnell, Caystile & Mathes, Printers, 1881.

Bieber, Ralph P., ed., in Collaboration with Averam B. Bender. "Cooke's Journal of the March of the Mormon Battalion, 1846–1847," in *Exploring Southwestern Trails 1846–1854 by Philip St. George Cooke, William Henry Chase Whiting, Francois Xavier Aubry*. Glendale: The Arthur H. Clark Company, 1938.

Boscana, Fr. Gerónimo. *Chinigchinich: A Historical Account of the Origin, Customs, and Traditions of the Indians at the Missionary Establishment of St. Juan Capistrano, Alta California; Called the Acagchemem Nation*. Translated by Alfred Robinson. In Alfred Robinson, *Life in California*. New York: Wiley & Putnam, 1846.

Botta, Paolo Emilio. *Observations on the Inhabitants of California 1827–1828*. Translated by John Francis Bricca. Los Angeles: Glen Dawson, 1952.

Brent, Joseph Lancaster. *The Lugo Case: A Personal Reminiscence*. New Orleans: Searcy and Pfaff, 1926.

Browne, Ross. *The Indians of California*. First published in 1864. San Francisco: The Colt Press Series of California Classics, 1944.

Caughey, John W., ed. *The Indians of Southern California in 1852: The B. D. Wilson Report and a Selection of Contemporary Comment*. San Marino: Huntington Library, 1952.

Coulter, Thomas. "Notes on Upper California." Reprinted from *The Journal of the Royal Geographical Society*, 1835. Chicago: Aldine Book Company, 1925.

Cowan, Robert Ernest, ed. "Bancroft's Guide to the Colorado Mines," *California Historical Society Quarterly*, vol. 12, no. 1 (March, 1933).

Crafts, E. P. R., assisted by Fannie McGehee. *Pioneer Days in the San Bernardino Valley*. Los Angeles: Press of Kingsley, Moles, and Collins, 1906.

Dana, Richard Henry, Jr. *Two Years before the Mast: A Personal Narrative of Life at Sea*. New York: Harper and Brothers, 1840.

Davis, William Heath. *Seventy-five Years in California*. San Francisco: John Howell, 1929.

Dillon, Richard, ed. *The Gila Trail: The Texas Argonauts and the California Gold Rush by Benjamin Butler Harris*. Norman: University of Oklahoma Press, 1960.

Dobyns, Henry F., ed. *Hepah, California: The Journal of Cave Johnson Couts from Monterey, Nuevo Leon, Mexico to Los Angeles, California During the Years 1848–1849*. Arizona Pioneers Historical Society, 1961.

Ellis, Arthur, ed. *Journal and Maps of Cave J. Couts*. Los Angeles: The Zamorano Club, 1933.

Ellison, William, and Francis Price, eds. *The Life and Adventures in California of Don Agustín Janssens 1834–1856*. San Marino: Huntington Library, 1953.

Fages, Pedro. *A Historical, Political, and Natural Description of California by Pedro Fages, Soldier of Spain*. Translated by Herbert Ingram Priestly. Berkeley: University of California Press, 1937.

Flint, Timothy, ed., *The Personal Narrative of James O. Pattie of Kentucky*. Chicago: The Lakeside Press, 1930.

Font, Fr. Pedro. "Diary of an Expedition to Monterey by way of the

Colorado River, 1775–1776." In Herbert Eugene Bolton, ed and
trans., *Anza's California Expeditions, Vol. IV, Font's Complete
Diary of the Second Anza Expedition.* Berkeley: University of California Press, 1930. Reprint. New York: Russell & Russell, 1966.

Foster, Stephen Clark. "Los Angeles on the Eve of the Gold Rush:
Remembrances of Men and Events in Southern California,
1847–1849, by the First American Mayor of El Pueblo." Told to
Thomas Savage in 1877. *Touring Topics,* vol. 21, no. 8 (August,
1929).

———. "Reminiscences: My First Procession in Los Angeles, March
16, 1847." *Historical Society of Southern California,* 1887.

Guinn, J. M., ed. "Origin of the Trouble Between the Yumas and Glanton, Deposition of Jeremiah Hill." In J. M. Guinn, "Yuma Depredations and the Glanton War," *Annual Publication of the Historical Society of Southern California and the Pioneers of Los Angeles
County,* vol. 6, pt. 1 (1903).

Heizer, Robert F., ed. *The Indians of Los Angeles County: Hugo
Reid's Letters of 1852.* Los Angeles: Southwest Museum, 1968.

Hill, Jane H., and Rosinda Nolasquez. *Mulu'wetam: The First People,
Cupeño Oral History and Language.* Banning: Malki Museum Press,
1973.

Jackson, Helen Hunt. "The Present Condition of the Mission Indians
in Southern California." *Century Magazine* (August, 1883).

Johnston, A. R. "Johnston's Journal," *Out West,* vol. 18 (January–
June, 1903).

Lugo, José del Carmen. "Life of a Rancher," *Historical Society of
Southern California Quarterly,* vol. 32, no. 3 (September, 1950).

Miller, Henry. *Account of a Tour of the California Missions, 1856: The
Journal and Drawings of Henry Miller.* The Book Club of California,
1952.

Painter, C. C. "A Visit to the Mission Indians of California." Philadelphia: Indian Rights Association, 1887.

Palóu, Fr. Francisco, O.F.M. *Historical Memoirs of New California.*
Edited by Herbert Eugene Bolton. Berkeley: University of California Press, 1926.

Robinson, Alfred. *Life in California During a Residence of Several
Years in that Territory Comprising a Description of the Country
and the Missionary Establishments, with Indians, Observations,
Etc., Illustrated with Numerous Engravings.* New York: Wiley &
Putnam, 1846.

Shinn, Hazen G. *Shoshonean Days: Recollections of a Residence of
Five Years Among the Indians of Southern California 1885–1889.*
Glendale: The Arthur H. Clark Company, 1941.

Tac, Pablo. *Conversion of the San Luiseños of Alta California.* Edited
and translated with Historical Introduction by Minna and Gordon
Hewes. San Luis Rey: Old Mission, 1958.

Tyler, Daniel. *A Concise History of the Mormon Battalion in the Mexican War, 1846–1847.* Glorieta, N.M.: The Rio Grande Press, 1964.

Wilbur, Marguerite Eyer, ed. *Duflot de Mofras' Travels on the Pacific
Coast.* Vol. I. Santa Ana: Fine Arts Press, 1937.

Wolcott, Marjorie Tisdale, ed. *Pioneer Notes from the Diaries of Judge Benjamin Hayes, 1849–1875.* Los Angeles: [privately printed], 1929.

Woodward, Arthur, ed. "Benjamin David Wilson's Observations on Early Days in California and New Mexico," as Dictated to Thomas Savage of Bancroft Library, Lake Vineyard, December 6, 1877. *Annual Publication of the Historical Society of Southern California* (1934).

———. "Notes on the Indians of San Diego County from the Manuscript of Judge Benjamin Hayes," *The Masterkey,* vol. 8, no. 5 (September, 1934).

———. *Journal of Lt. Thomas W. Sweeny 1849–1853.* Los Angeles: Westernlore Press, 1956.

"Yuman Indian Depredation on the Colorado in 1850, A Deposition," *Annual Publication of the Historical Society of Southern California,* vol. 7, pts. 2–3 (1907–1908).

SECONDARY SOURCES

Bancroft, Hubert Howe. *History of California Vol. II, 1801–1824.* San Francisco: A. L. Bancroft and Company, 1885.

———. *History of California Vol. III, 1825–1840.* San Francisco: A. L. Bancroft and Company, 1885.

———. *History of California Vol. IV, 1840–1845.* San Francisco: A. L. Bancroft and Company, 1886.

———. *History of California Vol. V, 1846–1848.* San Francisco: The History Company, 1886.

Barrows, David Prescott. *The Ethno-Botany of the Coahuilla Indians of Southern California.* Chicago: University of Chicago Press, 1900. Reprint. Banning: Malki Museum Press, 1967.

Bean, Lowell John. "Culture Change in Cahuilla Religious and Political Patterns." In Ralph Beals, ed., *Culture Change and Stability, Essays in Memory of Olive Ruth Barker and George C. Barker, Jr.* Department of Anthropology, University of California, Los Angeles, 1964.

———. *Mukat's People: The Cahuilla Indians of Southern California.* Berkeley, Los Angeles, London: University of California Press, 1972.

———. "The Wanakik Cahuilla," *The Masterkey,* vol. 34, no. 3 (July–September, 1960).

Bean, Lowell John, and Thomas F. King, eds. *Antap: California Indian Political and Economic Organization.* Anthropological Paper No. 2. Ramona: Ballena Press, 1974.

Bean, Lowell John, and Harry Lawton. "A Bibliography of the Cahuilla Indians of California." Banning: Malki Museum Press, 1967.

———. "The Cahuilla Indians of Southern California," *Malki Museum Brochure No. 1.* Banning: Malki Museum Press, 1965.

Bean, Lowell John, and Katherine Siva Saubel. *Temalpakh: Cahuilla Indian Knowledge and Usage of Plants.* Banning: Malki Museum Press, 1972.

Beattie, George William. *California's Unbuilt Missions.* [Privately printed], 1930.

———. "Development of Travel between Southern Arizona and Los Angeles as it is Related to the San Bernardino Valley," *Annual Publication of the Historical Society of Southern California*, vol. 13 (1925).

———. "Mission Ranchos and Mexican Grants," *San Bernardino County Historical Society*, vol. 2, no. 1 (Winter, 1942).

Beattie, George William, and Helen Pruitt Beattie. *Heritage of the Valley: San Bernardino's First Century*. Pasadena: San Pasqual Press, 1939.

Beattie, Helen Pruitt. "Indians of San Bernardino Valley and Vicinity," *Historical Society of Southern California Quarterly*, vol. 35, no. 3 (September, 1953).

Benedict, Ruth Fulton. "A Brief Sketch of Serrano Culture," *American Anthropologist*, vol. 26 (1924).

Berkhofer, Robert, Jr. "The Political Context of a New Indian History." *Pacific Historical Review*, vol. 40, no. 3 (August, 1971).

Bolton, Herbert. "The Mission as a Frontier Institution in the Spanish-American Colonies," *American Historical Review*, vol. 23, no. 1 (October, 1917).

Bowers, Stephen. *The Conchilla Valley and the Cahuilla Indians*. San Buena Ventura, 1888.

Bright, William. "The Cahuilla Language." In David Prescott Barrows, *The Ethno-Botany of the Coahulla Indians of Southern California*. Chicago: University of Chicago Press, 1900. Reprint. Banning: Malki Museum Press, 1967.

Bright, William, and Jane Hill. "The Linguistic History of the Cupeño." In Dell H. Hymes, ed., *Studies in Southwestern Ethnolinguistics*. The Hague: Mouton and Company, 1967.

Brown, John, Jr., and James Boyd. *History of San Bernardino and Riverside Counties Vols. I & II*. Chicago: The Lewis Publishing Company, 1922.

Brown, Paula. "Patterns of Authority in West Africa," *Africa*, vol. 21, no. 4 (October, 1951).

Caballeria, Fr. Juan. *History of San Bernardino Valley, from the Padres to the Pioneers*. San Bernardino: Times-Index Press, 1902.

Caughey, John. *California*. Englewood Cliffs: Prentice-Hall, 1953.

Clark, Dwight. *Stephen Watts Kearny: Soldier of the West*. Norman: University of Oklahoma Press, 1961.

Cleland, Robert Glass. *The Cattle on a Thousand Hills: Southern California, 1850–1870*. San Marino: Huntington Library, 1941.

———. *Pathfinders*. Los Angeles: Powell Publishing Company, 1929.

Collins, Harvey. "At the End of the Trail, The Mormon Outpost of San Bernardino Valley," *Annual Publication of the Historical Society of Southern California* (1919).

Cook, Sherburne F. *The Conflict between the California Indian and White Civilization: I, The Indian Versus the Spanish Mission*. Ibero-Americana 21. Berkeley: University of California Press, 1943.

———. *The Conflict between the California Indian and White Civilization: II, The Physical and Demographic Reaction of the Nonmis-*

sion Indians in Colonial and Provincial California. Ibero-Americana 22. Berkeley: University of California Press, 1943.

———. *The Conflict between the California Indian and White Civilization: III, The American Invasion, 1848–1870.* Ibero-Americana 23. Berkeley: University of California Press, 1943.

———. *Expeditions to the Interior of California Central Valley, 1820–1840.* Anthropological Records, vol. 20, no. 5. Berkeley and Los Angeles: University of California Press, 1962.

———. *Population Trends among the California Indians.* Ibero-Americana 17. Berkeley: University of California Press, 1940.

Crouter, Richard E., and Andrew F. Rolle. "Edward Fitzgerald Beale and the Indian Peace Commissioners in California 1851–1854," *Historical Society of Southern California Quarterly,* vol. 42, no. 2 (June, 1960).

Dale, Edward Everett. *The Indians of the Southwest: A Century of Development under the United States.* Norman: University of Oklahoma Press, 1949.

Davis, James. "Trade Routes and Economic Exchange Among the Indians of California." In Robert Heizer, ed., *Aboriginal California: Three Studies in Culture History,* University of California Archaeological Survey, no. 54. Berkeley: University of California Archaeological Research Facility, 1963.

DuBois, Constance Goddard. *The Religion of the Luiseño Indians of Southern California,* University of California Publications in American Archaeology and Ethnology, vol. 8, no. 3 (June 27, 1908).

Ellison, William H. "The Federal Indian Policy in California, 1846–1860," *Mississippi Valley Historical Review,* vol. 9 (1922).

Engelhardt, Fr. Zephyrin, O.F.M. *The Missions and Missionaries of California, Vol. II, Upper California, Part I, General History.* San Francisco: The James H. Barry Company, 1912.

———. *The Missions and Missionaries of California, Vol. II, Upper California, Part II, General History.* San Francisco: The James H. Barry Company, 1913.

———. *San Diego Mission.* San Francisco: The James H. Barry Company, 1920.

———. *San Gabriel Mission and the Beginnings of Los Angeles.* San Gabriel: Mission San Gabriel, 1927.

———. *San Juan Capistrano Mission.* Los Angeles: The Standard Printing Company, 1922.

———. *San Luis Rey Mission.* San Francisco: The James H. Barry Company, 1921.

———. *Santa Barbara Mission.* San Francisco: The James H. Barry Company, 1923.

Evans, William Edward. "The Garra Uprising: Conflict between San Diego Indians and Settlers in 1851," *California Historical Society Quarterly,* vol. 45 (1966).

Farmer, Malcolm F. "The Mojave Trade Route," *The Masterkey,* vol. 9, no. 5 (September, 1935).

Forbes, Jack. *Warriors of the Colorado: The Yumas of the Quechan*

Nation and their Neighbors. Norman: University of Oklahoma Press, 1965.

Frazer, Robert W. "Camp Yuma—1852," *Historical Society of Southern California Quarterly*, vol. 52, no. 2 (June, 1970).

Geiger, Maynard. *The Indians of Mission Santa Barbara in Paganism and Christianity*. Santa Barbara: Mission Santa Barbara, 1960.

Gifford, Edward Winslow. *Clans and Moieties in Southern California*, University of California Publications in American Archaeology and Ethnology, vol. 14, no. 2 (March 29, 1918).

———. *The Kamia of Imperial Valley*, Bureau of American Ethnology Bulletin 97, Washington: 1931.

———. "Miwok Lineages and the Political Unit in Aboriginal California," *American Anthropologist*, vol. 28 (1926).

Goffman, Erving. *Asylums: Essays on the Social Situation of Mental Patients and Other Inmates*. New York: Doubleday & Company, 1962.

Goldschmidt, Walter. "Social Organization in Native California and the Origin of Clans," *American Anthropologist*, vol. 50, no. 3 (July–September, 1948).

Guest, Florian F. "The Indian Policy under Fermín Francisco de Lasuén, California's Second Father President," *California Historical Society Quarterly*, vol. 45, no. 3 (September, 1966).

Guinn, J. M. *History of the State of California and Biographical Record of Coast Counties, California*. Chicago: The Chapman Publishing Company, 1904.

Gurr, Ted Robert. *Why Men Rebel*. Princeton: Princeton University Press, 1970.

Harvey, Herbert Raymond. "Population of the Cahuilla Indians: Decline and Its Causes," *Eugenics Quarterly*, vol. 14, no. 3 (September, 1967).

Heizer, Robert F. "The California Indians: Archaeology, Varieties of Culture, Arts of Life," *California Historical Society Quarterly*, vol. 41, no. 1 (March, 1962).

———. *Language Territories and Names of California Indian Tribes*. Berkeley and Los Angeles: University of California Press, 1966.

Heizer, Robert, and M. A. Whipple, eds. *The California Indians: A Source Book*. Berkeley and Los Angeles: University of California Press, 1965.

Hill, Joseph John. *The History of Warner's Ranch and Its Environs*. Los Angeles: [privately printed], 1927.

Hooper, Lucille. *The Cahuilla Indians*, University of California Publications in American Archaeology and Ethnology, vol. 16, no. 6 (April 10, 1920).

Hoopes, Alban. *Indian Affairs and their Administration with Special Reference to the Far West 1849–1860*. Philadelphia: University of Pennsylvania Press, 1932.

Hudson, Millard F. "The Last Indian Campaign in the Southwest," *The Pacific Monthly* 17 (January–June, 1907).

———. "The Pauma Massacre," *Annual Publication of the Historical*

Society of Southern California and the Tenth Annual Publication of the Pioneers of Los Angeles County, 1906.

Hughes, Tom. History of Banning and San Gorgonio Pass. Banning: Banning Record Print, 1938.

Hutchinson, C. Alan. Frontier Settlement in Mexican California: The Hijar-Padrés Colony, and Its Origins, 1769–1835. New Haven and London: Yale University Press, 1969.

———. "The Mexican Government and the Mission Indians of Upper California, 1821–1835," The Americas, vol. 21, no. 4 (April, 1965).

Iliffe, John. "The Organization of the Maji Maji Rebellion," Journal of African History, vol. 8, no. 3 (1967).

Ingersoll, Luther. Ingersoll's Century Annals of San Bernardino County 1769–1904. Los Angeles: [privately printed], 1904.

Jackson, Helen Hunt. A Century of Dishonor: A Sketch of the United States Government's Dealings with some of the Indian Tribes. First published in 1881. New edition, enlarged by the addition of the Report of the Needs of the Mission Indians. Boston: Roberts Brothers, 1886.

———. Ramona. Boston: Roberts Brothers, 1884.

James, Harry. The Cahuilla Indians: The Men Called Master. Los Angeles: Westernlore Press, 1960.

Johnson, Kenneth. K-344 or the Indians of California vs. The United States. Los Angeles: Dawson's Book Shop, 1966.

Johnston, Bernice Eastman. California's Gabrielino Indians. Los Angeles: Southwest Museum, 1962.

Johnston, Francis. "San Gorgonio Pass: Forgotten Route of the Californians," Journal of the West, vol. 3, no. 1 (January, 1969).

Johnston, Frank. "The Serrano Indians of Southern California," Malki Museum Brochure No. 2. Banning: Malki Museum Press, 1965.

Kroeber, Alfred L. Elements of Culture in Native California, University of California Publications in American Archaeology and Ethnology, vol. 13, no. 8 (November 21, 1922).

———. Ethnography of the Cahuilla Indians, University of California Publications in American Archaeology and Ethnology, vol. 8, no. 2 (June 20, 1908).

———. Handbook of the Indians of California. Smithsonian Institution, Bureau of American Ethnology Bulletin 78. Washington: Government Printing Office, 1925.

———. "The Nature of Land-Holding Groups in Aboriginal California." In Robert F. Heizer, ed., Aboriginal California: Three Studies in Culture History, University of California Archaeological Survey, no. 56. Berkeley: University of California Archaeological Research Facility, 1963.

———. Notes on Shoshonean Dialects of Southern California, University of California Publications in American Archaeology and Ethnology, vol. 8, no. 5 (September 16, 1909).

Landberg, Leif, C. W. The Chumash Indians of Southern California. Southwest Museum Report, no. 19. Los Angeles: Southwest Museum, 1965.

Loomis, Noel. "The Garra Uprising of 1851," *Brand Book No. Two.*
San Diego: The San Diego Corral of the Westerners, 1971.

Lummis, Charles F. "The Exiles of Cupa," *Out West*, vol. 16, no. 5.
(May, 1902).

Luomala, Katharine. "Flexibility in Sib Affiliation Among the
Diegueño," *Ethnology*, vol. 2, no. 3 (July, 1963).

MacEoin, Paudric. "Massacre at San Timoteo," *Frontier Times*, vol. 37,
no. 4 (June–July, 1963).

McGarry, Daniel. "Educational Methods of the Franciscans in California," *The Americas*, vol. 6, no. 3 (January, 1950).

McNickle, D'Arcy. *The Indian Tribes of the United States: Ethnic and
Cultural Survival.* London: Oxford University Press, 1962.

McWilliams, Carey. *Southern California Country: An Island on the
Land.* New York: Duell, Sloan and Pearce, 1946.

Mair, Lucy. *An Introduction to Social Anthropology.* London: Oxford
University Press, 1965.

Martin, Douglas D. *Yuma Crossing.* Albuquerque: University of New
Mexico Press, 1954.

Miller, Ronald Dean, and Peggy Jeanne Miller. "The Chemehuevi Indians of Southern California," *Malki Museum Brochure No. 3.* Banning: Malki Museum Press, 1967.

Mooney, James. *The Ghost Dance Religion and the Sioux Outbreak of
1890.* Bureau of American Ethnology Annual Report, 1892–1893.
Abridged with an Introduction by Anthony F. C. Wallace. Chicago:
University of Chicago Press, 1965.

Morrison, Lorrin. *Warner, the Man and the Ranch.* Los Angeles:
[privately printed], 1962.

Nasatir, A. P. "Pueblo Postscript: San Diego During the Mexican
Period 1825–1840," *Journal of San Diego History*, vol. 13, no. 1 (January, 1967).

Oswalt, Wendell. *This Land Was Theirs.* New York: John Wiley and
Sons, 1967.

Parker, Horace. "The Temecula Massacre," *The Westerners Brand
Book.* Los Angeles: Los Angeles Corral No. 10, 1963.

———. "The Treaty of Temecula," *The Historic Valley of Temecula.*
Librito 2. Balboa Island: Paisano Press, 1967.

Pourade, Richard. *The History of San Diego, Vol. III, The Silver Dons.*
San Diego: The Union-Tribune Publishing Company, 1963.

Quinn, Charles Russell. *The Story of Mission Santa Ysabel.* Downey:
[privately printed], 1964.

Raup, H. F. *San Bernardino, California: Settlement and Growth of a
Pass-site City,* University of California Publications in Geography,
vol. 8, no. 1 (1940).

Reading, June. "New Light on the Garra Uprising," Paper read before
the First Annual San Diego Historical Conference, San Diego, California, March 20, 1965.

Robinson, W. W. *The Indians of Los Angeles: Story of the Liquidation
of a People.* Los Angeles: Glen Dawson, 1952.

———. *Land in California: The Story of Mission Lands, Ranches,*

Squatters, Mining Claims, Railroad Grants, Land Scrip, Home-steads. Berkeley and Los Angeles: University of California Press, 1948.

Schusky, Ernest L. *Manual for Kinship Analysis.* New York: Holt, Rinehart and Winston, 1965.

Service, Elman R. *Primitive Social Organization: An Evolutionary Perspective.* New York: Random House, 1968.

Servín, Manuel P. "The Secularization of California Missions: A Reappraisal," *Southern California Quarterly,* vol. 47, no. 2. (June, 1965).

Smith, Gerald. "The Influence of the White Man Upon the Culture of the Indians of San Bernardino Valley." Master's thesis, University of Redlands, n.d.

Smith, Gerald, Raymond Sexton, and Elsie J. Koch. "Juan Antonio, Cahuilla Indian Chief, A Friend of the Whites," *Quarterly of San Bernardino County Museum Association,* vol. 3, no. 1 (Fall, 1960).

Smith, M. G. "On Segmentary Lineage Systems," *Journal of the Royal Anthropological Institute,* vol. 86, pt. 2 (1956).

Smythe, William E. *History of San Diego, 1542–1908, Vol. I, Old Town.* San Diego: The History Company, 1908.

Sparkman, Philip. *The Culture of the Luiseño Indians,* University of California Publications in American Archaeology and Ethnology, vol. 8, no. 4 (August 7, 1908).

Spencer, Robert F., and Jesse D. Jennings, et al. *The Native Americans.* New York: Harper and Row, 1965.

Stanford, Leland Ghent. *San Diego's LL.B. (Legal Lore and the Bar) A History of Law and Justice in San Diego County.* San Diego: Neyenesch Printers, 1968.

Strong, William Duncan. *Aboriginal Society in Southern California,* University of California Publications in American Archaeology and Ethnology, vol. 26 (1929).

———. "An Analysis of Southwestern Society," *American Anthropologist,* vol. 29, no. 1 (January–March, 1927).

Sutton, Imre. "Land Tenure and Changing Occupance on Indian Reservations in Southern California. Ph.D. dissertation, University of California, Los Angeles, 1964.

Temple, Thomas Workman, II. "The Founding of Misión San Gabriel Arcángel, Part II," *The Masterkey,* vol. 33, no. 4 (October–December, 1959).

———. "Toypurina the Witch and the Indian Uprising at San Gabriel," *The Masterkey,* vol. 32, no. 5 (September–October, 1958).

Thomas, Richard Maxfield. "The Mission Indians: A Study of Leadership and Cultural Change." Ph.D. dissertation, University of California, Los Angeles, 1964.

Underhill, Ruth. *Indians of Southern California.* A Publication of the Branch of Education, Bureau of Indian Affairs. Washington: Department of the Interior, 1941.

Walker, Edwin. "Indians of Southern California," *Southwest Museum Leaflets* 10. Los Angeles: Southwest Museum, n.d.

Waterman, T. T. *The Religious Practices of the Diegueño Indians,* University of California Publications in American Archaeology and Ethnology, vol. 8, no. 8 (March 30, 1910).

Wharfield, H. B. *Fort Yuma on the Colorado River.* El Cajon: [privately printed], 1968.

White, Raymond. *Luiseño Social Organization,* University of California Publications in American Archaeology and Ethnology, vol. 48, no. 2 (1963).

———. "The Luiseño Theory of 'Knowledge,'" *American Anthropologist,* vol. 59, no. 1 (February, 1957).

———. "A Reconstruction of Luiseño Social Organization." Ph.D. dissertation, University of California, Los Angeles, 1959.

Wolcott, Marjorie Tisdale. "The Lugos and Their Indian Ally—How Juan Antonio Aided in the Defense and Development of Rancho San Bernardino," *Touring Topics,* vol. 21, no. 12 (December, 1929).

Woodward, Arthur. "Bad Indians at Pauma," *Westways,* vol. 28, pt. 1, no. 8. (1936).

———. "The Garra Revolt of 1851," *The Westerners Brand Book,* Los Angeles Corral, 1947.

———. *Lances at San Pasqual.* Oakland: Westgate Press, 1948.

———. "Pauline Weaver of the Restless Feet," *Desert Magazine,* vol. 2, no. 5 (March, 1938).

Worsley, Peter. *The Trumpet Shall Sound: A Study of "Cargo Cults" in Melanesia.* Second, augmented edition. New York: Schocken Books, 1968.

Index